6236809    JENKINS,A.    THE STOCK
                          EXCHANGE
332.642                   STORY

D1582107

- 8

- 1 MAR 2006

-7 NOV 2008

4\12

**Hertfordshire**
COUNTY COUNCIL

Community Information

1 4 DEC 1999

4 JAN 00

1 0 MAR 2000

2 7 JUN 2000

Please renew/return this item by the last date shown.

So that your telephone call is charged at local rate, please call the numbers as set out below:

|  | From Area codes 01923 or 0208: | From the rest of Herts: |
|---|---|---|
| Renewals: | 01923 471373 | 01438 737373 |
| Enquiries: | 01923 471333 | 01438 737333 |
| Minicom: | 01923 471599 | 01438 737599 |

L32b

# The Stock Exchange Story

BY THE SAME AUTHOR

*Drinka Pinta*
*On Site 1921-71*

ALAN JENKINS

# The Stock Exchange Story

HEINEMANN : LONDON

William Heinemann Ltd

15 Queen St, Mayfair, London W1X 8BE

LONDON   MELBOURNE   TORONTO
JOHANNESBURG   AUCKLAND

Printed in Great Britain by
C. Tinling & Co. Ltd,
London and Prescot

# Foreword

by Sir Martin Wilkinson, Chairman of The Stock Exchange, 1965–73

For some years now The Stock Exchange has realized the need for its history to be written in what could be regarded as the popular idiom, and we are particularly glad, therefore, to welcome Mr. Jenkins's book. He tells the Stock Exchange story from its earliest origins in the time of the first Elizabeth up to the present day. There is much in this story that will be new to even the most well versed readers of City history, and it will entertain them too.

There have been many changes at the Stock Exchange since the last book was written about it, and it is a pleasure for me that one of my last duties before my retirement as Chairman should be to write the foreword to Mr. Jenkins's book. We have just seen the unification of all the Stock Exchanges in these islands and we look forward to a continuing growing together of the various regional interests; we have already come a long way since the first beginnings in London and the development of regional exchanges in the first half of the nineteenth century.

We have also just completed the move into the rebuilt Stock Exchange where the facilities for our Members – and for our visitors – are better than ever before. It is to be hoped that visitors who come to The Stock Exchange in the years to come will be interested in, and impressed by, what they see. I commend this book to them and to all who want to know about The Stock Exchange.

June 1973

Martin Wilkinson

# Contents

## Contents

# Illustrations

*The illustrations appear between pages 86 and 87*

Grateful acknowledgment is made to the following for use of copyright photographs: Radio Times Hulton Picture Library (Plates 5, 6, 8, 9, 10, 11*a*, 11*b*), London Express Pictures (Plate 13*a*), PA Studios (Plates 13*b*,15*b*), and Keystone Press Agency Ltd. (Plate 15*a*).

# 1

# Interesting Wallpaper

---

'Buy good securities, put them away, and forget them.'
—TIMOTHY BANCROFT, American financier

I do not suppose that any schools in the land still use Mr. Borchardt's *Arithmetic*. In a world of New Maths, and computer-programming, why should they? But to my generation of School Certificate ('O' Level) victims, Mr. Borchardt was indispensable. He was nothing if not practical. He required us to cover rooms with wallpaper, and calculate the cost; to fill plugless baths with water, and reckon how long they would take to empty; to work out the apparent speed of one train when seen from another proceeding in the opposite direction.

There were also chapters on Single and Compound Interest, and Stocks and Shares. These involved something called 'brokerage', which seemed invariably to be $\frac{1}{8}$ per cent. It was explained to me that this was a stockbroker's commission for investing my money. As I was unable to imagine a sum of money greater than £10, on which he would earn only 3 old pence, which would (even in those days) barely cover the postage, I was filled with pity for stockbrokers, that they should be so ill-rewarded. I was, many years later, to revise this opinion.

I was, from the age of three, a shareholder. Methodist families do not lay down a pipe of port for the boy to start drinking when he is twenty-one. They take a sterner view of the future. In my case, a generous uncle bought me £25 worth of 5 per cent War Loan, to enable my mother to start a Post Office savings account in my name.

This, and Mr. Borchardt, constituted my only experience of the stock market for many years. My father on the whole regarded

1

investment of this kind, like betting, as a mug's game, and never trusted anything but gilt-edged. He had been badly bitten, in his young days, by a bank manager who had enthusiastically recommended Chinese and Mexican Railways as the road to wealth; also the city of Nikolaev.

Nikolaev must have looked quite a proposition in 1914. It enjoyed a commanding position at the head of the estuary of the River Bug. Of course it needed icebreakers in winter to ensure access from the Black Sea twenty-four miles away, but look at its development potentiality: an extension to the Varvarovka jetty, new electric tramways, vodka and macaroni factories going up, a lively export trade for grain and timber, an equally promising import trade for foreign iron, steel, and machinery...

The political awareness of bank managers in 1914 could hardly be expected to foresee expropriations in China and Mexico, and a revolution in Russia which, together with frontier revisions, would lessen the importance of Black Sea ports in general. Father's bank manager was neither fool nor gambler: before the First World War, Russian credit was unchallenged; so, incredibly, was that of China, Mexico, Brazil, Greece. Where Father's bank manager went wrong was in recommending so many foreign eggs in one basket.

My father was the youngest of a family of six. His elder brother and sisters all made wills leaving their modest competences to each other and then died. Some forty years after the Nikolaev disaster, therefore, my father found himself the inheritor of fifty-four separate investments, some of them involving sums as small as £25. In exasperation he handed them over to my brother and me, to make what we could of them. The family solicitor introduced us to a stockbroker, and together we went through them. There were an extraordinary number of waterworks, I remember; and also a higher proportion of brewery shares than seemed proper for the portfolios of strict teetotallers. Perhaps the water was there just to dilute the beer. The broker's expression on seeing the original certificates of the City of Nikolaev and the Chinese and Mexican Railways was one I shall not easily forget, but he contented himself with describing them as 'interesting wallpaper'. Clearly, most of the portfolios had not been examined since the early 1920s.

We eventually reduced them to twenty-six sound holdings, prudently divided into equities and fixed-interest. Although I knew

2

little of the stock-market, I had learnt a thing or two about industry over the years, and was allowed to buy a mining share and a grocery chain for what my broker called 'a bit of spice'. I preened myself on having made an original contribution to the portfolio, and began to read *The Financial Times* regularly. Soon I was studying 'times covered' and yields, and foreseeing takeovers, like an old hand: not speculating, for trustees must not do this, but playing a sort of theoretical Stock Exchange war game whose fascination never palls.

I began to receive annual reports, some of which, being merely balance-sheets with a non-committal statement from the chairman, I did not understand. Others, got up like magazines with photographs in full colour and dramatic descriptions of the company's installations, made me feel one of the family: as a small shareholder, I was the salt of the earth. I was also sent periodic communications asking me to vote on matters of policy, or to nominate a proxy if I couldn't come. This was immensely flattering, and I did actually go to one or two annual general meetings. Nothing very exciting happened: nobody got up, like the dumb blonde in *The Solid Gold Cadillac*, and said: 'I think the Directors are paying themselves too much', and had to be made Stockholder Relations Manager to keep them quiet. My enduring memories are of a large wines-and-spirits company, whose annual general meeting was attended by some sixty convivial shareholders with pale puce noses who showed no interest in the agenda but enthusiastically sampled the products; and of a famous tea company whose chairman received us in carpet slippers, introduced us to all his aunts and brothers and cousins, and then gave us—a cup of tea.

These things I mention lest you should think that this book is a guide to quick riches, or to the workings of the Stock Exchange. There are many other books, and many financial experts who are infinitely better qualified to write such a book than I am. I am a social historian, not an economist, and what follows is the story of a national and international institution which, whether we know it or not, touches all our lives.

Five out of seven adults in Britain invest money through the Stock Exchange. Most of them do so indirectly, through life insurance, pension schemes, building societies, banks, and national savings. If you belong to a trade union, your union invests funds through the Stock Exchange. No industry, publicly or privately owned, can

3

develop without—directly or indirectly—making use of the Stock Exchange.

The Stock Exchange is a market place where, as the name suggests, stocks and shares are exchanged for cash, or for each other, and where their prices are controlled by speculation in its strict, professional sense. How and why this happens is best told by its history, which is an inextricable strand in our social history.

There are many views of the Stock Exchange. To F. E. Armstrong, author of *The Book of the Stock Exchange*, it is 'the Citadel of Capital, the Temple of Values. It is the axle on which the whole financial structure of the Capitalistic System turns. It is the Bazaar of human effort and endeavour, the Mart where man's courage, ingenuity and labour are marketed'. These ecstatic mixed metaphors are unfairly quoted from a standard work containing much humanity and learning lightly worn.

To others of a radical bent who have seldom actually seen the Stock Exchange at work, it may seem that behind all those stiff white collars and sober ties there lies a jungle where Eating People Is Right. If, in the following chronicle, there appears to be rather too much emphasis on the villains and paranoiacs of company promotion, that is because, as any reporter knows, such people make more column-inches of news than the unsung professionals who never, or seldom, put a foot wrong.

Moreover, the Stock Exchange, over two centuries, has necessarily learnt by its mistakes, and whenever it has been damaged by malpractice, it has closed one more loophole by taking quicker disciplinary action than the law itself can. The Hatrys of this world are necessary evils, and the line dividing legitimate business and larceny is a fine one.

To Maynard Keynes (to quote again out of context), 'when the capital development of a country becomes a by-product of the activities of a casino, the job is likely to be ill-done . . . (it) cannot be claimed as one of the outstanding triumphs of *laissez-faire* capitalism'. It has been suggested that these words, written in 1936, refer to the New York Stock Exchange; and that he was eating sour grapes after his own investments had gone wrong. The second charge is easily refuted, for Keynes's misfortunes had happened sixteen years before.

The late Harold Wincott, who first showed how to educate people in finance and business and investment by means of satire, and spread much hilarity among the bulls and bears, put it all much more simply: 'The Stock Exchange ' he wrote, 'is woven into the very texture of our national civilization, and could not be abolished without radically altering our national way of life.'

What follows is written with the wisdom of hindsight; and our story begins more than four centuries ago.

# 2

# Merchant Adventurers

---

'Which of the Kings of this land before her Majesty had
their banners ever seen in the Caspian sea? Which of
them hath ever dealt with the Emperor of Persia as her
Majesty hath done, and obtained for her merchants
large and loving privileges?... Who ever found English
Consuls and Agents at Tripoli in Syria, at Aleppo, at
Babylon, at Bokhara, and, which is more, who ever
heard of Englishmen at Goa before now? What English
ship did heretofore ... range along the coast of Chile,
Peru and all the backside of Nova Hispania, further
than any Christian ever passed ... ?'
—RICHARD HAKLUYT: dedication of his
*Voyages* to Sir Francis Walsingham (1589)

Falling exports; rising imports: it was time, City of London merchants felt, for exploration to go beyond the slaves-and-loot
exploits which had surrounded the names of Drake and Hawkins
with so much glamour. There was no true wealth without trade, and
in this the Spanish and Portuguese were fast outstripping us. Spain
had the best parts of America, and Portugal was the only European
power in India.

It so chanced that Sebastian Cabot, son of the Giovanni Caboto
who had mistaken Newfoundland for 'the territory of the Grand
Cham', was staying in London in 1553, when Hakluyt was two years
old. Cabot, now seventy-seven, was the most respected authority of
the age on travel. The North-West Passage had yielded little enduring
commercial gain: what, the London merchants asked him, was the
most likely way to approach the almost unknown land-mass in the
North-East?

Cabot's advice was to fit out three ships: with luck, one of them
might get through. 'And lest any private man should be too much

6

oppressed or charged,' Hakluyt tells us, 'a course was taken, that every man willing to be of the society, should disburse the portion of twenty and five pounds a piece: so that in a short time, by this means a sum of six thousand pounds being gathered, three ships were bought.'

The ships had to be practically rebuilt. In particular, says Clement Adam, writing in Latin, 'the bottom part of the vessels was further protected by a most ingenious contrivance. The merchants, it would seem, had come to know that in some parts of the ocean little worms are bred, which bore through the very stoutest oak and accordingly, the better to secure the sailors against this danger, they sheathed that part of the ship which sinks in the water with thin plates of lead.'

On Cabot's advice, they took provisions for eighteen months—six for the outward voyage, six for 'detention in port . . . in frightful cold', and six for the return voyage. 'Artillery' would be needed for dealing with unknown enemies. The captain-general of the expedition was Sir Hugh Willoughby, and his brief was to discover a north-east route to Cathay (China) and to pick up any trade he could on the way. He was provided with letters from Edward VI to any monarchs he might meet. Described as a man 'of good birth and singularly energetic character', he won his command against considerable competition, 'as he was not only a man of goodly person (being of great stature) but also an expert in military matters'.

He had little enough information to go on. Edward VI had two Tartar grooms in the royal stables, but even when sober they were not very communicative. They had heard reports of Moscow, which was believed to be about the same size as London, and of Novgorod, reputed to be even larger. Anthropophagi and 'men whose heads do grow beneath their breasts' were not ruled out, but wild animals were a certainty, possibly including the dreaded but unidentifiable *rossomacha*, which 'when filled with food and distended thereby, it seeks a couple of trees that stand close together, and squeezes itself through the narrow interspace in order to disburden its bowels, which it cannot do otherwise'.

On 10 May 1553 Willoughby sailed from Deptford with his own ship, *Bona Esperanza* (120 tons), and 35 crew; Richard Chancellor's *Edward Bonaventure* (160 tons) and 50 men; and the 90-ton *Bona Confidentia* (90 tons) under Cornelius Durfoorth with 28 men.

Chancellor, destined to be the survivor and hero of the expedition, may not have been of great stature, but he had a less noisy kind of leadership which comes from constant worrying and tenacity. He certainly did not lack daring: he had been brought up by Sir Henry Sidney (Philip's father) and was a friend of the King, who, in recommending him to the City merchants, said: 'While we are entrusting a mere trifle of money to the dice of fortune, he will be exposing what is sweetest to man, his very life, to the remorseless sea . . . he will entrust his safety to barbarous and unknown tribes, he will even expose his life to the monsters of the deep'.

But King Edward was not present when the three ships were towed in state down to Greenwich to cheers and salutes of guns, for he was ill with the consumption that was soon to kill him.

Willoughby's first port of call was Harwich, where they inspected their stores and found that some of the food was already rotten, and the wine casks were leaking. In mid-July they sighted the coast of Norway (it was actually one of the Lofoten Islands), and sailed due north.

They were now well into the Arctic Circle, and the sky looked threatening. Willoughby hoisted his flag to summon the other two commanders, and they agreed that 'should a storm of unusual violence fall upon them', and disperse their tiny fleet, they should all make for Wardhousium (or Vardö), a well-known haven at the north-eastern tip of Norway.

At four o'clock that afternoon, as Willoughby feared, the storm arrived and blew his and Durfoorth's ships out of Chancellor's sight. They and their crews are known to have reached a good harbour at the mouth of the Varzina, where they wintered, hemmed in by pack-ice. Next year, Russian fishermen found ships, bodies, Willoughby's will and his diary, which showed that some of them were still alive in January 1554. It is presumed that they all died of scurvy.

Chancellor, as agreed, waited for seven days at Vardö. While he was there, 'certain Scotsmen' warned him of the dangers of proceeding further. But he had come nearly 1,700 miles from London and was not going to turn back now. Ignoring them, Chancellor ventured alone into the White Sea. In the weird light of the midnight sun, the *Edward Bonaventure* reached 'a large gulf about 100 miles wide' which we now know to have been the Bay of Archangel.

As they sailed up an estuary, they sighted a fishing smack, and approached it, wishing to inquire where they were, and to find out if

8

the natives were friendly. The crew of the smack, however, were terrified, and tried to escape. Apprehended, they threw themselves on the freezing earth and kissed Chancellor's feet. He, 'winding his arms about them as they lay prostrate, raised them to their feet. This act of kindness won him astonishing goodwill.'

The Russian fishermen—for so they were—quickly spread along the coast a report of a strange people of unexampled humanity, and brought food. They said they could not trade with the English because they were 'not allowed to buy foreign goods without consulting their Prince', whose name was Ivan Vasalivich, one day to be known as Ivan the Terrible.

The local headmen offered Chancellor safe conduct to Ivan, but secretly dispatched a courier to the Czar, who, seeing that it was a long way to Moscow (about 650 miles) and that they would need provisions en route, gave permission to trade with the English mariners. He also agreed to pay for the post-horses which would be needed to pull the sledges.

By this time many of Chancellor's men were 'fainting with cold', and we do not know how they survived the journey. But they did, and arrived at a Moscow of fir-wood houses surrounded by city walls with an arsenal looked after by monks.

Ivan kept them waiting twelve days, and then summoned them to his palace, where they were received by 'a hundred courtiers, arrayed in golden apparel which reached down to their very ankles'. They were then admitted to the Presence Chamber, where they saw 'the Emperor of the Russians seated aloft upon his throne, wearing the Robe of State, a marvellous product of workmanship in gold, and holding in his right hand a golden sceptre embellished with gems'. Next to him stood his Chief Secretary and his Grand Usher.

Chancellor, 'without any change of countenance' and with only a perfunctory bow, delivered a letter from Edward VI. This demeanour suited Ivan, who had always liked merchants and 'men of lowly origin', preferring them to the bearded boyars who were supposed to advise him. How was the King? Ivan asked. 'Well' replied Chancellor, not knowing that Edward had died the day after his departure from Deptford, and presented the Czar with a royal gift. Ivan, already ill and neurotic, badly wanted outlets to the West, and would one day offer Queen Elizabeth an alliance and even a half-hearted proposal of marriage.

The English mariners were invited to a banquet in the Golden Palace, at which the Czar and his entourage wore silver robes. The English noted the great display of gold plate and 'four vases of gold nearly five feet high'; also that the Court wore 'outwardly linen, but costly furs next to the skin'. The Czar made the sign of the cross every time he took knife or bread in hand, and there was a ceremonial 'presenting of bread' while seven carvers served roast cygnet. Chancellor's men observed that 'a hundred and forty servants, arrayed in robes of gold or silver, changed their dress three times in the course of the banquet', and that the Czar 'addressed each guest and each servant by name'. They learnt, among other things, that the Czar had an army of 900,000, 'all cavalry'; that the Flemings already had a company of merchants in Novgorod; and that there were prospects of trade in furs—marten; white, black, and red fox; ermine and sables.

The outcome of all this barbaric magnificence was a treaty giving freedom of trade to English ships, which Chancellor took back with him when he rejoined his ship the following spring. He made a second journey to Moscow in the summer of 1555, wintered there and, in July 1556, sailed for home, only to be wrecked and drowned on 10 November in Pitsligo Bay off Aberdeenshire.

It is thus that the history of the Stock Exchange begins in the pack-ice of the White Sea; that the 'Mysterie and Companie of the Merchant Adventurers for the Discoverie of Regions, Dominions, Islands and Places unknowen' became the Muscovy Company. What Professor Trevelyan has called 'the adventurous spirit of the capitalists of the City of London' was allied to 'the quality of the new school of sailors and sea-captains'. The journey to Moscow had required courage and faith of an almost unimaginable order. It had also required money and the spreading of risk. The Muscovy Company was in fact the first known 'joint stock company'. Its members no longer traded on their own account, but contributed money or goods to a joint 'stock'. It was managed by a Governor, Deputy-Governor and assistants (later called Directors and Managers). Thus control and ownership were separated, and the capital was divided into shares which were freely transferable.

The royal fleet could not protect everyone; so single ships and traders, for security and to maintain remunerative prices against competitors, banded together in joint stock companies to equip armed fleets of their own, with Royal Charters giving them privileges and monopolies of certain regions.

So the Muscovy Company penetrated to the Caspian and beyond, to Bokhara, Turkestan, and Persia. The Eastland Company of 1579 enjoyed a monopoly of the Baltic; the Turkey Company was established in 1581, and two years later Ralph Fitch and five other merchants started on a series of hazardous journeys to Aleppo, Baghdad, and Basra; visited the emperor Akbar in India and even reached Pegu and Malacca in the South Seas. In 1599 William Adams arrived in Japan by way of the Magellan Strait, married a Japanese girl, and taught her people to build ships. He was buried on a hill overlooking Yokohama, and a street in Yeddo still bears his name.

Most sea-captains returning from voyages were interviewed by the Rev. Richard Hakluyt, now rector of Wetheringsett, Suffolk, and lecturer in geography at Oxford. His *Principall Navigations, Voyages and Discoveries of the English Nation* became required reading when planning new companies, and his cousin (also called Richard), a lawyer, was economic adviser to the Muscovy Company (he is presumably the 'man learned in cosmographie' to whom a contemporary account refers). The City merchants were insisting on sound intelligence before planning new enterprises. Only rarely were there backslidings, such as Frobisher's Company of Cathay, established after he had reached Baffin Land and brought back samples of 'black earth' which were thought to be gold ore. Because the Queen was interested (she was at Deptford to wave goodbye to Frobisher's two tiny ships as he set off), the Muscovy Company had to support the enterprise.

The need to coordinate the work of the Eastern adventurers, together with the dangers of the land route through Turkey, led to the formation of a Company to trade with India and the East Indies via the Cape of Good Hope. The Dutch were already enjoying a near-monopoly of trade with the Spice Islands, and had raised the price of pepper from three to eight shillings a pound. (Not until the activities of Mr. Bishirgian, in 1936, was the British public to be so worried about the price of pepper). Thus, on the last day of 1600, the old Queen granted a Charter to 'The Governor and Company of Merchants of London trading into the East Indies' (218 people in all), eventually to be known as the East India Company.

It was proposed to raise money separately for each voyage, in the

11

usual way. For the first voyage at least £60,000 (ten times as much as Chancellor's first voyage to Russia) would be needed. Shares of £200 were offered, and bonuses for prompt payment. Eventually £68,373 was scraped together. The two ships of the fourth voyage were wrecked, and finance remained a constant headache until 1613, when the Company managed to raise £418,700, which in 1617 was increased to £1,609,000, an astronomical sum for the day. It had, at last, a permanent joint stock, subject to three years' notice of cancellation of the Charter if it should prove unprofitable to the realm.

The East India Company built its own dockyards at Deptford, to build ships—East Indiamen, bigger and better armed than other ships (its sixth voyage used a vessel of 1,100 tons), dominated the world's merchant shipping until the middle of the nineteenth century. In the seventeenth century they had to be prepared at any moment to fight Malay pirates or the armed trading ships of their Portuguese, Dutch, and French rivals. They had also learnt how to deal with scurvy by issuing crews with 'lemon water' and oranges.

They were careful to avoid quarrels with the Indian Princes, and Sir Thomas Roe, James I's ambassador and the Company's agent at the court of the Mogul, laid down its policy thus: 'A war and traffic are incompatible. Let this be received as a rule that if you will profit, seek it at sea, and in quiet trade; for without controversy it is an error to affect garrisons and land wars in India.' This good advice lasted as long as the Mogul Empire kept its authority.

Charles I accused them of neglecting English interests and granted a licence to a rival association known as the Assada merchants, whose piratical methods brought disgrace to everybody. Eventually Cromwell re-granted the original charter, provided that Indian trade should be in the hands of a single joint-stock company; and Charles II granted the Company no fewer than five charters, giving it the right to acquire territory, coin money, negotiate alliances, make war and peace, and generally do as it pleased.

The Company was now in an immensely strong position. The profit on the original stock went as high as 40 per cent per annum, and the price of £100 stock reached £500 in 1685. The Company could raise short loans at interest as low as 3 per cent, and turn them all into large profits. It was said that Sir Josiah Child had a bribery fund to influence both Court and Parliament in favour of the Company's monopoly.

There were other interlopers, and another serious rival company in 1698 which led to an amalgamation four years later—at a price, for the new company was asked to lend the nation £3,200,000. The stage was now set for the Indian Raj.

However, the times were not yet ready for a stock market or specialist dealers in stocks. We were still very far from the age of the small investor. There were not yet enough companies or enough capital, and the atmosphere of monopoly in charters of incorporation tended to restrict membership. If you were neither a member nor the son of a member aged twenty-one or more, you generally had to pay an entrance fee as well as to pay for your shares. Moreover, shares were sometimes so large that subscribers sometimes took 'under-adventurers' into partnership to split the cost. It was probably by these informal, not to say haphazard, means that joint-stock companies were formed, in the first twenty-five years of the seventeenth century, to colonize Virginia, Bermuda, Guiana, New England, and Nova Scotia.

Company development was not all based on foreign adventure. At home we see the beginnings of industry and its capitalization. In 1568 two related companies—the Mines Royal and the Mineral and Battery—had been born. The second used raw material provided by the first. The Mines Royal produced and sold copper in Nottingham and London. The Mineral and Battery (of which My Lords Burghley and Leicester were both shareholders) bought copper from the Mines Royal to alloy with its own zinc mined in Somerset, and owned iron works and a wire-making factory in Monmouthshire. Finance was also raised (by Francis, Earl of Bedford, with £100,000 of his own money and a company of 'adventurers') for draining the Fens, and for giving London its first fresh water supply. 'The Governor and Company of the New River brought from Chadwell and Amwell to London', founded in 1609, continued as a water company until 1904, when it was taken over by the Metropolitan Water Board, but still exists as a property concern and is thus the oldest company still quoted on the Stock Exchange.

The second oldest company still listed is the Hudson's Bay Company (1668). The troublous times of Charles I and Cromwell were not good for business, and few new companies were formed: one of them, John Jervase, Molyns, Richardson & Co., supplied gunpowder to Cromwell's armies, just as the City of Birmingham made most of his swords.

13

For gunpowder, you need saltpetre, and this was one of the chief commodities brought to England by the East India Company. London was mainly Parliamentarian in the Civil War, and so the Roundhead policy of keeping monopolies for overseas trading companies was pleasing to the City, which was thus free to finance industrial enterprises at home, even though it was difficult to raise the cash. This very freedom, a century later, was to lead the world in an Industrial Revolution.

With the Restoration, confidence and wealth began to increase. In 1661 came the Royal Fishery Company, and next year an Act of Parliament, for the first time in our history, formulated the principle of limited liability and applied it to the new Fishery Company and the old East India and Africa Companies. Six years after this, and one year after the Great Fire, we find one Nicholas Barbon, doctor, M.P., builder, and property speculator, starting a company 'for the insurance of houses against fire'. Soon there were several new water companies, one of them in Newcastle-upon-Tyne; Samuel Hutchinson's 'Proprietors of the Convex lights' for lighting London streets by means of mirrors; a Company of White Paper Makers and a Royal Lustring Company.

There had been considerable competition to buy shares in the East India and other companies, and the urge to invest was waiting to be released.

For what, as Professor Trevelyan has asked, *could* a man do with his spare cash in those days? Well, he could buy land, lend it at interest, or bury it. When Samuel Pepys fled before the Fire of London, he had to bury his gold and valuables. When the fourth Earl of Bedford died in 1641, his son paid his father's funeral and other family debts out of a 'great trunk' at Bedford House in the Strand, wherein he found the sum of £1,557 14*s*. 1*d*. During the following year rents and the sales of farm produce filled the trunk with £8,500. When Alexander Pope's father fled London, terrified of the Bloodless Revolution, he took with him £20,000 in a box.

There were no banks. There was no stock market, no national savings, no building societies. You could give your non-earning daughter a handsome dowry and so buy her a husband. You could start a cottage industry employing local labour, but it could never grow very big. You could start a local transport service with horses and carts. But suppose you wanted to carry out major development or engineering works?

We have seen, in the schemes to drain the Fens, the beginning of a modern economic principle: in Trevelyan's words, 'the accumulation of capital and its application to an enterprise conceived beforehand on a large scale by men who were ready to risk great sums of money and wait twenty years or more for a return'.

Lending money at interest had only recently become both legal and respectable. From the Middle Ages down to the middle of Elizabeth's reign, when the usury laws were relaxed, it had been regarded as foreign, even immoral. And borrowing was something the reprobate Squire did when he had gambled his wealth away. Generally you went to a goldsmith in Lombard Street for money. You could even *lend* money to a goldsmith, and he would give you up to 6 per cent. The first cheques were hand-written notes to one's goldsmith asking him to pay out so much money to a creditor. The first bank notes (containing the words 'promise to pay') were 'notes accountable' issued by goldsmiths.

What the goldsmiths were really doing, we should now call banking. The idea of a bank was far from new: Venice, Hamburg, Amsterdam and other cities had had Giro-type banks since the early 1600s. Who would first start one in England—and how?

# 3

# The Pernicious Art

---

'Fancy giving money to the Government! . . .
Ten to one they'll start another war.'
—A. P. HERBERT

After the comfortably-named 'glorious bloodless revolution' of 1688,
England acquired its first and only Dutch king. Nobody liked him
much, but he came from a great commercial nation with a sophisticated knowledge of finance acquired from Venetians and Lombards,
and some of his economic experts followed William of Orange to
London, shrewdly perceiving that it was about to become a developing money market. Whether we liked it or not, the Dutch, who were
our rivals in the East Indies (but had helped us to drain East Anglian
marshes), were now our friends and allies.

The new king, of course, needed money. Not only must he settle
matters in Ireland and Scotland, but we were at war with France,
having entered the Grand Alliance, and nobody knew how long this
costly involvement would last. It was to cost £40 million.

The bad old way of raising cash—especially royal cash—was
borrow and default, or to pay interest without repaying much of the
principal (as Queen Elizabeth, who raised loans in Antwerp, was
reputed to do). Sometimes the Lord Mayor, Common Council and
Livery Companies of the City of London were expected to come to the
rescue. Charles I, unable to get finance for a Royalist army, had even
seized the £200,000 of bullion which City merchants had deposited
at the Mint for safety. No wonder that merchants, after this, preferred to use the goldsmiths' strong rooms. But some of those
goldsmiths who lent money to Charles II either lost heavily or went
bankrupt, and only a few, such as Child's and Hoare's, survived and

16

eventually became private banks. Most goldsmiths were reliable, but some, like bad money, tended to drive out the good, and there was a general yearning for a trustworthy national banking institution. A joint-stock bank, in fact.

Charles I, Cromwell, Charles II, James II, civil and foreign war—all the convulsions of the past fifty years had established two important principles: in future, no monarch could rule without Parliament, and Parliament held the purse-strings. There was now a clear distinction between royal income and Government revenue. Before 1689, most Government borrowing had been temporary, and most of it had been incurred by the King, who pledged revenue from certain duties as security for the repayment of principal and interest. Now, since Parliament could impose taxes, longer-term borrowing could be envisaged. The expression 'National Debt' was about to enter the language.

Among many schemes for a war loan was that of Charles Montague, Earl of Halifax, who had gained royal favour by a fulsome poem on William III's victories in Ireland. His plan was to raise £1 million on annuities for ninety-nine years. But both King and Government preferred William Paterson's plan for a national bank. It had been put forward twice before, but had not found enough support. The financial crisis of the French war, and an atmosphere of high prices and inflation, now made it a matter of urgency. It was Halifax who introduced the bill for the incorporation of the Bank of England, and he was rewarded with the Chancellorship of the Exchequer.

Paterson, a Scot and a member of the Merchant Taylors' Company, who had gained some renown as a writer on politics and economics, resigned from the Bank after a year 'owing to a disagreement on policy', failed to start a rival bank, promoted a Hampstead Aqueduct Company, and devoted much of the rest of his life to a disastrous scheme for colonizing the Darien isthmus as New Caledonia and filling it with cities called New Edinburgh and New St. Andrews. After several expeditions, the venture was defeated by Spaniards and fever, and Paterson returned to England to make his other great contribution to economic life—the idea of the Sinking Fund, which we shall meet in Chapter 6.

The Bank of England, backed by some of the foremost City men of the day—Sir John Houblon (who eventually became its first Governor), his brothers James and Abraham, Sir William Scawen, Sir Gilbert Heathcote, and Sir Theodore Janssen—sought a subscribed capital of £1,200,000. This sum was to be lent to the King immediately at 8 per cent. The King, for his part, agreed to give the Bank a royal charter granting, among other privileges, the right to issue notes payable on demand up to the amount of the loan. A 'perpetual fund' of interest of £100,000 was to be secured by duties on wines, spirits, and ship's tonnage, and £4,000 was to be set aside to pay the expenses of staffing and running the Bank. Apart from Governor and Deputy Governor, there were twenty-four directors, seventeen clerks and two doorkeepers.

On 1 June 1694 subscription lists were opened; on 13 June they were closed again, for the entire sum had been subscribed. To realize its size, Professor E. Victor Morgan says, we should reflect that a capital of £1,200,000 represented more than a quarter of the total tax revenue for 1694–5—or £1,500 million in today's terms. The Bank opened in the Mercers' Hall in August 1694, and before Christmas moved to the Grocers' Hall where it stayed until it was transferred to Threadneedle Street in 1736.

The goldsmiths, of course, were furious: they had lost trade, and interest rates were down. In a petition to Parliament they maintained that 'the said Bank is ruinous and destructive to trade in general and is only a private advantage to the said Corporation'. But it was useless: the Bank had come to stay.

Other companies had also come, but not all had stayed. Those concerned with metal, armaments, explosives, and mining tended to survive; the company to make 'hollow sword blades' will be met again when we come to the South Sea Bubble; but others, for raising wrecks, for diving equipment, for burglar alarms, and for making a fire engine invented by one John Loftingh (which was said to work on the 'sucking worm' principle), sank with little trace. The important thing was that new enterprises, encouraged by the Bank of England, could now be financed by joint-stock companies, of which there were now nearly 150, compared to about 15 only six years ago.

Money for private enterprise, and money for the Government: obviously the time was ripe for the emergence of some kind of middleman who would bring promoters and subscribers together. Such middlemen were not yet likely to enjoy any great social standing, for investment was not only still regarded as a form of gambling, it was literally mixed up with gambling. The word most generally used was 'adventure'. Thus, in 1694, we find the Million Adventure, the first of many lottery loans. The word 'lottery' had not yet been legally defined, so that it bore no stigma. Parliament asked for £1 million, to be divided into £10 tickets which anyone could buy. £40,000 a year was set aside as prize-money for the lucky winners; and whether you won or not, you still got 10 per cent for sixteen years, at the end of which time there were no further payments, and you did *not* get your capital back.

Does this scheme sound vaguely familiar? The Premium Bonds introduced by the Conservative Government in 1956 are comparable, except of course that you can withdraw your money at short notice. The reader may amuse himself working out which scheme he prefers. But historically the Million Adventure was of great importance, for this was the origin of our National Debt. The money raised by taxation to administer the lottery loans became known as 'the funds', and eventually this was the popular word for the National Debt itself until, for reasons which will appear later, the word 'Consols' took over.

Two other vitally important words, 'broker' and 'jobber', appeared in the last thirty years of the seventeenth century. They did not mean precisely what they mean today. The *Oxford English Dictionary* traces the word *jobber* back to 1670, where one of its meanings was a man who 'turned a public service or trust to private gain or party advantage'. Other meanings were 'a broker, a middleman, a small trader or salesman', a man who 'worked by the piece'. There was no doubt at all about what *jobbery* meant: it was corruption. From the start, therefore, and quite unfairly, jobbers have been considered slightly less 'U' than brokers.

We know that there was an Act of Parliament in 1673 for the regulation of brokers, but—while they may well have been broking stocks and shares—there is no actual evidence of such a specialized meaning. Twenty years later it was a very different story. A certain John Houghton, Fellow of the Royal Society, who seems to have set up as a kind of one-man Neddy, had for ten years been publishing weekly economic advice to all and sundry under the title *Collection of Letters for the Improvement of Husbandry and Trade*. In the summer of 1694, even as subscriptions for the Bank of England were pouring in, he began printing a series of articles on 'Joint Stocks and the various dealings therein, *commonly called Stock Jobbing*'.

Houghton is our main source of evidence for the existence of an already highly-organized stock market in London. Clearly stock-broking began, like insurance and almost all the institutions of the modern commercial city of London, in coffee-houses.

'The manner of managing the trade is this,' Houghton writes: 'the Monied Man [who corresponds to the wholesaler or jobber] goes among the Brokers (which are chiefly upon the Exchange, and at Jonathan's Coffee House, sometimes at Garraways and at some other Coffee Houses) and asks how Stocks go? and upon information bids the Broker buy or sell so many shares of such and such Stocks if he can at such and such prices. Then he tries what he can do among those that have stock, or power to sell them; and if he can, makes a bargain.'

To many men of the turn of the eighteenth century, jobbing was bound to smell a little of 'rigging the market'. Jobbers, stockjobbers, brokers, call them what you would, had no trade association or institute to regulate their professional conduct and so offer some guarantee against sharp practice. Words and bonds were not yet synonymous.

Brokers had attained a certain degree of respectability. But they were by no means necessarily *stock*-brokers. They could deal in anything they liked—stocks, gold, haberdashery, fish, bread, carpentry, spectacles, even bows and arrows, anything represented by City Guilds or Livery Companies, and many things represented by no official body at all. And of course there were many unlicensed brokers who brought disrepute on the rest.

Jobbers and brokers were fine fellows when things were going well, but instantly became scapegoats when anything went wrong. During 1696, which was a slump year, Parliament saw fit to appoint a Commission 'to look after the Trade of England'.

'The pernicious art of Stock-jobbing,' it reported, 'hath, of late, so wholly perverted the end and design of Companies and Corporations, erected for the introducing or carrying on of manufactures, to the private profit of the first projectors, that the privileges granted to them have commonly been made no other use of . . . but to sell again, with advantage, to ignorant men.' Some promoters were wont, having sold a great deal of stock at inflated prices, to get out of the company they had founded and leave its management to the 'unskilful hands' or

men allured by the noise of great profit', who knew nothing of laws
and patents.

For example, the Commissioners said, look at the paper and linen
industries 'which, we fear, feel the effects of this stock-jobbing
management, and are not in so thriving a condition as they might have
been'. There was even a case for nationalizing certain staple industries
or at least bringing them under direct Government supervision. The
home fishery, for instance: a 'private stock and the scattered endeavours of men acting separately' were simply not good enough to
rescue this important source of food which would never flourish until
'the hands of the poor be all brought to labour'.

John Houghton, who by his publications had been 'looking after
the trade of England' for nearly twenty years, came out on the side of
the jobbers and brokers. He was one of the few men of his time who
understood that markets were bound to fluctuate, or that there was
such a thing as the law of supply and demand. Hardly anyone had yet
applied mathematics to business, and the study of economics barely
existed. Newton used his logarithms to help formulate laws of
physical science. Edward Halley, discoverer of the comet, took time
off from astronomy to draw up the first statistically-based mortality
table, thus becoming the first actuary.

It seems, therefore, that the sharpest critics of stockjobbing were
those who knew least about it, or who had suffered from it. 'May we
not as well prohibit the use of wine,' Houghton wrote, 'because we see
men wallowing in the kennels by drinking too much of it? . . . I know
many worthy persons of great honour and probity who deal in stocks
that do abominate the least unjust action, and would not for the
world have an ill-gotten penny among the rest of their estates; and it
is a great hardship on such gentlemen to undergo the censures of
mankind, who inveigh against all traders and trading in stock,
though at the same time they know little or nothing of it.'

Moreover, brokers could hardly be blamed for the activities of
unscrupulous company promoters. However, it is clear that certain
people were 'rigging the market'. In particular, they were rigging
dealings in options by a practice which John Houghton called 'the
mystery of buying more than all'; 'Some rich men will join together
and give money for refuse . . . strive to secure all the shares in a stock,
and also to give guineas for refuse of as many shares more as folk will
sell, that have no stock! . . . and then such takers for guineas of

21

refuse as have no stock must buy of the other that have, so many shares as they have taken guineas for the refuse of, at such rates as they or their friends will sell for; though ten or twenty times the former price.'

'Buying more than all': we shall see this principle at work in many doubtful share issues, many swindles which no amount of restriction and regulation can entirely avoid, right up to comparatively recent times. However rapid and accurate the available information, the risk persists. We shall find it in the South Sea Bubble, the Railway Mania, Horatio Bottomley, and Clarence Hatry (in whom it did not stop short of forgery).

No wonder, then, that Parliament at last, in 1697, brought in an act 'to restrain the number and ill practice of brokers and stock-jobbers'. By it, no broker in commodities or share dealings could trade without being 'admitted, licensed, approved and allowed by the Lord Mayor and Court of Aldermen'. There were to be no more than one hundred such brokers. Each was to take an oath that he would 'truly and faithfully execute and perform the office and employment of a broker between party and party ... without fraud or collusion ... according to the tenor and purport of the Act ... So help me God'.

These official brokers were given silver medals bearing the Royal Arms on one side and the City Arms, with the broker's name, on the other. They were designed and struck by Milton, Assistant Engraver to the Royal Mint. Several such medals (presented to the Stock Exchange in March 1931) are displayed in the Council Anteroom, on the twenty-third floor of the new building. A new medal based on the same design was issued to Members in 1972 to commemorate its opening.

There were admission fees of up to £2 and a deposit of £500, to be forfeited if they were found guilty of malpractice. Registers of brokers were to be kept at the Royal Exchange and Guildhall. Brokers were to keep books strictly, list every deal in them, and take not more than 10 shillings per cent commission. They were to deal only for clients, not on their own behalf. Options were not to be held open for more than three days—penalty for infringement: permanent expulsion. Dealers in Government business would need a special licence from the Treasury.

Penalties were very severe—a £500 fine for acting as a broker with-

22

out a licence, and, for clients, a £50 fine for knowingly using an unlicensed broker. Unlicensed stockbrokers were singled out for special punishment: three days in the pillory.

The 1697 Act ran for three years, and then for seven more. Eventually it was allowed to lapse, nobody knows precisely why. We know that there was a good deal of resistance against it in the City, largely because of the restriction to only one hundred brokers. A petition to Parliament in 1704 complained that this restriction was 'a great prejudice to the petitioners and others who understand trade and might be employed as brokers, yet cannot, by reason of the said Act, though many . . . through losses in the late way and otherwise are reduced and want business'.

But this, the lucky hundred quickly replied in another petition, was the very reason why one hundred was enough, since there was already not enough business to go round, and 'many . . . do not get a subsistence for themselves and families'. The hundred won.

We have said that stockjobbers and brokers were meeting in coffee-houses by now; yet many still met in the Royal Exchange, where all sorts of commodities were bought and sold. Sir Thomas Gresham, member of the Mercers Company and financial adviser to Edward VI and Queen Elizabeth, had originally founded his 'burse' as a copy of the Amsterdam Bourse. It became the home of Flemish bill-brokers and exchange dealers, but scarcely justified its existence until gradually it became a general rendezvous for merchants—including jobbers. By the end of the seventeenth century jobbers and brokers had what was known as a 'walk' there, in the new building which had been opened in 1669 after the burning of the old one.

Charles Duguid, who published a history of the Stock Exchange in 1902 (to celebrate its centenary), reproduced an old print showing the various walks—Irish Walk, Dutch and Jewellers', Scotch Walk, Clothiers', Salters' (all these were on the north side). On the south side were Virginia, Jamaica, Spanish, and Jews' Walks; on the west, Norway, Silkmen's, East India, Grocers', Druggists'; and on the east, French, Italian, American, Portugal, and—last, and rather despised—Brokers etc. of Stocks. By 1696, the unhappy year of the anti-jobber Commission, stock dealers had apparently moved nearer the centre of the building between 'Salters, Italian merchants and the Canary merchants'.

One complaint against the stock dealers seems to have been that they were too noisy. Duguid quotes a contemporary account which says: 'The stockbrokers caused the walls of this Royal Exchange to resound with the din of new projects'. Yet this was in an atmosphere of multilingual jabber where 'the grave Fleming might be seen making a bargain with the earnest Venetian ... the Frenchman with his vivacious tones, the Spaniard with his dignified bearing, the Italian with his melodious tongue, might be seen in all the variety of national costume'.

The contemporary witness goes on: 'The noise of the screech-owl, the howling of the wolf, the barking of the mastiff, the grunting of the hog, the braying of the ass, the nocturnal wooing of the cat ... all these in unison could not be more hideous than the noise which these beings make in the Stock Exchange ... I know not why the jobber who contracts to buy is styled a bull, except that he appears, when a loser, as surly as that animal: the term can have no classic origin, as these beings are in general illiterate and have never heard of the bull offerings to Apollo'.

Fine writing, but it does not explain why the stockbrokers left the Royal Exchange for the coffee-houses. The Corporation of the Royal Exchange certainly wanted to get rid of them, on the grounds that they were a diversion from the objects of the founder; a thin enough excuse. *Were* they thrown out? There were now a considerable number of them, so that some kind of overflow seemed necessary. It is, anyway, a great deal pleasanter to conduct business in a coffee-house. Some brokers certainly migrated—if the term may be used of such a short distance—to Exchange Alley, and were then attacked by the City in proclamations (1700 and 1703) for 'presuming to meet in 'Change Alley', where they probably caused a traffic hazard. Meanwhile the Corporation of the Royal Exchange seems to have repented, and actually tried to stop them from leaving by inserting conditions in their bonds, by which they undertook not to assemble in 'Change Alley.

We may take one last look at the Royal Exchange in a venomous portrait of Sir Josiah Child (the same Governor of the East India Company who had been accused of bribing the Court of Charles II; a considerable writer on economic subjects in his day, whose family was one day destined to found Child's Bank). It is to be found in *The Anatomy of Exchange Alley*, believed to be by Daniel Defoe. It may well have been, for Defoe's own business experiences had generally been disastrous. Writing in 1719, twenty years after Child's death, he has no hesitation in calling him a 'capital cheat' who 'kept it in his power to set the price to all the dealers. Every man's eye when he came to the market was upon the brokers who acted for Sir Josiah: does Sir Josiah sell or buy? If Sir Josiah had a mind to buy, the first thing he did was to commission his brokers to look sour, shake their heads, suggest bad news from India . . . Immediately the Exchange . . . was full of sellers; nobody would buy a shilling, till perhaps the stock would fall six, seven, eight, ten per cent, sometimes more. Then the cunning jobber had another set of men employed to buy, but with privacy and caution, all the stock they could lay their hands on, till by selling ten thousand pounds at four or five per cent cost he would buy a hundred thousand pound stock at ten or twelve per cent under the price.'

# 4

# All the Rage and Fashion

'Never be afraid of missing the boat: it may turn out to
be the *Titanic*.'
—ELLIOT JANEWAY (February 1971)

It has been thought by historians that the emergence of the joint-stock
company, and investment in Government funds, were a bulwark
against revolution in that they gave people a personal stake in what
we now call The Establishment and created a useful distrust and fear
of change.

From this attitude of mind it was easy to conclude, at the beginning
of the eighteenth century, that anything sanctioned by the Government must be sound. This was no doubt how the investing public
viewed the South Sea Company when it was founded in 1711. Moreover, it sounded romantic and adventurous: after civil war, revolution, rapid changes of monarch, and religious squabbling, it must
have stimulated visions of a rip-roaring return to the piratical glory of
Drake and Raleigh.

Society—the people who 'mattered'—was then very small. Gossip
and rumour were often indistinguishable from news, which travelled
fast by private letter, or by after-dinner talk among gentlemen after
the ladies had withdrawn, and the port bottles (and the silver
chamber-pots from the dining room sideboard) went round. Gambling
was almost a point of honour in gentlemanly behaviour, and the line
between gambling and investment, or between business and fraud,
was a thin one.

Foreign ventures had suffered a setback. The East India Company
had not performed well—as a chartered company. The Government
therefore started a new and separate one in 1698, just a year before the

death of the competent but devious Sir Josiah Child, called The General Society, which required two million pounds 'for the service of the Crown of England'. This was to be a joint-stock company entitling subscribers to share in what benefits there might be, at a dividend of 8 per cent. In this form it lasted four years, and was then merged with the old company to form the United East India Company.

Meanwhile the War of the Spanish Succession had started; like all wars, expensive, and bringing the National Debt once again to the forefront. Both Government and businessmen hoped that the war would end with a treaty under which trade with Spanish America might be opened. Trade meant chiefly slave trade, which was dominated by the Portuguese, who had the concession (called the Assiento) for supplying slaves to the Spanish American colonies. However, it was mainly British merchants who found and captured West African slaves and transported them to the slave market in Jamaica, where Portuguese dealers paid up to £22 each for them.

Robert Harley, first Earl of Oxford, in 1711 found himself Chancellor of the Exchequer in a coalition government, very insecure among political enemies, and with a National Debt of nine million pounds. His cousin Abigail Masham was about to become Queen Anne's close adviser, replacing the Duchess of Marlborough. He was never to be able to control the scheme he was about to set in motion, for with the accession of George I he was to be thrown into prison and narrowly escape impeachment, and his last years would be spent in amassing his library, the Harleian manuscripts which are in the British Museum.

On 7 March 1711, Harley announced in Parliament his plans to discharge the National Debt by converting it into shares in a new joint-stock company whose full title was 'The Governor and Company of Merchants of Great Britain trading to the South Seas and other parts of America, and for encouraging the Fishery'. We shall not hear very much about the Fishery. The company was to be given a monopoly of trade to South America and the Pacific, in which holders of navy and ordnance bonds were offered stock with a guaranteed interest of 6 per cent (for which the Government provided £568,000 a year).

Harley became a Governor of the Company, with St. John and others. St. John issued a reassuring statement that 'for the public good of the nation and the particular advantage of this Company, Her Majesty has been pleased to assist them with a sufficient force in order to their making a settlement with the South Seas for their security and better carrying out the trade to these parts'.

Was the South Sea Company a serious enterprise? The war was not yet over, and when peace came in 1713, the Treaty of Utrecht gave only a very limited trading concession—one ship a year, which could *not* enter the Pacific; and the right to operate the slave-trade. But by 1718 we were at war with Spain again, which made nonsense of the Company's original aims. Certainly there were optimists who genuinely believed in the Company's prospects—in 1711. Men like Sir Theodore Janssen, who was a Governor of the Bank of England, and one of several prominent financiers who put up large amounts of money. Some of them were to become as mad as all the rest, once the maelstrom began to go out of control.

John Blunt, or Blount, was a different creature altogether, a Dissenter who had made money as a scrivener but was always inveighing against 'the luxury of the age'. We first hear of him as secretary of the Hollow Sword Blade Company which had been manufacturing sword blades for about fourteen years before becoming a bank—a bank which provided some of the money for the new South Sea Company, which had several Hollow Sword Blade directors on its board. There is little doubt about Blunt's motives: they were the same as those of Horatio Bottomley two centuries later, who was to use the title 'John Blunt' for his last disastrous journalistic enterprise. Blunt, like Bottomley, was to provide much of the emotional patriotic appeal that made South Sea investors feel they were back in the golden age of Drake, Raleigh, and foreign conquest.

Subscriptions began to pour in at the Mercers' Hall, Cheapside, on 14 July, and afterwards at a new South Seas headquarters in Threadneedle Street. The first shareholders' meeting was held on 14 September 1711; and on 12 November we find Dean Swift, attracted by a prospectus which promised free trade with Spanish America, writing to Stella: 'I am resolved to buy £500 South Sea stock, which will cost me £380'; from which we can reckon that it was then quoted at 76.

Swift, a shrewd speculator, had hitherto concentrated on Bank of England stock. His letters to Stella are sprinkled with references to it: 'The Bank . . . is rising now, and I knew it would; it fell from 129 to

96 . . . I was a little too late for the cheapest time, being hindered by business here; for I was so wise as to guess to a day when it would fall . . . Bank stock is fallen 3 or 4 per cent by the whispers about the town of the Queen's being ill, who is however very well.' Poor Queen Anne died many times in her lifetime, and caused several panics. A certain Sir Manasseh Lopez was said to have started some of the rumours, so that he could buy heavily during the panic.

Dean Swift obviously expected the South Sea Company to behave in much the same way as the Bank of England; and indeed there was no obvious cause for alarm for some years. An Act of 1715 raised the capital to £10 million, and two years later a further £2 million was added. This was at a time when the whole share capital of all joint-stock companies, including the Bank of England (over £5,500,000) and the United East India Company (nearly £3,200,000), amounted to only £20 million. More than half the invested wealth of the country was in a single company.

What, it may well be asked, was that Company actually doing? Its first two ships, *Bedford* and *Elizabeth*, had been badly treated by the Spaniards. Of two more annual ships allowed by the Treaty, the *Royal Prince* and the *Royal George*, one never sailed because of the Anglo-Spanish trouble which was to bring war again. The Company, though having a theoretical monopoly, found itself to some extent in rivalry with the Royal African Company, from whom it found it convenient to buy slaves rather than go to the trouble of getting them in Africa or Jamaica. From Jamaica many slaves escaped, and it was often found more profitable to sell an uncaught runaway than to spend money on recovering him. All this, in the Company's early days, was arranged by Harley and St. John, and public opinion did not turn a hair.

So far, the Company was over-capitalized, but you couldn't actually call it a fraud. For that matter, you couldn't yet call the operations of John Law in France fraudulent—and these were being watched intently by Blunt (now *Sir* John). Law, in many ways a financial genius, came, like William Paterson, from Scotland. The son of an Edinburgh goldsmith, he might indeed have made his name in London had he not killed one Edward Wilson in a duel in 1694 and found it convenient to flee to Amsterdam, where he studied banking. Returning to Scotland eleven years later, he submitted a scheme for a national bank—not to the Government in London, but to the

Scottish parliament. But Paterson used his influence against it, and the scheme was rejected.

During the next decade, Law living by gambling (which earned him over £100,000) hawked his idea round other European capitals, and at last found favour in France. In 1716 he established a Banque Générale in Paris with a capital of six million livres. The Banque could issue notes payable on demand, and these notes could be used to pay taxes. Soon the rate of interest fell to $4\frac{1}{2}$ per cent, and the note issue rose to sixty million livres. Henceforth Law could do no wrong.

He now originated the famous Mississippi scheme, which began with a merger between the French Louisiana Company and the Canada Company to run the whole trading area of the Mississippi, Ohio, and Missouri rivers. The new company also bought the tobacco monopoly. Subscriptions (paid in at Rue Quincampoix, the 'Change Alley of Paris) were plentiful; but unfortunately the Company was not in itself a monopoly, and soon a rival company was formed and Law's shares dropped. By now he had managed to convert the Banque Générale into the Banque Royale, with himself as Director: the bank's notes were now guaranteed by the king (Louis XV was then 10 years old). Meanwhile the Louisiana Company had taken over the French East Indies and China Company, under the general title of the India Company, and was now allowed to manage both the mint and the coin issue, and the national revenue as a whole—anything and everything, as long as it paid the National Debt.

The speculation fever was on, and in 1720 Law brought off what was intended to be his master-stroke by amalgamating the India Company with the Banque Royale. He might, at this point, have said with his late Majesty 'L'état, c'est moi'. But he had now frightened the investing public, who started withdrawing their money. On 21 May came a decree reducing the value of bank notes by half—and a week later the panic was so great that all payments were suspended. The whole system collapsed, and Law disappeared.

Now there was an interval of a few months between what was happening in France and the stages by which the South Sea Bubble in England plunged into its worst excesses. Time enough, surely, for the Directors of the South Sea Company to see clearly what could happen in England. There was some excuse for what Law did; there was none for what the South Sea Company did; and when at last they did try to control what they had started, it was too late.

They had tried raising money by lottery tickets, redeemable at 5 per cent interest; but this was small beer. They now, inspired by Sir John Blunt and, in turn, by John Law, conceived the greatest financial design in human history: incorporating the funds of the Bank of England, the East India Company, the Exchequer, and the South Sea Company. Blunt, however, went one better: he invented a new scheme—to merge the National Debt with the South Sea Company.

There is no present-day parallel to this. We cannot imagine anyone proposing to amalgamate Unilever with Consols, or ICI with National Savings, with the Queen or the Duke of Edinburgh on the board. To understand how such a scheme was possible, we must forget modern economics entirely and look at the eighteenth-century doctrine of ingrafting. Merging the National Debt into the capital of big companies (and bigness was reckoned to be synonymous with soundness) was thought to make for stability. It had worked perfectly well with the Bank of England and the East India Company: why should it not work also with the South Sea Company? Why, the King himself was a Governor of it!

Part of the National Debt, however, was not so ingrafted, and this consisted of three kinds of stock—'long annuities' of up to ninety-nine years, and 'short annuities' of thirty-two years (both regarded as 'irredeemable'), and the 'redeemable' 4 per cent and 5 per cent stocks. The whole lot amounted to £31 million. Sir John Blunt and his friends wished to convert all of it into South Sea stock, and 'corner' it.

This was the proposition which he placed before John Aislabie, Chancellor of the Exchequer, and James Craggs (the elder) who was Joint Postmaster-General. The Bank of England tried to outbid the Blunt faction, who merely offered still more for the stock—without having the money to pay for it. Sir Robert Walpole, the Prime Minister, supported the Bank of England's offer of '£1,700 stock for every £100 in the long annuities', and opposed the South Sea Bill, which he said savoured of the 'pernicious practice of stockjobbing, by diverting the genius of the nation from trade and industry', and published a pamphlet to reinforce his views. He had nevertheless already done very well out of South Sea stock, buying cheap and selling at the top of the market.

There were many critics of the South Sea Act of April 1720, Sir Richard Steele among them. Yet astonishingly few saw the fundamental economic, or arithmetical, fallacy of it. It was easy to be

31

blinded with science, to be influenced by the great names associated with it, especially through the manipulations of the Blunt gang, who gave fictitious parcels of stock to prominent people for the use of their names. The only thing most people seem to have feared was the *power* of a corporation with £43 million. How could it ever have made a profit? No matter—the Government supported it, and if one did not understand it, anyone could believe anything.

The behaviour of South Sea shares during 1720 forms a kind of graph of euphoria and panic. They stood at 128½ in January, rose to 330 in March, 550 in May, 890 in June, 1,000 in July; plunged insanely to 175 in September and sank to 124 in December.

Five days after the passing of the Bill, the Directors invited the public to subscribe £1 million at £300 for every £100 capital. The issue was 100 per cent oversubscribed and the stock advanced to £340. A dividened of 10 per cent was then announced, and a second subscription of £1 million was opened at £400 per cent; in a few hours £1,500,000 had been subscribed. Among the first subscribers were the King and the Prince of Wales. Others—incredibly—were foreign noblemen who hoped to recover some of the money they had lost in Law's Banque Royale.

'Change Alley, Cornhill and Lombard Street were impassable for 'lords and ladies in their carriages', and according to a ballad sold in the streets—

> 'Then stars and garters did appear
> Among the meaner rabble,
> To buy and sell, to see and hear
> The Jews and Gentiles squabble.
> The greatest ladies thither came
> And plied in chariots daily,
> Or pawned their jewels for a sum
> To venture in the Alley.'

In 'Change Alley the stockbrokers, we are told, 'were in perpetual hurry, being tossed about between hopes and fears, upon the different accounts they received almost every minute from their agents and friends in Westminster'.

Edward Harley (junior), writing to his Aunt Abigail, confirmed the ballad: 'South Sea is all the rage and fashion; the ladies sell their jewels to buy, and happy are they that are in . . . There are few in

32

London that mind anything but the rising and falling of the stocks . . .
so that unless I bring South Sea, African Bank, cent per cent, par,
etc. and such stuff into my letter I shall neither be fashionable nor
fill it up.'

The Duke of Chandos was said to have £30,000 in Africans. John
Barter (Dean Swift's printer and afterwards, in 1733, Lord Mayor of
London) invested £20,000 in South Sea, and speculated until he
became a millionaire, but lost most of it in other 'bubbles'.

And yet, in May 1720, Edward Harley wrote to Lord Oxford from
Paris: 'Some say Mr. Law is committed, others that he is fled'. He
*had* fled—to Brussels, en route for Venice, where he was to die.

In June came the Bubble Act; not so much an act, more an attempt
to discourage competing issues by making illegal any company
formed without a charter; and forbidding any broker to deal in such
shares on penalty of a £500 fine. Nobody took it seriously.

Many speculators got out in time; others were ruined. Who, after
all, was really in the know? All great swindles rely to some extent on
confusion, and this was what Blunt was doing. Mrs. Howard, mistress of the Prince of Wales, lost money. A Director of the South Sea
Company, James Edmondson, seemed genuinely mystified when he
was asked at Garraway's coffee-house whether it was true that the
third subscription would be opened at 1000: 'Truly, gentlemen seem
to strive to take us into some such price, whether we will or not'.

On 15 July, James Craggs (the younger) wrote to Lord Stanhope:
'The crowd of those that possess the redeemable annuities is so great
that the Bank, who are obliged to take them in, has been forced to set
tables with clerks in the street'. It was computed that, about this
time, 'the advanced prices of all those stocks . . . amount to about
£500 million sterling; or about five times as much as the current cash
of all Europe'.

'All those stocks' including nearly 100 other 'bubble' companies
with a theoretical capital of £300 million—companies for 'paving the
streets of London', 'importing timber', and insuring people against
highway robberies. The company for 'importing Spanish jackasses' to
improve the breed of British beasts of burden has been held up to
ridicule, but the clergyman who started it had actually gone to the
trouble of acquiring marshlands near Woolwich for the purpose. At
least it made more sense than some of the projects—for example, 'a
Company for carrying on an undertaking of great advantage but

nobody to know what it is', by which each subscriber of £2 deposit was entitled to £100 per annum per share, disposed of 1,000 shares in six hours.

The technique was simple: you took a room near 'Change Alley, put an advertisement in the papers, and investors queued up for as big a parcel of shares as they could afford. The legendary Sudanese who was sold a tramcar in the streets of Cairo was not easier game. Naturally it helped to have a lord on the board; better still, a duke. The Duke of Rutland was known to be a Governor of the Copper Miners of the Principality of Wales, and the Duke of Bridgewater was Governor of a company 'for building houses' in London and Westminster.

Is satire ever any use in stemming the follies of mankind? It certainly wasn't in the first quarter of the eighteenth century. William Rufus Chetwood, bookseller and dramatist, wrote several comedy-farces about the South Sea Company. In one, *Exchange Alley*, the leading role was 'Mississippi, a merchant dealing in stocks', and he was supported by Messrs. Bite, Cheatall and Bubble. Similar characters appear on a contemporary pack of 'Bubble playing cards'. It was almost as if people *knew* they were being swindled, and enjoyed it, like Chico Marx in the famous Marx Brothers' skit on encyclopedia salesmanship.

Colley Cibber, in *The Refusal* (1720), has a scene in 'Change Alley where 'you'll see a Duke dangling after a Director: here a peer and a 'prentice haggling for an eighth; there a Jew and a parson making up differences; here a young woman of quality buying bears of a Quaker; and there an old one selling refusals to a lieutenant of the Grenadiers'.

Mrs. Centlievre, another dramatist of the time, who was married to Queen Anne's 'yeoman of the mouth' and might be supposed to know what was going on, sets one scene of her comedy *A Bold Stroke for a Wife* in Jonathan's Coffee House (Act IV, Scene I). In it, a stockbroker says: 'I would fain bite the spark in the brown coat. He comes very often into the Alley, but never employs a broker.'

A new stratum of *nouveau riche* middle class was being produced by the Bubble: 'City ladies buy South Sea jewels, hire South Sea maids, take new country South Sea houses'; and this in turn bred a new race of estate agents, known as land jobbers.

As late as 24 August 1720, the Fourth Money Subscription for the

South Sea Company was opened, and the entire issue was taken up in three hours. People might be wary of small bubble companies, but they still seemed infatuated with the big one: indeed, there is evidence that many investors gambled in small bubbles so as to invest their profit in the big one, and that it was largely fears about the little ones that led anyone to suspect that there might be something wrong with the big one.

Archibald Hutcheson, M.P. for Hastings and a strong advocate of refinancing the National Debt (though not by means of the South Sea Company), has left us his interpretation of the human greed that motivated the Bubble. It reads rather like a chain-letter scheme. Let A be the First, B the Second, C the Third and D the Fourth Subscription. 'A, having a £100 stock in trade, though pretty much in debt, gives it out to be worth £300, on account of many privileges and advantages to which it is entitled. B, relying on A's great wisdom and integrity, sues to be admitted partner on those terms, and accordingly brings £300 into the partnership. The trade being afterwards given out or discovered to be very improving, C comes in at £500, and afterwards D at £1,100. And the capital is then completed to £2,000.

'If the partnership had gone no farther than A and B, then A had got, and B had lost, £200. If it had stopped at C, then A had got, and B had lost, £200, and B had been as he was before; but D also coming in, A gains £400 and B £200, and C neither gains nor loses, but D loses £600.'

It was therefore D who was invariably the fall-guy. Six days after the Fourth Subscription, Lord Bathurst wrote to Lord Strafford: 'Some of the Directors have been playing the rogue and have endeavoured to run down the stocks after having sold their own out, in order to buy in cheap again. This has put people in a fright.' There was also the old trap of 'small print': at the top of each page of the subscription book there was a paragraph awarding power of attorney to 'certain persons' so that subscribers had no claim if anything went wrong.

Thomas Brodrick, a businessman who like Hutcheson was suspicious, said to Lord Middleton on 13 September that he thought the Directors, 'with their fast friends the Tories, Jacobites and Papists', had 'drawn out in good time ... Thousands of families will be reduced to beggary'.

The Directors themselves were beginning to panic, and asked the

East India Company for a merger. Prime Minister Walpole used his influence to set up a meeting with the Bank of England, which sent the stock up for a week or two. Sir Gilbert Heathcote, one of the Bank's founders, would give no definite assurance of rescue. Could the Sword Blade Company help? No: it was bankrupt. Besides, Heathcote said, 'if the South Sea Company is to be wedded to the Bank, it cannot be allowed to keep a mistress'.

The Bank did nothing, because there was nothing it could do. Wild rumours broke out, and the hunt for scapegoats began. Alexander Pope was one of thousands who lost their investments (in Pope's case, only half): with more oil than vinegar, he told the Bishop of Rochester on 23 September: 'methinks God has punished the avaricious'. John Gay, who had been given some shares by Craggs, could have sold for £20,000 (Dr. Johnson tells us) but did not—he lost them all, and did not recover his fortunes until the success of *The Beggar's Opera*. Thomas Guy, on the other hand, had sold out for £234,000 before mid-June and so could afford to endow Guy's Hospital. Guy was a broker who specialized in Seamen's Tickets, the paper vouchers with which the Navy was paid instead of cash. He used to buy them cheap and convert them at the Treasury.

Walpole himself had speculated on a vast scale, sold out at the top of the boom, made a fortune with which he rebuilt his stately home at Houghton, and started his collection of pictures. Guided by him, the Prince of Wales had bought £20,000 stock and sold at a high price. So did the Duke of Argyll. But Sir David Hamilton, the Royal physician who had delivered many of Queen Anne's nineteen children, lost £80,000 through hanging on too long.

'Director' had become a dirty word: at cards, the Knave was called the Director. In cartoons, Directors were often represented as foxes. Hogarth's first caricature was on the South Sea Bubble.

It was noted that four of the thirty-one Directors were M.P.s— Theodore Janssen, Francis Eyles, Sir Robert Chaplin, and Jacob Sawbridge. A Mr. Walker had already moved in the House of Commons 'that a Committee be appointed to address the Parliament, to bring to justice the betrayers of their country'. In the House of Lords, a peer, finding that there was no law for punishing Directors, wished them to be tied up in socks and thrown into the Thames.

Not until 4 January 1721 was a really specific motion put before the House of Commons. Sir Joseph Jekyll, M.P. for Lymington and

Master of the Rolls, proposed: 'That leave be given to bring in a Bill for restraining the Sub-Governor, Deputy-Governor, Directors, Treasurer or Cashier, and Accountants of the South Sea Company from going out of this kingdom for the space of one year, and until the end of the next session of Parliament; and for discovering the estates and effects, and preventing the transporting or alienating the same.' William Shippen, M.P. for Newton and a Jacobite, said he was prepared to name 'some men in great stations' who were 'no whit less guilty' than the Directors. James Craggs (the younger) was unwise enough to stand up in the House and challenge Mr. Shippen to a duel.

A week later the names of a Committee of Secrecy were announced to investigate the Bubble. The Chairman was Thomas Brodrick; the other members were Archibald Hutcheson, William Clayton (M.P. for Bletchingley), Edward Jeffreys (M.P. for Droitwich), Sir Joseph Jekyll, Nicholas Lechmere (former Attorney-General), Lord Molesworth (M.P. for St. Michael, Cornwall), Sir Thomas Pengelly (Serjeant-at-law and M.P. for Cockermouth), General Ross (M.P. for Ross), William Sloper (M.P. for Bedwin), Colonel Thomas Strangeways (M.P. for Dorset), the Hon. Dixie Windsor (M.P. for Cambridge University), and the Hon. Edward Wortley Montague (Lady Mary's husband, and M.P. for Westminster).

What was the Committee *for*? To 'roast the South Sea Directory' —or to 'ingraft South Sea stock upon the stocks of the Bank and the East India Company'? If the latter, then, wrote Lady Elizabeth Lechmere to Lord Carlisle, it would be 'two months' stockjobbing, and then all sink together'. But the public wanted blood. Lord Stanhope had moved 'that the estates of the criminals, whether Directors or not, ought to be confiscated to make good the public losses'.

Yes, but who *were* the criminals? One made himself obvious: on 23 January, Robert Knight, Cashier of the South Sea Company, fled in disguise to Calais, leaving a letter in which he admitted 'indiscretions' but not guilt. The key witness was already gone.

Orders were given to seize the books of Knight, Robert Surman (Deputy-Cashier), John Grisby (Accountant), Elias Turner & Co. and Sir George Caswell & Co.; and to arrest Sir John Blunt, Sir John Lambert (Directors), and Sir John Fellowes (Sub-Governor). The House of Commons quickly expelled the four Director-M.P.s. The same evening, John Aislabie, Chancellor of the Exchequer, resigned. £2,000 reward was offered for the capture of Knight, who was now in Antwerp castle, from which he could not be extradited. (He eventually escaped to Paris, and was pardoned twenty-one years later.)

The Committee, after sitting behind locked doors, said in the first of seven reports that books had been falsified, and fictitious stock distributed to members of the Government to induce them to pass the South Sea Bill. The Earl of Sunderland (First Lord of the Treasury) had had £50,000, Mr. Secretary Craggs £50,000, Charles Stanhope (one of the Secretaries to the Treasury) £250,000, and Aislabie's account showed an enormous profit of £794,451.

What kind of man was this Aislabie? 'A man of good understanding,' says a contemporary, 'no ill speaker in Parliament, and very capable of business; but dark, and of a cunning that rendered him suspected and low in all men's opinions'. When examined, he pleaded ignorance, blaming the Directors. Unfortunately he had burnt the books showing his own dealings. He was found guilty of the 'most notorious, dangerous and infamous corruption', expelled from the House and committed to the Tower. His imprisonment was celebrated by bonfires in the City. All the property he had acquired since becoming Chancellor of the Exchequer was confiscated, though he was allowed to keep his estate at Studley Royal. Possibly Walpole's plea 'that it would seem hard to put a person of Mr. Aislabie's eminence and distinction on the same level with the Directors' had something to do with this mitigation. Walpole himself was only acquitted by sixty-one votes.

Sir George Caswell, head of a jobbing firm, tried to blame the absent Knight (it was he who had sold stock to Charles Stanhope, who was given the benefit of the doubt and acquitted by three votes). He was expelled from the House and joined Aislabie in the Tower while his estates were held liable for his illegal profit of £250,000. There was daily uproar in Parliament: the Duke of Wharton and Lord Stanhope attacked each other so fiercely that Stanhope broke a blood vessel and died next day. The younger Craggs died of smallpox (aggravated, gossip says, by a drinking-bout at the Duke of Newcastle's). His father, not long afterwards, fell into 'a lethargick fit' and died, either of sheer terror or suicide, before his examination. A potentially brilliant man, he had risen from small beginnings. Most of his £1½ million estate went to alleviate ruined shareholders.

Among those (relatively) ruined men were the Duke of Portland, who had to ask for the Governorship of a distant colony. The price of lodgings in Bath fell as impoverished holiday-makers hurriedly left. Lord Lonsdale applied for the Governorship of the Leeward Islands, and Lord Irvine for Barbados—tantamount to exile.

The investigations dragged on through March and April 1721—and still there was talk of 'hanging the Directors', still nothing had been done about the National Debt. First, public fury had to be appeased. Surprisingly, the South Seas Directors' estates were valued at only £2,014,123. Sir John Blunt, whose 'petition of innocence . . . moved the House to laughter', was allowed to keep £1,000, despite a motion that he 'should have but a shilling'. Francis Hawes, Cashier of the Customs, was allowed to keep the odd £31 out of his £40,031 estate. Not until 29 July did the South Sea Sufferers' Bill receive Royal Assent.

Following the broad application of Walpole's original suggestion, that the Bank of England and the East India Company should take over £9 million each of South Sea stock, the Company continued to trade under its new Directors. It was never very successful. Seven years after the Bubble, it fitted out twenty-three ships, not for the South Seas, but for the Greenland Whale Fishery: they returned with only eighteen whales. In 1732, twenty-one ships brought back only twenty-four whales. In the eight years between 1724 and 1732, it made a loss of £177,782. Its trade with America was always obstructed by Spain and by its own dishonest agents. Only one ship, the *Royal Caroline*, ever made a decent profit—£70,000 in 1733, with a cargo of pieces of eight, cochineal, and indigo. In 1748, by the Treaty of Aix-la-Chapelle, the Port of London lost the slave-trade (which however still went on from Bristol and Liverpool); and the South Sea Company ceased to be a trading company. It meandered on for more than a century, dealing in Government securities, and Charles Lamb, who was a clerk in 'the South Sea House' in the 1790s, gives it a somnolent personality typified by an accountant named Tipp, who always had plenty of time to practice the violin in office hours.

# 5

## Wrote Over The Door

'One must go into the market as into a cold bath—quick in and quick out.'
—SALOMON ROTHSCHILD (1774-1855)

The typical business man's day, in the first quarter of the eighteenth century, has been described for us by one Ned Ward in *The Wealthy Shopkeeper* (1706). He has little time for his wife and family. He gets up at five, spends three hours in his counting house, and then has breakfast (toast and Cheshire cheese). He looks after his shop or office for another two hours, then goes to a coffee-house for news and gossip. Back to the shop for a short while, then upstairs for dinner at twelve on 'a thundering joint'.

At one o'clock he goes to the Exchange, or perhaps 'Change Alley, and at three he is in Lloyd's Coffee House 'to read the letters and attend the sales', and if he is in insurance, to transact business; dashes back to the shop for an hour, then to another coffee-house for relaxation, then to a 'sack shop' for a drink with friends; then home for a light supper and so to bed, 'before Bow Bell rings nine'.

If he is interested in the stock market, he will call at Garraway's to see the latest quotations, which since 26 March 1697 had been published by John Castaing, a broker, who had an office at Jonathan's before moving to Garraway's, where the list (*The Course of the Exchange and Other Things*) was produced by his son. A single sheet, ten inches by four, it gave more than twenty prices, including India Stock, Hudson's Bay, gold, silver, wheat, red and white rye, barley, oats, and cochineal; and it was issued on Tuesdays and Fridays. Castaing's sister continued it after his death from an office in Pope's Head Alley, Cornhill, in partnership first with Richard Shergold and later with Peter Smithson, both brokers. This, in an unbroken line, was the ancestor of the present *Stock Exchange Daily Official List*.

In an age that had as yet no pubs and clubs, the coffee house was a social leveller. It served wines, spirits, sandwiches, biscuits, and cheese. Each tended to have its speciality: you went to Will's, near Covent Garden, to meet writers and critics, to the Grecian for philosophers, to White's Chocolate House to gamble. In City coffeehouses men of all ranks met to do business 'as if they had left their quality and degrees of distance at home'. Lloyd's already specialized in shipping and marine insurance: there was a rostrum for auctions and for reading out shipping news. At the time of the South Sea Bubble, company promoters advertised that shares were on sale in about thirty different taverns and almost as many coffee-houses.

Historians tend to regard the Bubble as having 'crippled the joint-stock company' for the next half-century. Economists lean rather to the view that joint-stock ventures were no longer very much needed. Unless you wanted to start a bank, an insurance company or a waterworks, or dig a canal, there was little incentive to seek money by subscription. Most industries were still at the local or cottage level, and could be financed by one man's capital.

The modern idea of healthy competition had not yet been born, and there was a feeling that few businesses were really safe unless their owners had a monopoly.

However, there were always 'the funds'. The Premiership of Walpole gave the country twenty-one years of peace. For the rest of the century we were generally at war, and the National Debt, although Walpole managed to reduce it by over £6 million, was over ten times larger at the end of the century than it had been at the beginning. There might have been a market in foreign lotteries, but these were forbidden—they savoured too much of Bubbles. There were also a few foreign loans, which Walpole tried to regulate by an act requiring a royal licence for engaging in such business. The occasion was a request from the Emperor Charles VI for a loan of £400,000. There had been other loans to Spain, Chile, Peru, Russia, Austria, Portugal, Brazil, Mexico.

We had much bigger business of our own, brought about by bigger and costlier wars which banks alone could not finance. Lotteries were often the bait by which investors were persuaded to put their money into 'the funds'. After the South Sea Company was reorganized, 'the

41

funds' yielded 4 per cent. The issue of a Government 3 per cent annuity in 1726 had a lottery attached. There were a number of these 'carrots' during the next hundred years: sometimes lottery tickets were given away free like trading stamps; sometimes the subscriber bought his tickets cheaper in proportion to the amount of his investment; sometimes annuities were offered as well.

The year 1781 gave us a word which most people with a television set today associate with Uncle Timothy Forsyte: 'Consols'. Prime Minister Henry Pelham, better at sound finance than at prosecuting war, gathered together several 3 per cent annuities into 3 per cent Consolidated Bank Annuities, destined to become the largest part of Britain's 'funded debt' right up to 1914, and to be known ever after as 'Consols'.

The War of the Austrian Succession had raised the National Debt to £71 million, and we had just entered the Seven Years' War which was going to make it £128 million. These were 'modern' land-and-sea wars, almost 'world' wars in their ramifications—India, Canada, the West Indies, all mixed up with privateering at sea—which may indeed have 'laid the foundations of the British Empire' (do not ask which school history book this comes from) but were damnably expensive. Could the Government go on borrowing at 3 per cent? It seemed not (though if you already held 4 per cent stock, you could buy Reduced Annuities at 3½ per cent up to the end of 1787 and 3 per cent thereafter).

Sir John Barnard, in that same year of 1787, brought in a bill to convert 4 per cents to 3 per cents. One of the reasons why it never succeeded was the fear that it would hit the smaller investor. Already lists of shareholders were revealing a preponderance of holdings under £1,000 (there were 17,196 of them), and the typical small investors of the next century—the trustee, the widow, the businessman putting by for his retirement—were already emerging.

So was a new kind of stockbroker—the Government contractor, who had to tender against others for the right to sell Government stock, usually bought a block of it for himself, and was able to guarantee a number of subscribers in advance. The Bank of England, the South Seas Company, the East India Company, other banks, and smaller stockbrokers were among them. This tight little network made for fairness and the protection of the small investor. The best-known banker-contractor of this era was Sampson Gideon, an extremely popular Portuguese Jew who was to be seen every day at Jonathan's Coffee House, and whose claim to fame was the coolness with which he had bought cheap during the panic of 1745, when it was feared that the Young Pretender would march on London to unseat the House of Hanover.

Gideon (whose real name was Abudiente) was one of about a dozen Jews who were allowed to practise as brokers (normally brokers had to be Freemen of the City). He probably worshipped at the Sephardic Synagogue of Bevis Marks, which had been built in 1701. His was one of many foreign accents to be heard in coffee houses and 'Change Alley. Others were Dutch, and went to the new Dutch church in Austin Friars. There was already a firm connection between the Amsterdam Bourse and the London stock market, and a large proportion of British government loans (more than a third) was held by Dutch investors. The Netherlands were losing prosperity, and the Dutch, and Dutch Jews, who arrived in London during the second half of the eighteenth century had much to offer the City—including capital, for they were not rags-to-riches immigrants.

They added new words to the jargon of the stock market. One was *rescontre* or *rescounter*—settling day every three months, following the practice of the Amsterdam Bourse. *Contango* also appears at about this time: no two dictionaries agree on its derivation. It may come from the Spanish *contante*—ready money, or it may be connected with the words 'continue' and 'contingent': it means commission which the buyer of stock pays to the seller to postpone transfer to the next settling-day. The words 'bull' (one who buys for a rise), 'bear' (one who speculates for a fall), and 'lame duck' (a defaulter) were in common use, the first two dating back to the first decade of the eighteenth century. 'Backwardation' can be traced to 1755, when there was a little boom in 'funds', and 'bulls', instead of paying for contango facilities were being paid, while 'bears' were doing the opposite.

Meanwhile, how was Average Stockbroker faring? He still had to take the oath, sign a bond, and receive a medal from the City of London. The same Sir John Barnard, who failed to cut 4 per cents down to 3 per cent, had succeeded in 1733 in getting through Parliament a stringent bill 'to prevent the infamous practice of Stockjobbing'. This title was less insulting than it sounds. It was designed to stop any kind of dealing that was 'in the nature of a wager' or which involved 'any premium or consideration' that inflated stock or might give rise to the dangerous nonsense of the Bubble. Whether you were a broker or not, you were liable to a fine of £500 if you entered into any such arrangement, and another of £500 for selling stock which you did not actually possess, and another £100 for 'knowingly executing' such a contract. It caused temporary fury in 'Change Alley, because time-bargains were what many brokers lived on. It was full of loopholes, and difficult to enforce, but it does seem to have discouraged wild speculation by increasing brokers' risks.

It had one useful and important by-product: the need for, and importance of, trust and a good City reputation, which would one day be expressed in the Stock Exchange motto: My Word Is My Bond. Once you had been expelled from Jonathan's or Garraway's, you might still be able to pick up a little business here and there, but you were out in the cold.

The stockbroker's 'image', however, had not improved very much. Ever after the South Sea Bubble, satire still pursued him. We do not know how seriously to take *The Bubbler's Mirrour of England's Folly*, first published in 1725, which used the technique of mixing fact with fiction. Were there really quotations for companies for the bleaching of hair, the insurance of horses, manufacturing radish oil, curing the gout and stone, importing Italian padlocks, extracting butter from beech trees, insuring against divorce? How was an 'air pump for the brain' supposed to work? Why should not somebody seek money to develop 'a flying engine', which was only two centuries away? Or to 'trade in human hair', in an age of wigs? Did it really require a capital of £1 million 'to provide a wheel of perpetual motion?' Yes, it probably did.

The brokers, feeling the need to become a profession, began to close ranks. It really wasn't good enough, popping in and out of coffee-houses and taverns, sheltering from the rain in 'Change Alley, Birchin Lane and Lombard Street, where one could be button-holed by all sorts of riff-raff. The Bank of England had (in 1765) built a Rotunda where dealers in government funds apparently made so much noise and ragged the unhappy clerks so unmercifully that they occasionally had to be thrown out. Clearly, as in so many businesses, the faults of the few brought disrepute on the many. Incredibly, this sort of thing went on well into the 1830s.

Besides, there was a new school of thought which regarded brokers as an unnecessary evil. Its voice was one Thomas Mortimer, in a book called *Every Man His Own Broker*.

Mortimer is valuable if only as a source of information about the stock market in the latter half of the eighteenth century. He was a regular customer at Jonathan's, and while we need not take his dislike of brokers too seriously, his general advice on investment is sound: 'Never remove your money at a loss but in cases of absolute necessity; but, instead of believing idle reports of bad news, wait patiently till the situation of public affairs has brought your stock to the value at which you bought it, or higher. . . . Never follow the advice of a man who would persuade you to be continually changing the situation of your money, for he is certainly influenced by some private motive.'

The 'better sort' of brokers therefore formed a club, with a (for those days) fairly hefty subscription of £8 a year. There were 150 of them, and for their benefit Jonathan's Coffee House became, for a year or two, all their own. Unfortunately, they were not legally covered against gate-crashers. Old customers of Jonathan's no doubt felt they had the right to go there for refreshment, whether they were members or not, and one of them sued the management for wrongful ejection and won his case.

A decade later, we find the brokers in a building of their very own at last. It seems to have been known as 'New Jonathan's'—possibly because Old Jonathan's had been burnt down; but there had been several disastrous fires in the district, the worst in 1748, and it is not clear whether the proprietors were the same. It was in Threadneedle Street; there does not appear to have been a fixed club subscription, but there was an entrance charge of sixpence a day.

This was the first building actually to be known as *The* Stock Exchange, and it is confirmed by the *Gentlemen's Magazine* of 15 July 1773: 'Yesterday the brokers and others'—and others, notice—'at New Jonathan's came to a resolution that instead of its being called New Jonathan's, it should be called The Stock Exchange, which is to be wrote over the door'.

That which is 'wrote over a door' tends to become established. There were two committees, one representing the coffee-house owners, the other—called, historically, the Committee for General Purposes—representing the customers or members. As membership does not seem to have been defined, it is difficult to see how they were elected except by the personal recommendation of friends. Who were those 'others' if they were not brokers? We do not know. The Stock Exchange, shakily enough, existed; and in this form it continued for nearly thirty years.

# 6

# Funds and Founders

'It makes a strange confusion now that brokers are so
much concerned in the events of war. How Scipio would
have stared if he had been told that he must not demolish
Carthage, as it would ruin several Aldermen who had
Punic actions!'

—HORACE WALPOLE (1761)

We have seen the social mixture of the coffee-houses. It could also
be said that the joint-stock company was bringing the landed
aristocracy closer to the business middle class. 'The landed magnate,'
Trevelyan says, 'could, without becoming that abhorred thing, "a
tradesman", meet on the board the City man and act with him, so
that the political influence of the one could be joined to the business
brains of the other.' Banks, especially outside London, had sprung
up, some of them small family concerns, but still useful sources of
capital for middle-sized enterprises.

Some of these banks were owned by Quaker families, such as the
Gurneys of Norwich: 'honest, quiet, liberal and peace-loving, they
had a steadying effect on the excitable violences and Jingoisms of the
financial world'. Richardsons, Barclays, Overends, Frys, Lloyds,
Hoares—'the silence in meeting,' says Paul H. Emden, the Quakers'
historian, 'is such that the drop of an eighth in Consols is clearly
audible'.

The Jews, too—many of them from Amsterdam—brought their
particular virtues to the City, and especially to stock-broking. The
Jew, says C. R. Fay, 'was ubiquitous and enterprising, persistent but
not pugnacious; he ran after customers without regard to his
dignity. . . . For international finance the Jews had a special bent,
overcoming by their tribal bonds the boundaries of nations, and yet as
individuals retaining that mental detachment which is so necessary to
financial analysis.'

47

In 1770 Levi Barent Cohen arrived in London from Holland. One of his daughters married Nathan Mayer Rothschild, who came to England in 1798, and another married Moses Montefiore. Other Cohens married Samuels, and a son married the niece of Abraham Goldsmid, one of the Government loan contractors and a spectacular financier who, however, took one risk too many, crashed in 1810 and committed suicide, having first entertained his creditors to a banquet at his Surrey house. His cousin Isaac became the first Jewish baronet, and his grandson became the first Jewish barrister.

All these families had moved to London between 1750 and 1800. By 1850 many of them, says Chaim Bermant in *The Cousinhood*, would have become 'nature's own Victorians, pious, God-fearing, high-minded worthies, industrious, sober, practical'.

Jews and Quakers got on well together, formed companies together, even (in the case of David Ricardo) intermarried—having abandoned the Jewish faith, Ricardo became a Unitarian and married a Quaker.

Cazenove, de Zoete, Antrobus, Capel, Vigne, Ricardo—familiar City names were beginning to appear among the broking and banking concerns of the last few years of the eighteenth century. Many of them banked with Coutts, and there seems to have been a two-way traffic of personnel between banking and broking, probably because the Stock Exchange used brokers to distribute Exchequer bills. In 1777 one of the three Edmund Antrobuses (all from Cheshire), perhaps yearning for security, gave up his broking business and joined Thomas Coutts; he afterwards wrote thus to Coutts: 'I would much rather hold the respectable situation of a partner in your House, and the power of serving my friends, with half the money I possess, than to have continued in the City with three times the sum . . . but I was fully sensible of the advantages I was giving up'.

London was now on the way to becoming the financial capital of the world. The foreigners who settled here came, not as ragged immigrants, but bringing money with them. In the seventeenth century, as we have seen, London had begun to compete in international finance with Antwerp, Amsterdam, Genoa, and Venice. Now only Amsterdam survived as a serious competitor, and when Napoleon's wars cut off continental Europe from most international trade, they were only completing the claustrophobia which many European finance houses were feeling. In Britain, *laissez-faire* was the order of the age; the expansion of British economy in the Industrial Revolution was producing a reserve of wealth which could be used for financing the City's activities at home and abroad.

Foreign businessmen liked the liberal, tolerant, informal way in which commerce was conducted in London. They brought to London, among other things, long experience and international connections. They paid well for intelligence: there was a highly-organized secret news service during the Napoleonic wars. While Napoleon tried to exclude British trade from Europe, a merchant ship carrying contraband goods to a French or Dutch port would often sail back with information from an agent abroad; and if you had a Dover office, you could sometimes get news ahead of your rivals and make appropriate purchases on the Stock Exchange.

How did Britain finance the Napoleonic Wars? Our National Debt after the War of American Independence stood at £243 million. William Pitt proposed in 1786 to reduce it by a Sinking Fund, an idea which had been suggested by William Paterson and tried by Walpole in 1716, but which Pitt seems to have got from a moral philosopher, Dr. Richard Price, who in 1772 had published *An Appeal to the Public on the Subject of the National Debt*. It would nowadays be regarded as bad economics, but it commanded great public confidence at the time. It also brought a lot of business to the Stock Exchange.

The Commissioners for the Reduction of the National Debt were to invest the same sum of money every year in government stock, and then to re-invest the interest in more stock, and to go on doing this until there was no more National Debt. The sum to be invested was £250,000. Benjamin Cole, who had been a stockbroker for nearly twenty years, was appointed broker, and was told to invest not more than £5,000 at a time, buying as cheaply as he could. However, he had to get through his £250,000 in a year, so he could seldom choose his time according to the state of the market. It was an interesting scheme, but did very little to pay off the Debt. And it is historically significant, because Benjamin Cole was the first Government Broker, and his firm—which survives today as Mullens & Co.—still performs this office.

The Debt was destined to reach the breath-taking total of £820 million by 1815. Unlike the Sinking Fund, it did not bring much business to members of the Stock Exchange. The contractors handled most of it—firms like Boyd, Benfield & Co., who parcelled out the shares to the Bank of England, the South Sea Company, other bankers and smaller brokers. Sir Francis Baring & Co. and Sir J. Esdaile & Co. were other contractors. As they had to tender for contracts, they were at considerable risk, and were not above manipulating the market by rumours: we have seen what happened to one of them, Abraham Goldsmid. However, it was possible for members of the Stock Exchange to form a syndicate, as David Ricardo did with Messrs. Barnes and Steers. They managed to get the whole of the 1807 loan and farmed it out to their Stock Exchange colleagues (who seem to have numbered 222). So pleased were their friends that all three were presented with silver vases, which must have been pretty large, since Ricardo's was engraved with a 68-word testimonial of 'unanimous approval of his conduct as joint contractor on that occasion, whereby the just and equitable principle of mutual participation between contractor and subscriber has been so manfully asserted. . . .'

In the last three years of the War, the competitive tender system seems to have broken down, and contractors found it less fatiguing to share the business out among themselves.

We left the Stock Exchange, at the end of the last chapter, in its new premises in Threadneedle Street, on the corner of Sweetings Alley opposite the Post Office. Its organization, we have seen, was informal if not vague, and by the turn of the century there was a general feeling that things could not go on like this. Something more practical, and better financed, was needed. The records show a resolution, dated 7 January 1801, 'for converting the Stock Exchange into a Subscription Room'. The two Committees—the Proprietors and the General Purposes—were merged into a United Committee, under the chairmanship of John Barnes, which drew up rules and instituted a ballot system for electing members, who were to pay an annual subscription of ten guineas. On Friday 7 February it was shut down as 'the Stock Exchange', and on Tuesday 3 March it reopened as 'the Stock Subscription Room'.

Among the rules was one which imposed a fine of two guineas for 'disorderly conduct'. The fines, rather like a swear-box, were to go to charity. What 'disorderly' meant is not altogether clear, but in its anxiety to 'preserve the most respectable character' the Committee had obviously excluded certain faces it did not like. It is not difficult to imagine the resentment of old customers of New Jonathan's who had not been elected to membership, and, as had happened at Jonathan's, there was probably a certain amount of gate-crashing.

Worse, there was trouble on the Committee itself. The amalgamation of committees has seldom promoted harmony, and the new Chairman, a senior stockbroker named John Battye who had done well out of the 1796 loan (Boyd, Benfield had allowed him £93,000 worth), led a number of resignations over a case of 'disorderly conduct'. We do not know exactly what happened, but there seems to have been a row between Proprietors and members of the old General Purposes Committee, largely about voting rights on the election of members and on the making of new rules.

Perhaps inevitably, the United Committee broke down. It had made certain regulations: had these regulations any validity if the Committee no longer existed? Instead, the governing body, without the Battye group, seems to have been called simply 'Proprietors of the new Stock Exchange'. Various little groups met in odd corners, trying to smooth over the breach between resigners and stayers, apparently with little success.

All this in-fighting seems to have happened in about two days; for on 4 March 1801, the first full meeting of the new senior management took place at the Antwerp Tavern. The chairman was now William Hammond, who seems to have played it cool, since we hear little of him (except as a member of the old General Purposes Committee) until now. With him were John Barnes, John Bruckshaw, John Capel, William Grey, Isaac Hensley, Griffith Jones, Thomas Roberts, William Steer, and Robert Sutton.

It is odd that David Ricardo was not among them: he had been active in Stock Exchange affairs until now, but in recent weeks had been a frequent resigner. It may be that, successful stockbroker though he was, and still only 30, his economic theories were unpopular. As his subsequent writings show, he was critical of the funding system, believing that nations should pay their debts rather than raise loans. He held heterodox views on the relationship between wages, profits, and the cost of food. He thought bank notes were depreciating, and that the Bank of England was inefficient. One supporter of the spirit of the age, self-help and *laissez-faire*, called him 'that stupid, bothering stockbroker'. However, we find his name among the ordinary members of the Committee, together with such famous names as Antrobus and Ellis.

51

The meeting was told that because the present Subscription Room was 'too small for the accommodation of the members who frequent it' and could not be extended, a new building had been acquired in Capel Court, Bartholomew Lane. It would cost about £15,000 to buy and convert, and the money was to be raised by 300 shares of £50 each, of which no one was to have more than four. Leaning over backwards to be decent, the committee wrote to the old Proprietors 'that the interest of the Old Proprietors of the Stock Exchange should not be forgotten, and we therefore offer to you, as managing proprietors, one hundred shares, being one third of the new concern'.

The old proprietors, to whom this was so much workhouse Christmas pudding, replied, with a curtness seldom found in contemporary business correspondence, in a single sentence: 'I am directed by the Proprietors of the Stock Exchange Subscription Room to inform you that they decline accepting your offer of 100 shares'. This letter was signed 'E. Wetenhall'—Edward Wetenhall, who, sixteen years before, had taken over from Peter Smithson the publication of the official Stock Exchange list of quotations, *The Course of the Exchange*, which appeared twice a week.

Soon the estimated cost, like so many estimates, had risen to £20,000. The Committee needed more land than it had thought. There would have to be a certain amount of demolition and alteration of adjacent buildings. Daniel Mendoza's boxing room next door, unfortunately, would have to go. This Portuguese Jewish middleweight prize-fighter had, seven years before, been defeated by Gentleman Jackson, a heavyweight who numbered Lord Byron among his pupils, and who was allowed by the rules of those days to grab Mendoza by his long hair in order to deliver the knock-out blow. Mendoza, generally called 'the first scientific boxer', famous for his lightness on his feet, taught young noblemen—and no doubt young stockbrokers—the art of bare fisted self-defence.

If it was sad to lose Mendoza's boxing room, it was pleasant to be able to enter, and leave, the new Stock Exchange building by the Hercules Tavern, which had to be adapted for the purpose, and served as a ready-made members' bar. The two official doors gave on to Capel Court, in Bartholomew Lane, and New Court, in Throgmorton Street.

At the Capel Court door an old woman kept a stall where she sold buns and other refreshments; but she soon retired because, she said, 'the Stock Exchange is such a wicked place'. Probably members needed more solid fare, and it seems to have been about this time that they formed the habit of bringing their own chops and steaks, which were grilled at a nearby cookshop for a penny, vegetables and bread being provided free.

The design of the new building was dominated by the lofty Exchange room, which was surrounded by a gallery furnished with desks, chairs, and bookshelves, mainly for the use of clerks, who, we are told, to save time and energy, threw books down to their masters on the floor when required, rather than use the stairs. The gallery was supported by pillared arches above the trading floor. There was a special 'pitch' for the Reduction of the National Debt, and a notice board for 'lame ducks'.

On 18 May 1801 the foundation stone was laid. It was made of copper, and would have been lost to posterity had not additional vaults been constructed in 1883. Frequenters of what we now call the 'old' Stock Exchange will remember some stairs (between the Boer War memorial in the South wall and the Great War memorial in the West wall) leading to the strong rooms. It was down here that the original foundation stone was at last discovered. It recorded that 'at this era, being the first year of the Union between Great Britain and Ireland, the Public Funded Debt had accumulated in five successive reigns to £582,730,924', and ended—with a time-capsule message for the future, if ever there was one—'the inviolate faith of the British nation and the principles of the Constitution sanction and secure the property embarked in this undertaking. May the blessings of that Constitution be transmitted to the latest posterity.'

The names of the founders follow—the ten names we have already noted (including poor Mr. William Grey, who had meanwhile died), and also James Peacock, the architect. The wording emphasizes that the building 'was erected by private subscription for transaction of business *in the public funds*'. The *Gentleman's Magazine* in 1802 gives a list of stocks dealt in—Bank Stock, Consols, Navy, Long and Short Annuities, India Stock, India Bonds, Exchequer Bills, Funds, South Sea Stock, Old Annuities, Omnium (parcels of stocks offered, as incentives, with loan stock), Irish 5 per cent, Imperial 3 per cent, English lottery tickets, English prizes. Foreign funds business, however, still went on in the Royal Exchange, and continued so until 1822.

These original ten managers, with twenty-one other Committee members, were men of foresight who 'put their financial world on a paying basis'. They disclaimed any intention of creating a monopoly for their 500 members. They resisted attempts of others to bring in legislation opening the Stock Exchange to all and sundry, on the grounds that they did not wish to 'shelter convicted defaulters and afford new facilities to the criminal designs of notorious and unprincipled gamblers'.

Writing to the M.P. for Lancaster, John Dent, in 1810 to thank him for his support in Parliament, John Hammond, the Chairman, refers mysteriously to 'the treachery of Mr. Hemming, who has been ignominiously dismissed'. John Hemming was the Secretary of the Committee: he had been extremely inefficient for about eight years, but there seems to have been a curious lack of vigilance. Was it really treachery? A sub-committee, chaired by Francis Baily, was appointed to inquire into his activities, or lack of activities: it consisted of William Hammond, Charles Nairne, Francis Wakefield, Charles Laurence, Benjamin Oakley, and Marmaduke Langdale.

'Your Sub-Committee,' it reported, 'experienced considerable difficulties, owing to the very loose and careless manner in which the minutes of the Committee for General Purposes were kept by the late Secretary, Mr. John Hemming. Not only are the transactions of the several meetings entered in the book in the most slovenly and disgraceful mode, with such frequent interlineations and erasures as to render the subject extremely doubtful and confused, but likewise many resolutions appear to have been passed by the Committee which have never been entered on the journals.'

Sins of omission, certainly, to the impoverishment of our history. Why were they not discovered before? Did not the Secretary read the minutes of each last meeting, so that they could be 'signed as correct'? However, an excellent young man called Robert Watson Wade was found to succeed Hemming, and it is not long before we find a resolution praising his 'zeal, assiduity and abilities', which are described as 'voluntary and gratuitous', during the period of the Hemming investigation.

Perhaps it was this fiasco that made the Committee want to look closely at the whole constitution of the Stock Exchange, or it may have been the reappraisal that revealed Hemming's 'treachery'. Anyway, in 1811 a sub-committee, consisting of the same seven members as the Hemming sub-committee, was appointed to 'inspect the journals and papers of the Committee to make extracts of those rules and regulations they may think worthy of being preserved as the fundamental laws of this house, and to propose such new rules, or such alterations in any old rules as they may think ought to be adopted for the good government and safety of the members of this house'.

The sub-committee began by examining the original Deeds of Settlement of the old Threadneedle Street Stock Exchange, and made them 'the foundation of all the subsequent proceedings of your sub-committee'. They then considered all minutes and records of the old Exchange from 19 December 1798 to March 1802, and also of the new Exchange up to the present. Every possible resolution, every case-history which might serve as a precedent was sifted. The result, boiled down to a short list, was unanimously adopted by the General Purposes Committee on 17 February 1812. It forms the basis of the rules governing the Stock Exchange today.

Those rules fixed the admission and conditions of membership, which resembled those of a respectable club, and made the point that neither members *nor their wives* must engage in any other business. Since the middle of the last century there had been an increasing trend towards specialization. We read of a Mr. Morgan Vaughan of Finch Lane, Cornhill, who was in business during the 1760s as a 'hatter, hosier and stockbroker', and as late as 1814 a Mr. J. M. Richardson was said to be 'a bookseller, but occasionally acting as a stock-broker'. This suggests that some existing members *were* allowed to go on trading in other directions.

But for new members the rules of entry were strict: you had to be put up by two members; your name was posted on the notice board; objections, if any, were sent to the Committee within eight days before the ballot.

There were rules about dealing with non-members and disputes over bargains, which were to be settled by arbitration; and failures must be publicly announced (on the notice board under the clock) so that the 'lame duck's' assets could be fairly divided among his creditors. (There had been a crude 'defaulters' board' as long ago as 1787, when there were twenty-five failures.)

There were rules about the recording of quotations, and an 'earnest recommendation' about speculation. 'Those gentlemen of the Stock Exchange who transact business on commission for time' were asked

c                                      55

'to regulate the extent of such dealings (unless with sufficient security) as much as possible by their own ability to fulfil their engagements: being of opinion that every material deviation from this rule (unless for persons of well known property) is nearly as unwarrantable as if they had entered into such speculations on their own account.'

There was, finally, one of those despairing recommendations which keep cropping up in Stock Exchange records, that members should give up 'rude and trifling practices which have too long disgraced the Stock Exchange'. What were they? The kind of horseplay we shall see again a century later? Or the wilder japes which caused the resolution of 2 February 1818, 'respecting the disgraceful practice of knocking off hats'?

Speculation, in an age of slow and unreliable communications, could still get out of hand. There were two main kinds of rumour: 'Napoleon is dead' and 'the French have invaded'. When in 1797 it was reported that French troops had landed in Wales, 3 per cent Consols fell from $97\frac{1}{4}$ to $47\frac{3}{8}$. Six years later, Lord Hawkesbury repeated to the Lord Mayor a forged report that the negotiations at Amiens had succeeded. Funds shot up from $63\frac{3}{4}$ to $71\frac{1}{4}$. The Committee of the Stock Exchange closed the doors of the House pending confirmation; then declared all bargains void, and offered a reward for information about the forger.

We have seen that some smart brokers found it worthwhile to keep an agent in Dover in an effort to get earlier news from the Continent. As almost the only person making news at this time was Napoleon, and the 'funds' financing our conduct of the war affected many thousands of investors, the breathless arrival on 21 February 1814 at the Ship Hotel, Dover, of a Colonel du Burgh in full red uniform, announcing 'the fall of Paris' and the death of Napoleon, was sure to rock the Stock Exchange.

Du Burgh was nothing if not circumstantial. He was, he said, A.D.C. to General Lord Cathcart. He had crossed the Channel in a French ship, *L'Aigle*, whose master he named as Pierre Duguin. He vividly described the final battle: Napoleon had been butchered by Cossacks, who had actually cut up his corpse and 'divided it between them'. All this he told to the Port Admiral at Dover, desiring him to semaphore the news to London. But the weather was too foggy for the signals to be seen, and so 'Colonel du Burgh' went by coach, which he had planned to do anyway.

He was in fact one Charles de Berenger, and his middle name was Random. He had brought with him handbills announcing the 'news', and threw them, followed by handfuls of French money, into the crowds as he drove along his prearranged route—London Bridge, the City, and Blackfriars Bridge. This, we are told, 'sent Omnium up six points' (it was down to 27½ after the Battle of Montmirail). The scheme was not as successful as he and his fellow-conspirators had hoped, but they sold over £700,000 of stock at a profit of £10,000.

Peanuts, you may think, comparing it to the enormous deals of the South Sea Bubble. The Stock Exchange, having offered a reward of £250 for the discovery of 'du Burgh', appointed a sub-committee of inquiry of its own, and on 24 March posted a notice in the House announcing that a Thames waterman had brought them pieces of a red uniform such as Colonel du Burgh was said to have worn. Could any member give further information? 'It does not appear that any Member of the Stock Exchange has been implicated in the knowledge or participation of a measure which would have inevitably rendered him liable to expulsion from the House'.

With its own hands clean, the Stock Exchange demanded a public inquiry, and sought the help of the Government and the Bank of England. Two of the names involved were Members of Parliament, Admiral Lord Cochrane and his uncle, the Hon. Cochrane Johnstone. All the defendants were sentenced to twelve months' imprisonment and fined £1,000.

Most students of financial history assume the guilt of Admiral Cochrane. The judge, Lord Ellenborough, obviously disliked him, and was no doubt prejudiced by the fact that Cochrane disdained to be present at the trial in Guildhall, and only defended himself with any vigour in an attempt to get a re-trial.

Lawyers think differently. Sir Travers Humphreys, in his reminiscences, points out that during his lightning coach tour of London de Berenger called at Cochrane's house at breakfast time, but found he had gone to see his uncle. Would he not have avoided all contact with de Berenger for a few days if he had been guilty? He had freely admitted to the Stock Exchange Committee that he knew de Berenger. (This was, in fact, the first time the Committee had ever heard of the man, and it enabled them to prosecute.) In an affidavit Cochrane had described de Berenger as wearing a green uniform, not a red one. Was there not a reasonable doubt . . . ?

Was it, indeed, likely that the Admiral would risk his reputation for such a small gain? 'His name,' said his biographer Fortescue, 'will go down to history printed in capital letters by the side of Nelson's, Collingwood's, and Exmouth's.' He had commanded the *Pallas*, a 32-gun frigate, in the year of Trafalgar; he was the hero of the Basque Roads attack on the French fleet; he was M.P. for Westminster, and had radical views on election bribery; he would one day fight for Chile against Spain, for Brazil against Portugal, plan to use steamships in the Greek war of independence, invent new processes for gas, tar, tubular boilers and screw-propulsion, the use of smoke-screens in war; reinstate himself in the Navy, and be buried in Westminster Abbey.

This was the man whom Lord Ellenborough imprisoned, fined and ordered to be exposed in the pillory at the Royal Exchange between 12 and 2 p.m. (He was in fact spared this indignity by the personal intervention of the Prince Regent.)

Had he really benefited by 'the rise in the funds'? The Cochranes, like everyone with money to spare, had gambled heavily on the rise or fall of Government Stock. We know that on 21 February 1814, the day of 'du Burgh's' appearance at Dover, Lord Cochrane had £139,000 of stock which he had bought on 12 February at a premium of 28½. He had given instructions to sell on a rise of one per cent, and it was sold on an average at 29½ premium. Guilty or not guilty? The reader must decide for himself.

When, at last, the Battle of Waterloo was won, the Funds did not react as violently as might have been expected. Is it true that the Rothschilds, instead of buying Consols, sold and sold, and then quickly bought while the panic was on? Is it true that they were the first to know, through their agent Mr. Rothworth in Ostend? Was there really a carrier-pigeon bearing the message *il est mort* in cipher? (Many brokers *did* use pigeons, but they only really worked in good weather.) It is an attractive story, and excellent film material. The sober facts are that in January 1815 Consols stood at 66; in June they went down to 54, and by Christmas they were up to 60 again. Perhaps too many people had cried wolf too often.

# 7

# Persons of Known Respectability

'With loves and doves—at all events,
With money in the Three Per Cents.'
—BROWNING

How, meanwhile, was Average Investor getting on? He, or she, was probably a fundholder (there were about 250,000 of them) receiving an annual interest of £200 or less. Many fundholders, like the good ladies in Mrs. Gaskell's *Cranford*, had no other source of income. William Cobbett denounced them as 'bloodsuckers eating the taxes of the people', almost as objectionable as stockjobbers. Landowners, clergymen, retired officers, farmers, were among their number.

We may search contemporary fiction in vain for much reference to investment—it was after all vulgar to talk about the *sources* of money. Jane Austen tells us that Miss So-and-So, with her £10,000, is considered quite a catch; people's wealth is measured by their property, and everyone knows how much that is worth. Old Mr. Woodhouse, subsisting on lightly-boiled eggs and thin gruel, must have had a good deal of money invested, but in what? Young Frank Churchill disappears to London to buy Jane Fairfax the unsuitable gift of a piano, but we do not hear that he called on his broker while he was there.

Most of these fundholders would have had their money in 3 per cent Consols, which were by far the most popular of the four principal Government stocks. (Lord Stowell, admiralty judge and friend of Dr. Johnson, famous for the phrase 'a dinner lubricates business', praised 'the elegant simplicity of the three per cents'.) The more adventurous investors might also have a few shares in canals, docks, roads, waterworks, or—if they were pure visionaries—in the Gas, Light & Coke Co, which had been founded in 1810. If you lived in the

59

provinces, say Cheshire, you might be more interested in canals than a London investor would be. The Chester Canal in 1777 offered the first preference shares on record.

But you would not necessarily have bought your canal shares through a member of the London Stock Exchange. When the Duke of Bridgewater in 1761 wanted to transport coal from his mines at Worsley, Lancashire, to Manchester, eleven miles away, he borrowed £25,000 from Child's Bank, added the rest of the cost from his own money, and engaged James Brindley, a man who could barely read and write, to dig a canal: he never bothered to form a company.

To build the Grand Junction, linking the Mersey with the Trent and the Severn, Josiah Wedgwood the potter and his friends had to raise more than £1 million. This still did not mean that the company was necessarily quoted on the Stock Exchange: in some cases, canals were financed by local shareholders. However, as more and more canals were built, and the dividends were seen to be good, the shares came to market, and the early 1790s saw a boom in them: in three years, there were eighty-one Acts allowing canals to be built.

Once you have started a canal, you have to finish it. What we should now call 'feasibility studies' generally under-estimated costs, fresh capital was invariably needed, and the speculation was such as to constitute a warning for the future—a warning that had not the slightest effect half a century later when the country was plunged into the Railway Boom. Many brokers outside the London Stock Exchange did well out of canal shares: the Kennet & Avon Canal Co. shares were sold mostly at the Exchange Coffee House in Bristol and Garraways in London.

Coal had stimulated the first canals, and coal likewise brought the first railways—horse-drawn, or operated by steam winches. Soon the steam-engine would take to wheels, and a whole new era of speculation would open—much of it well outside the Stock Exchange.

But the Stock Exchange, determined to preserve the standards it had set itself in the 1812 rules, was suspicious of everything except the funds. There was still a good deal of broking business done at the Bank of England, the Royal Exchange, 'Change Alley and coffee-houses. Unauthorized brokers, with lower standards of practice and no inhibitions about advertising, were having the effect of a kind of Gresham's Law; not actually driving out the good coinage, but debasing it.

One hopes (but does not really believe) that members of the Stock Exchange were not the direct target of Cobbett's diatribe in *Rural Rides* (1823). 'Mark the process,' he snarled. 'The town of Brighton, in Sussex, fifty miles from the Wen, is on the seaside, and is thought by the stockjobbers to afford a salubrious air. It is so situated that a coach which leaves it not very early in the morning reaches London by noon. . . . Great parcels of stockjobbers stay at Brighton, with the women and children. They skip backwards and forwards on the coaches and actually carry on stockjobbing in 'Change Alley though they reside at Brighton.'

Members of the Stock Exchange could say with a clear conscience that they had relatively little to do with the outbreak of dubious company promotion in the ten or twelve years following the battle of Waterloo. In 1827 a stockbroker named Henry English published a report on all joint-stock companies set up in 1824 and 1825, which were boom years. There were 624 of them, seeking £372 million. Some were for enterprises abroad, especially mines; others for canals, railways, and new insurance companies. Less than a quarter of them survived, and many of these failed to raise enough money. There were rigs and corners and bubbles, and one recorded case of a member being expelled by a special Stock Exchange subcommittee for forging share certificates in the Lower Rhine Steam Navigation Company.

Two famous insurance companies date from this time—the Guardian and the Alliance, both backed by big banking names such as Baring, Rothschild, Gurney, Montefiore: they joined the respectability of the Atlas and the County Fire Office, founded during the Napoleonic Wars, and were approved of by the Stock Exchange.

Foreign loans had become an increasing problem after 1815. Should they be quoted on the Stock Exchange or not? They were to be regarded with caution, and the greedier investor should perhaps be protected from them—if indeed you can ever protect a greedy investor. Barings had been handling American securities for some years. Boyd, Benfield had raised a loan for the Austrian Government in 1796, and when it went wrong, it went through the usual process of being merged with the National Debt. Barings were said to be making millions out of French reparations, and the Rothschilds handled loans for both Russia and Prussia. No authentic record of the Rothschild family has ever been published, but they are believed to have raised

£100 million for the European governments during the Napoleonic War—Nathan in London, Anselm in Frankfurt, Salomon in Vienna, Karl in Naples, and Jacob in Paris. They all became barons, with the right (in Germany and the Habsburg Empire) to use 'von' before their names.

Brazil, Peru, Mexico, Colombia, Chile, Argentine, Guatemala—all sought loans. Then there was Greece, seeking independence from Turkey. The British upper classes, with their classical educations, have always tended to be what have been called 'boo-hoo Phil-Hellenes' —and the bad Lord Byron was their figurehead in 1821. There was an inadequate £800,000 loan issued in 1824, and another £2 million in 1825. There was to be an expedition led, as we have seen, by Lord Cochrane, who demanded an enormous sum for leading it. All the Greeks got was two ships and the original £200,000.

As if the dismal experience of his fellow-Scot William Paterson in Darien had never happened, the 'Cacique of Poyais' suddenly appeared in London. 'Cacique' means three things in Spanish: political boss, one who leads an easy life, and native chieftain. Gregor MacGregor no doubt wished to be the second, but for the present claimed to be the first and third. His victims were mostly his own countrymen. He had invented the fertile, gold-paved land of Poyais, which was in fact an area of malarial swamp in what we now call British Honduras. He did not actually own any of it, but published travel brochures and sold parcels of land to would-be colonists, who went there and were never heard of again. The swindle would hardly be worth recording but for the fact that the Stock Exchange found itself involved: it somehow failed to show its new-found vigilance, and members dealt in a loan of £200,000 at 80 per cent. The South Sea Bubble was threatening to ride again. . . .

Foreign loans were destined to make London the first financial centre of the world; but not yet. In the years following Waterloo, they were dealt in, often by non-members of the Stock Exchange, on the floor of the Royal Exchange. Why should not they be offered at the Stock Exchange, in conditions of respectability? Six brokers, all members of the Stock Exchange, therefore wrote to the Committee in July 1822 saying that they were 'fully sensible to the advantages of dealing with persons of known respectability', and had 'experienced the want of an open fair market for Foreign Securities'; might they, please, have such a market inside the Stock Exchange, which would 'afford great convenience and profit to the House at large'.

This letter was supported by another, in September, signed by thirty members, some of them representing stockbroking firms with such eminently respectable names as Vigne, Marjoribanks, Capel, Sir John Easthope, and Allen.

They had not long to wait. After taking legal advice as to whether they could allow it under their Deed of Settlement, the Committee gave their permission on 4 October. But now came the old troubles of committees and membership rules. The foreign loan dealers seem to have taken it for granted that they would be allowed to form their own Foreign Stock Market Committee straight away. But how could they, unless certain rules of the existing Stock Exchange were bent? Some of the foreign dealers engaged in business other than stockbroking. Some of the existing Stock Exchange Members were tempted to cut themselves a slice of the foreign securities boom, but were forbidden to. Discussions went on until March 1823, when the constitution of the Foreign Stock Market Committee was settled and eighty-nine members were admitted. Others followed, and the membership at full strength seems to have reached about two hundred.

Two years later, the boom showed signs of faltering, there were resignations from the Foreign Stock Exchange, and the remaining members humbly begged to be allowed to join the Stock Exchange. They were even willing to give up their own Committee. There was fresh trouble over the rules, and a new ruling that there should be three classes of membership, those with five years' membership, those with three, and those with less. The General Purposes Committee had, besides the enforcement of rules and professional ethics, another worry: the House was simply getting too crowded. A separate Foreign Room for a declining number of foreign dealers was a luxury that could not be afforded, and in 1835 it was abolished.

Was this wise? Many foreign loans had gone wrong, but some of the business was sound, and some of the best of it tended to go to merchant banks and country banks, by-passing the Stock Exchange altogether.

There was a little panic in 1835 over Spain and Portugal, with the simultaneous revolts against Don Carlos in Spain and Dom Miguel in Portugal. Portugal was already in default, yet she received £2,800,000 in loans while Spain got £4 million.

For a time, it looked as if America was the direction in which foreign investment ought to go. Names not heard of in financial circles since the Bubble and Law began to dominate after-dinner conversation: Louisiana, Michigan, Mississippi, Florida; there were not many issues, but they seemed to be doing sound things, such as building railways and canals, just like us. The names of far-off places fascinated a certain type of investor, just as Muscovy and Bombay and the Spice Islands had done centuries before. The collapse of the Second Bank of America started a chain reaction of disaster. Individual States defaulted with little more than a shrug, and there were wretched bondholders who had been waiting for up to twenty-five years for a dividend.

But listen to the Rev. Sydney Smith, Rector of Combe Florey, Somerset, a co-founder of the *Edinburgh Review*. No lover of stock-jobbers, he was yet grateful, in his old age, for the money he had inherited from his brother Courtenay—'After buying into the Consols and the Reduced, I read Seneca *On the Contempt of Wealth*'. But when the State of Pennsylvania, in which he had a modest investment, repudiated its debt, his fury knew no bounds. In a series of letters to the *Morning Chronicle*, he said that America had become 'the common sewer of Europe, and the native home of the needy villain . . . This new and vain people can never forgive us for having preceded them 300 years in civilization.' No doubt they wished to start another foolish war? 'The warlike power of every country depends on their Three per Cents. If Caesar were to reappear upon earth, Wetenhall's list would be more important than his Commentaries; Rothschild would open and shut the Temple of Janus; Thomas Baring, or Bates, would probably command the Tenth Legion, and the soldiers would march to battle with loud cries of "Scrip and Omnium, Consols, and Caesar!" '

But now the Americans, in the whole habitable globe, could not borrow a guinea, and could not draw a sword because they had no money to buy it. If they came to Europe, they ought to wear a uniform with 'S.S.' on it, to show they came from Solvent States.

'And now,' he concluded, echoing the feelings of hundreds of disappointed British investors, but displaying just as little wisdom, 'having . . . sold my stock at 40 per cent discount, I sulkily retire from the subject, with a fixed intention of lending no more money to free and enlightened republics, but of employing my money henceforth in buying up Abyssinian bonds, and purchasing into the Turkish Fours, or the Tunis Three-and-a-half per Cent Funds.'

# 8

## It's Quicker by Rail

'Railroads will only encourage the lower classes to move
about needlessly.'

—THE DUKE OF WELLINGTON

Sydney Smith died in the year of the Railway Mania, 1845. He had
on the whole welcomed railways, especially the Great Western, which
had reached Somerset three years before. It enabled him to get to
London in six hours, instead of a three-day coach journey: 'Railroad
travelling is a delightful improvement of human life. Man is become
a bird; he can fly longer and quicker than a Solan goose. The mamma
rushes sixty miles in two hours to the aching finger of her conjugating
and declining grammar boy. The early Scotsman scratches himself in
the morning mists of the North, and has his porridge in Piccadilly
before the setting sun.'

But people would, drunk or sober, step out of trains while they were
moving, and the Great Western insisted on locking carriage doors
between stations, so that if the train caught fire, you would see
'bishops done in their own gravy', or 'three ladies of quality browned'.
Sydney Smith, so far as we know, had no railway shares: he stuck to
Consols.

Not so the very much poorer Brontë family. Brother Branwell, of
course, had actually held down a job for a few months as a clerk on
the Leeds & Manchester Railway, and in his sober intervals should
have been able to warn his sisters about railways as an investment.
The three sisters had been left £350 each by their aunt Miss Branwell.
It was Emily who insisted on investing it; Charlotte who worried
about the wisdom of doing so. Writing to her old schoolmistress and
friend Miss Wooler on 30 January 1846, Charlotte says: 'I thought

65

you would wonder how we were getting on, when you heard of the railway panic, and you may be sure that I am very glad to be able to answer your kind inquiries by an assurance that our small capital is as yet undiminished. The York & Midland is, as you say, a very good line; yet, I confess to you, I should wish, for my own part, to be wise in time. I cannot think that even the very best lines will continue for many years at their present premiums, and I have been most anxious for us to sell our shares ere it be too late, and to secure the proceeds in some safer, if, for the present, less profitable investment.'

The trouble was that her sisters, especially Emily, who had been managing the family finances while Charlotte was away in Brussels, would not agree. Emily was always the one for hanging on too long. Three years later Charlotte is telling her publisher Mr. Smith that the shares have gone down so far that she dare not tell her father: 'Many, very many, are by the late strange railway system deprived almost of their daily bread'.

Commenting on this, Charlotte's biographer, Mrs. Gaskell, says: 'They were in the York & North Midland Company, which was one of Mr. Hudson's pet lines, and had the full benefit of his peculiar system of management'.

The case of George Hudson (it was Sydney Smith who called him the Railway King) is worth examining in some detail if only because he exposed all the contemporary weaknesses of company law and accounting, and in the end produced a strong and historically important reaction from the Stock Exchange.

In 1846, the year of Charlotte Brontë's despair, Hudson already controlled 1,450 out of Britain's 5,000 miles of railway. The son of a farmer at Howsham, Yorkshire, and uninhibited by education, he was apprenticed to Bell & Nicholson, drapers, and in true Room-At-The-Top style married the boss's daughter, Elizabeth Nicholson, who was five years older than himself. Somewhere along the line he inherited £30,000 which he was determined to use for not only promoting, but *amalgamating* railways. This was one reason why his defenders have claimed that Hudson gave his country 'much of the benefit of a railway *system*, in place of a railway *anarchy*'.

At the age of 33, in 1833, we find him establishing a joint-stock bank, the York Union Banking Co., which would operate, with the help of Glyn's bank, in London as well as in the North. For a man who had taken as his slogan 'Mak' all t'railways coom t'York' this was far-sighted. It was assumed from the start that people wanted railways because they wished to travel (hardly anyone visualized railways being used for freight, for which canals were thought to be adequate). There had to be railways—it almost didn't matter where they went. But it mattered to George Hudson: he was about to build an empire in which railways, docks and industry were all inter-connected and linked to banking, landed property and, finally, his own political career, both local and national.

He built big new docks at Sunderland and Monkswearmouth and Hull. He became director and principal shareholder of a glass works at South Shields (to make glass roofs for stations), and had an interest in George Stephenson's collieries at Clay Cross. He was a wholesaler of iron, reselling to his own and other railway companies.

In London he had a City office to guide his brokers in buying and selling shares which he wanted to push up or down the market—not only in London but also in York, whose own local stock exchange was founded in 1845. His City office also ran rumour and intimida-tion campaigns to further his amalgamation schemes or discourage rival interests.

He developed Scarborough and Whitby as holiday resorts, and bought a great deal of land in the East and North Ridings so that rival railways should not have it. He became a Member of Parliament largely in order to pilot his own railway bills through. He was part-owner of the *Yorkshire Gazette*, the *Sunderland Times* and the *Railway Chronicle*, thus buttoning up press approval of his actions.

At the time when Hudson started the York Union Bank, the joint-stock company was becoming popular again. Was there not some-thing democratic about it, in tune with the Reform Bill? It seemed the best way to ensure strong banks and well-built railways. Railway companies were attracting the capital of middle-class merchants, tradesmen, landed gentry, doctors, and lawyers. They liked the feeling that they were voting shareholders who could actually take part in running the companies, even if that participation consisted largely of 'applauding extravagant estimates, then urging parsimony, and always shouting for dividends'.

How were these early railways financed? Henry Burgess, secretary of the Country Bankers' Committee, thought that they had 'ad-vanced ... almost wholly without the assistance of the Stock Exchange'. (He was writing ten years before the Boom.) The money was coming from big local industrialists, who advertised the issue of shares, held local enthusiasm meetings, sought loans from local banks, and enlisted the aid of provincial stock exchanges which were now springing up. Yet we know, from Wetenhall and London Stock Exchange records, that Burgess was not entirely right about this. The Birmingham & London Railway (1833), the Liverpool & Manchester Railway (1825) and the Grand Junction Railway which linked them, all issued shares which were dealt in on the London Stock Exchange. For one thing, railway company promoters liked to have London stockbrokers' names—Hammond, Hichens, Moxon, Hanbury, Peppercorne—on their prospectuses.

However, the atmosphere was speculative, and there were reasons why the Stock Exchange should be wary. There were charges of 'allotment rigging'. There was an alarming amount of business done at coffee-houses and in the street after the Stock Exchange had closed. And a new word joined the Stock Exchange vocabulary: *stag*, one who applies for an allotment of shares without any real intention of keeping or paying for them.

One important effect of the Railway Boom was that share-owning spread more deeply into the provinces than it had ever done before. As with canals, small investors took an intense interest and pride in their local railways.

Having founded his Bank, Hudson got John Rennie, the engineer of London Bridge, to survey the country between York and Leeds. Rennie was all for railways, but could see no long-term future in steam: he recommended horses. Possibly Hudson shared these thoughts at first, but after he had met George Stephenson while on holiday at Whitby, he was a steam man for good. He managed to raise £300,000 for the York & North Midland Railway, mostly in London. The £50 shares started to attract speculative attention in 1836, with a premium of £4 on each. Hudson was Chairman of the company, and by now also Lord Mayor of York. The new line was opened on 29 May 1839, with 12½ columns of publicity in the *Yorkshire Gazette*. The Minster bells were rung in his honour. There were a few brawls, due partly to the Liberals, who were anti-railway; but in most respects Hudson was at the height of his regional popularity.

On 6 June 1840, there was a grand ceremonial opening of the whole North Midland line. Henceforth you could travel from York to

London (217 miles) in ten hours, and there were four trains a day. During the following year there was a fatal accident—and a 6 per cent dividend. Certain shareholders began to get worried: they could not understand the accounts—could auditors please be appointed?

Hudson behaved in a hurt, even shocked, manner: did they not trust the directors to do their own auditing? One shareholder, who happened to be a director of the Great North of England Railway, said solemnly: 'Nothing, next to religion, is of so much importance as a ready communication'.

Hudson might own the *Railway Chronicle*, but the *Railway Times* could say what it liked, and it was turning satirical: in October 1843 it invented a new opera called *Midas*, whose opening chorus, 'to be sung at a *grand amalgamation* meeting', went—

> 'George, in his chair,
> Of railways Lord Mayor,
> With his nods
> Men and gods
> Keeps in awe.'

There was a growing suspicion that railways were over-capitalized and wastefully constructed. There was criticism, on the grounds of both humanitarianism and safety, of the fact that Hudson used boys to work the points. He replied that he used boys because they were cheaper. In his *Latter-Day Pamphlets*, Thomas Carlyle, who disapproved of so much, looked back on railway promotion with the wisdom of hindsight: 'You find a dying railway: you say to it, live, blossom anew with scrip; and it lives, and blossoms into umbrageous flowery scrip . . . Diviner miracle what God ever did?'

'I consider Mr. Hudson a shrewd, *honest* man,' said a correspondent in the *Railway Times*, 'but for pity's sake, sir, call the attention of shareholders to the sway this person is obtaining.'

Branch lines were considered very saleable. In recommending one to Scarborough, then only a fishing village, from York, over a stretch of flat country with very little population, Hudson warned investors that of the nineteen railways authorized by Parliament in 1836, only three had kept their shares above par. One of these was his York & North Midland, whose shares were at a premium. Would investors neglect a chance like this? A branch line of a proven success? Nobody listened to a disgruntled shareholder who called it 'the calving of the cow'.

But Mr. Gladstone, President of the Board of Trade, was feeling uneasy. In February 1844 he set up a Committee of Inquiry into railways. He agreed with George Hudson on the virtues of amalgamation, but he would go further—almost to nationalization. The Railway Bill he proposed wanted third-class fares to cost only a penny a mile; but the sting in its tail was a provision that the Government should be able to purchase certain lines after twenty-one years.

Hudson meanwhile had opened thirty-nine miles of a new Newcastle & Darlington Junction Railway with all his growing flair for publicity. On 18 June, the anniversary of Waterloo, trains from all directions converged on Darlington, including one from London, 303 miles away, bringing copies of that morning's issue of *The Times*. Everyone then repaired to a six-hour banquet in Newcastle.

Down in London, the Stock Exchange was also uneasy. The York & North Midland wanted to buy the Leeds & Selby line. Hudson had told York & North Midland shareholders that to raise the necessary capital he was going to create 6,700 £50 scrip-shares which he would offer them in proportion to their original holdings. He would 'guarantee' a 10 per cent dividend, but at first would call up only £15 per share. By temporary borrowing he reckoned he could pay 6 per cent on capital not yet called up. What happened? Something very curious. The shares rose—and were sold to a group of Hudson's friends. Speculators on the London Stock Exchange who had been 'bears' suffered considerable losses.

To get a quotation on the Stock Exchange, railway promoters had to show that three-quarters of their capital was already subscribed. There were quick, ruthless methods of doing this: shares were given to the contractors who were going to build the line, and it was said that in order to secure the names of Members of Parliament on prospectuses, they too were given parcels of shares.

To bring in new premiums, promoters kept pushing branch lines. The interests of promoters and investors were drifting wider and wider apart. Shareholders like the Brontës just wanted a safe investment. Preference shares were issued; but only the richer shareholders could afford them, and the poorer ones, who had the biggest stake in profitability, bore the biggest risk. They cannot be blamed, because no proper accounts were published. In 1849, when the Government

auditors inspected railway accounts as best they could, they concluded that promoters habitually raised more capital than they
needed.

*Punch*, which had jeered at railways from the start, (but seems not
to have been read at Haworth Parsonage) said on 8 March 1845:

> 'Believe me, if all those extravagant lines
> They talk of so wildly today,
> Were each made in the way its projector defines,
> They're none of them likely to pay.'

But *Punch* was a London magazine, and York and London did not
trust each other. Hudson seemed genuinely surprised that anyone
should want to go to London at all, except on business.

The mere rumour that Hudson wanted to buy a line sent its shares
up. In 1843 the £100 shares of the Great North of England line were
quoted at a discount of £40. Two years later they rose to a premium
of £45. The total earnings of the line were only £75,000 a year—yet
he wanted £3½ million to buy it. Why? Because amalgamation was
for the public benefit and this was supposed to justify the whole
operation. It was about this time that Hudson, to float another
scheme, boasted: 'I'm going to ask the shareholders to give me 2½
millions of money, and I won't tell a soul of them what I'm going to
do with it!'

The sum he sought to raise for the London & York Railway in
1844 was £4½ million. The prospectus said it would go from Penton-
ville through Barnet, St. Neots, Peterborough, and Lincoln. Hudson,
who bragged that his legal advisers were costing him £3,000 a day, was
simultaneously piloting other railway bills through Parliament, some
of them for extending the Midland by branch lines to the east. He also
found time to obstruct the Committee appointed to examine Mr.
Gladstone's Bill: it sat for seventy days in a small, hot, fetid, temporary room near the new Houses of Parliament which could not be
used because they were still being built. Lord Brougham, who
thought it quite improper that Hudson should be there, remarked:
'The only Sovereign entitled to be present is Her Majesty'.

Matters were not helped by Hudson's discovery that there were a
number of oddities in the subscription list for the London & York
Railway: £29,000 worth of shares had been earmarked for persons

who had no addresses; £44,000 for people who had no property qualification; and the son of a charwoman had been put down for £12,000.

Thus ridiculed, he returned to Yorkshire, to the Sunderland Conservative Association, whose chairman praised him as a public benefactor who had 'provided business for the citizen, employment for labour, trade for the shopkeeper, and markets for our manufacturers'.

He now bought estates in his home county so that his sons George, John, and William could all become country gentlemen: Octon, near Bridlington, with more land at Baldersby, in the North Riding. In two weeks (September 1845) he bought two more stately homes—Earl de Grey's Newby Park, next to Baldersby, and the Duke of Devonshire's 12,000-acre Londesborough Park (costing £500,000) where he planned to build his own railway station, reckoning that any railway from York to Hull must pass through it.

More trouble, this time on the 150-mile Eastern Counties line from London to Norwich. It was badly run, and shareholders were angry. Hudson took over as chairman, and proposed to solve everything, Bubblewise, by issuing £4½ million of Eastern Counties Extension Shares. Extending where? To Yarmouth, no doubt. One extraordinary feature of the whole boom was the apparently unlimited willingness of banks to lend money for railway investment. Economists of the time seemed to reason that anything which created a demand for labour, employed plenty of solicitors, stockbrokers, and estate agents, and gave rise to twenty new railway magazines must of itself be good.

*The Times* did not think so. It warned its readers that schemes for new railways would need £200 million—'more than the whole public revenue'. Consider the figures: in 1844, 1,950 miles of railway were in operation and 800 more had been approved at an estimated cost of £20 million; in 1848, 2,150 miles were open, and a further 2,700 planned with a capital of £59 million; in 1846, 2,400 miles were open, and 4,500 more were planned at a dumbfounding cost of £132 million. (One of the reasons *The Times* attacked Hudson, it is said, was the belief that he had a financial interest in Charles Dickens's *Daily News*.)

The Government now asked for more facts and figures. They showed that a cross-section of people who had invested more than

72

£2,000 in railways included, besides land-owning aristocrats and big industrialists, 900 lawyers, 364 bankers, 287 clergymen, and 157 Members of Parliament.

The bubble began to break when Bank Rate was raised in October 1845. The Board of Trade moved in swiftly and fixed 30 November as the last date for new railway prospectuses. There was an indecent rush of 800 promoters; but already frightened investors were rioting in Preston and Mansfield, and others were madly trying to get to London by coach or train. (One train, folklore claims, set up an average speed record of 78 m.p.h.)

In all this pandemonium, Hudson posed, and was accepted by many people outside London, as the only stable element. His admirers got up a £30,000 testimonial for him. Among the subscribers were Emily and Anne Brontë, who gave £1 each. Charlotte did not contribute.

It was time, Hudson now felt, to conquer London. He moved into Albert House in Knightsbridge, which was then still a kind of Green Belt suburb. The mansion, built by Sir William Cubitt, cost £15,000 and he spent nearly as much again on decoration and furnishing. He enjoyed a kind of film-star fame (but, Lady Dorothy Nevill said in her memoirs, 'the Hudsons were never in Society'). There were sniggers about Mrs. Hudson's Malapropisms, and their daughter was having a bad time at her Hampstead finishing school because of her accent.

The Duke of Wellington called on them: his sister's railway shares were doing badly, he said; could anything be done? Hudson bought into the company, the shares went up, the Duke's sister took her profit. In gratitude, the Duke called on Miss Hudson in Hampstead, and the accent mattered no more.

Meanwhile, George Hudson had been elected Lord Mayor for the third time: Yorkshire's Dick Whittington. (His Sheriff was G. T. Andrews, who had built many of the stations on his lines.) This no doubt consoled him for the appalling state of the Midland Railway (£30 million liabilities) and the Eastern Counties (£13½ million liabilities). He tried to boost the latter by a publicity stunt—a special train to Cambridge for Queen Victoria and the Prince Consort, who was Chancellor of the University. 'Beautiful,' said the Queen. 'Most gratifying.'

The year 1848 was a terrible one in Hudson's life. His enormous exertions and too many banquets were producing warning symptoms of heart disease. His old friend George Stephenson died. In the autumn, railway shares began to plummet. He found himself in the classic company promoter's hell of robbing Peter to pay Paul, it was discovered that he had 'lent' nearly £150,000 belonging to three northern railway companies to the Sunderland Dock Company, apparently not knowing that, apart from the duty of informing shareholders, he was supposed to have Government permission to do it.

It was now that the London Stock Exchange moved in for what seemed to be the kill. Two members, Horatio Love and Robert Prance, both shareholders of the York, Newcastle & Berwick Railway, set a trap for Hudson. They had done a great deal of homework on him, and were planning a surprise visit to the annual general meeting in 1849. They had noticed, about eight weeks before, an anonymous letter in the *Railway Times*. Whoever was the author of the letter seemed to have had access to Hudson's books. He wished to remind shareholders of the Great North of England Railway that Hudson had promised them that they would be paid off at £250 for every £100 share. But how could this be, since, to the writer's certain knowledge, the money raised for this purpose had in fact been used to pay for new construction work on the York, Newcastle & Berwick line?

Mr. Prance and Mr. Love looked at each other with a wild surmise, and asked that most scientific and creative of all questions, *Why*? In the best tradition of the Stock Exchange on the warpath, sharpened by their personal anxiety as shareholders, they minutely examined all the York, Newcastle & Berwick figures they could get hold of, and found that some of the shares had been bought at absurdly high prices. Why? Why had £15 shares been bought at £23 10s? Combing through old Stock Exchange lists they noted that since 1846 these shares had never stood higher than £21.

*Why*? asked Prance and Love; and this time they were putting the question at a shareholders' meeting, and putting it to Chairman Hudson himself. 'The company says it has bought 3,790 shares,' said Prance, spokesman of the duet. 'I am sure that no more than the odd hundreds were bought by the public, so that *someone* has received great benefit by selling them at this extravagant price to the Company.'

Hudson's attitude was one of bored impatience—a man with his many interests could hardly be expected to carry all the details in his head—but, yes, he *had* 2,800 of the shares, he believed, and if there had been 'a slight overcharge' it was probably the fault of his co-director Nathaniel Plews.

Not good enough, said Prance; and he insisted on a Committee of Investigation. Hudson retreated to Newby Park; no, he would not see anybody, nor could he be contacted through the new electric telegraph he had installed because it was unfortunately out of order. There was no law under which he could be prosecuted so the Prance Committee made him buy back the shares he had sold and make good the losses, all of which cost him £9,000.

Meanwhile another Committee of Investigation had been set up, this time into the Eastern Counties company. The chairman was William Cash, a Quaker, who arraigned Hudson in the language of the seventeenth century: 'Didst thou ever, after the accountant had made up the yearly accounts, alter any of the figures? Wilt thou give the committee an answer, yea or nay?' What had happened to a sum of £9,000 described in the accounts as 'Parliamentary expenses'? Was it by any chance the same £9,000 used to appease the Prance Committee? Mr. Cash found it difficult to press this point, as he had been accused of political bribery himself. But he attacked everyone within sight—directors, auditors, even shareholders—they *all* knew the accounts had been cooked to raise the value of the shares.

'How was Midas ruined?' asked Bernal Oxborne, M.P. 'By keeping everything but his accounts.'

The *Railway Times*, which was in a splendid position to say, 'I told you so,' on 30 September looked back in anger: 'From the fall of dividends . . . and continual pressure of calls, the distrust of railway property became such that towards the autumn of 1849 large masses of it were practically unsaleable. The retrospect of the third quarter of 1849 is the most dismal picture that it has ever been our duty to lay before our readers. Gloom, panic and confusion appeared to have taken possession of the railway market, and a commensurate depression in the value of all lines, good, bad and indifferent, has been the result. . . . Within the last few weeks the stock of the London & North-Western Company has fallen 20 per cent. . . .'

Everything now went wrong for Hudson. His brother-in-law Richard Nicholson drowned himself in the river Ouse. Why? His York bank manager was suddenly dismissed. It was discovered that

Londesborough Park had been bought with York & North Midland money. Newby Park was sold. Albert Gate became the French Embassy. Greville, in his *Journal*, wrote of Hudson: 'In the City all seem glad of his fall, and most people rejoice at the degradation of a purse-proud, vulgar upstart'.

In August 1855 he went to Spain to build a new railway, but fell ill again. The following year found him taking a cure in Germany. In 1857, incredibly, he managed to get re-elected M.P. for Sunderland, just before the Sunderland Dock Co. finally failed. His daughter Anne married a Polish Count, his son John was killed in the Indian mutiny.

Hudson, gouty and on crutches, commuted between London and Paris to evade creditors. Showing his face in Whitby, he was arrested for debt and jailed for three months in York Castle. But he still had a few friends, and they subscribed to buy him an annuity, and, best of all for his self-esteem, enabled him to rejoin his old London club, the Carlton, where he was elected 'Chairman of the smoking room'. He lived on until 1871, and was buried in the family grave at Scrayingham, Yorkshire.

Crook or genius? Both? George Stephenson never stopped trusting him; of the Quakers, very active in railway promotion, only William Cash ever attacked him. His biographer, R. S. Lambert, says: 'He had acted neither better nor worse than the directors of hundreds of other railway companies at the time'. Company law being still in its infancy, he was never prosecuted. Like Bottomley after him, he claimed that he had been misunderstood, that his only weakness was carelessness about detail. Today he would have been jailed for misappropriation of shares, and publishing false balance sheets.

Even after his downfall, Gladstone called him 'no mere speculator, but a projector of great discernment, courage and rich enterprise'.

From the viewpoint of the Stock Exchange, all was not lost. The Committee had, in 1847, brought in a new rule which was a direct result of the Railway Mania: it concerned Special Settlements, and enforced fixed dates for payment for shares bought, and for delivery of shares sold. Somehow, the railway market was already stabilizing itself even before the disappearance of Hudson. The *Stock Exchange Official List* in 1845 quoted 280 different railway shares. By 1849 there were only 160. George Hudson and his rivals had started something that was eventually to serve both investors and members well—Home Rails, for many years 'the safest thing next to Consols'.

# 9

# Home Notes and Foreign Loans

---

'The trouble in this world is not caused by what people
don't know, but what they do know that ain't so.'
— JOSH BILLINGS, American sage

In more than one way, George Hudson was the expression of what
was happening to industry in the mid-nineteenth century, in the later
stages of the industrial revolution. It was no longer possible for one
man to start a railway—or any other concern needing that amount of
capital—as a father to son to grandson family business. Railways
never found their Sainsburys—they had to 'go public' from the start.

Family firms tended to lose their vitality in the third generation; to
become inefficient, however comfortable; to need a new kind of
management. Mr. Gladstone's view that railways, established by Act
of Parliament, would eventually need to be controlled by the State
was beginning to extend to other public utilities—gas, tramways,
local government bodies, electricity.

The stage was set, in fact, for the Limited Liability Company.
Company law was being tightened up in an effort to prevent fraud, and
even in the middle of the Railway Boom the 1844 Companies Act had
made compulsory the registration of all new joint-stock companies. It
also tried (not very successfully) to stop dealing in shares before
registration—a longish process—had been completed. From the viewpoint of industry, what was lacking in company organization was
what we now call professionalism of management. Professor
Trevelyan sees it as 'a step . . . towards collectivism and municipal and
State-managed business'. A Marxist might even see it as a step
towards 'the confrontation of capital and labour'.

A new class of shareholder was emerging—one who knew very little of the company he or she was investing in beyond its financial reputation. These shareholders were dependent on their dividends; often they had no other source of income, and it is possible to see the growth of comfortable seaside towns like Eastbourne and Bournemouth and Torquay as being partly due to people who lived there on the interest from their investments. Such people wanted security, and would more readily invest their modest capital if they were free from the fear of losing all of it if a company failed. 'What we pray,' the Warmley Company had said as long ago as 1768 when asking for a charter, 'is that shareholders may not be liable beyond what they have subscribed'.

After three attempts—in 1855, 1856, and 1862—limited liability was established. All you now had to do was to assemble at least seven people, state the objects of the company, and register it. Soon there was an increase in the number of companies, and it is not too much to say that the limited liability company helped to build the Empire, for much of the capital went to Africa, India, and Australasia as well as to Europe and America. London was becoming the greatest financial centre in the world.

More companies, more investors, more Stock Exchange members. There were 864 members in 1850, the annual subscription was still only £10, and they were dealing in less than 300 securities. Yet the 1802 building had become uncomfortably crowded even thirty years after it was opened. The Committee decided, in 1853, that they needed more than twice as much accommodation. They hired Thomas Allason to design it and William Cubitt to build it; spent £6,000 on extending the site, estimated £10,400 for the cost of building, and soon found that it was going to cost £20,000. Demolition began in June 1853 and members (who had temporarily occupied the Hall of Commerce in Threadneedle Street) moved into the new building in March 1854. Such speed more than justified the cost. The new House (which in the next century would be known as the Old House) had a restaurant in the basement known as Mabey's, and if it was full, you could always go next door to Porch's and lunch by candlelight in the wine-cellar. For additional refreshment, there were Elphinstone's Bath Bun shop, and Mr. Moth's steak-house: Mr. Moth's customers were mainly clerks who liked to make him drunk and fill his pockets with mustard.

The Crimean War, a relatively 'cheap' conflict, had added a mere

£32 million to the National Debt, and Consols were still the favourite stock for security. But limited liability was making Average Investor a little more venturesome, and he was beginning to put money into coal, steel, engineering, shipping—Cammell, John Brown, Stavely, B.S.A. are all names which date from the 1850s and 1860s.

The Stock Exchange, in pursuance of its 1802 Deeds of Settlement and its 1812 Rules amid the almost ten-yearly cycle of boom and slump, was touchy about its honour. It disliked Government intervention and was always keen to show that it could keep its own house in order. Picture, therefore, the dilemma of a Chairman of the Committee who found forgery going on in his own office. Robert Hichens, founder of Hichens, Harrison & Co. who had been a member since 1806 and was Chairman of the Stock Exchange 1838-42, discovered that for five years one of his clerks, J. Beaumont Smith, had been circulating forged Exchequer Bills to the tune of more than £270,000.

Hichens, who could have sidled more or less gracefully out of the whole affair, went straight to the Chancellor of the Exchequer, and together they decided to bring the whole affair out into the open by getting both the Treasury and the Committee of the Stock Exchange to conduct inquiries. Beaumont Smith was transported for life, and Robert Hichens was presented by his colleagues with a suitably-inscribed silver punch-bowl to commemorate the occasion.

The honour of the Stock Exchange suffered a temporary blow, followed by a swift vindication, in November 1858. No member was blamed; but an outside broker named William Lemon Oliver seems to have made a packet out of a bogus share issue, whereupon someone wrote a letter of complaint to the Lord Mayor, who of course could do nothing because Mr. Oliver was not a licensed broker. The case would be hardly worth mentioning but for the fact that it inspired a thundering sermon from the pulpit of *The Times*, which recommended investors always to deal through the Stock Exchange: 'The commission charged by the true broker is inconsiderable in itself, and trifling indeed when set against the security derived from his position and responsibilities. . . . The final decision of the Committee in the case of every defaulter is posted up in the Stock Exchange for thirty days. An adverse decision of the Committee is far more dreadful to a member of the Stock Exchange than any sentence of a court of law.'

Far more serious for the City as a whole was the Overend, Gurney

79

crisis of 1866. These good old Quaker names had always seemed rock-solid. It had been a well-respected discount house until 1865, when, we are told, it fell into the hands of 'young and imprudent partners' who proceeded to diversify in all directions at once, and very speculatively—corn, shipping, iron, railways: pouring capital into everything they could see, and leaving no reserves. Needing more capital, they relaunched themselves in 1865 as a limited company, with a capital of £5 million, enthusiastically tipped by the *Bankers' Magazine*, which called them 'the triumph of limited liability', this being the new economic panacea.

In the 1860s it was said of Overend, Gurney that 'they ploughed the seas with their ships . . . they covered the earth with their railways'. But they also had 'the unsound habits of buying unrealizable stock like railways and shipping lines', and of 'selling out bills representing such securities over the head of the original owner'. This happened to a Mr. Stefanos Xenos, a shipowner, who had borrowed £80,000; and also to Sam Beeton, husband of Mrs. Beeton who wrote the cookbook, whom Overend, Gurney had helped to start such magazines as *Boy's Own* and *Queen*, and who was bankrupted and forced to resign his directorship of Ward, Lock & Tyler, his publishing company.

Overend, Gurney had been foolish enough to put money into the London, Chatham & Dover Railway, apparently without doing any research into why it was doing badly. They were also heavily speculating in bank shares; and on 10 May 1866, the crash came. Uncle Timothy Forsyte, who would then have been rising 46, must have been beside himself, for Consols fell to 84, the lowest point in the whole of the nineteenth century. Less than a year after their relaunching, Overend, Gurney went bankrupt with liabilities of £19 million and assets of about £11 million. Six directors were tried before the Lord Mayor at the Mansion House, and charged with 'conspiracy to defraud'; and although they were acquitted, the ramifications went on for nearly thirty years, for it was not until 1893 that Overend, Gurney Ltd. was finally liquidated.

More than a century after the crash, it is difficult to see why it should have had such a shattering effect on the stock market and the prestige of the City. True, there had been 'scandalous irregularities in the financial conduct of the London, Chatham & Dover and the North British Railways' which took everyone right back to the age of

George Hudson, and this was a pity, since Home Rails had become pretty respectable. But, looking back on the whole episode, *The Times* saw fit to thunder again: 'No single bankruptcy has ever caused so great a shock to credit. The following day produced the greatest agitation which has ever been known in the City, and the Government was compelled . . . to authorize the Bank of England to issue notes beyond the legal limit. . . . For some months after the panic, English credit fell into entire disrepute on the Continent.'

Well, there had been no lack of smaller agitations. Two years before, on 26 April 1864, news of the assassination of President Lincoln had plunged American securities into gloom. After the Civil War, however, American securities did well, especially Erie Rails, promoted by Jay Gould, a rather nastier version of George Hudson, who flourished until his arrest in 1872.

Turning to domestic matters, there had been occasional complaints about Members' dress. Contemporary pictures of the House in those times generally show a uniform of tail coat, silk hat, and cravat. Mr. Wilkins Flasher, described with a colleague in the *Pickwick Papers* some thirty years before, was 'a very smart young gentleman who wore his hat on his right whisker and was lounging over the desk killing flies with a ruler . . . balancing himself on two legs of an office stool, spearing a wafer-box with a penknife which he dropped every now and then with great dexterity into the very centre of a small red wafer that was stuck outside. Both gentleman had very open waistcoats and very rolling collars, and very small boots, and very big rings, and very little watches, and very large guard-chains, and symmetrical inexpressibles, and scented pocket handkerchiefs.' (It is rather as if Malcolm Muggeridge were to describe a young public relations executive today.)

By the 1850s, younger members were still upsetting the Establishment by being 'peculiar in their dress, which occasions a rage now and then among them for strangely-fashioned hats, deep-striped shirts, long-waisted coats'. There were also older members who went on dressing in pre-Victorian style. Edward Callow, who became a Member in 1844 and lived on till the turn of the century, says in his memoirs that he knew brokers who wore top boots and breeches, a blue coat with gilt buttons, pure white neckerchief and ruffles, and had their back hair in a sort of pig-tail, like the sailors in *H.M.S. Pinafore*. They did not appear to work very hard by twentieth century standards, and seemed to have plenty of time for taking their families to Ranelagh or Hampton Court. They tended to live in 'a nice villa at Norwood or Clapham', which were then on the fringe of the country; and many of them took a 'businessman's quick lunch' at Birch's (a basin of soup and a glass of Madeira) or at the Auction Mart Coffee Room (which also kept sherry for celebrating a bargain).

They were having to pay more for membership of the Stock Exchange. The £50 shares originally stipulated in 1802 had begun to pay £10 per annum dividends from 1805 onwards, so that one 1802 share would have accumulated £571 in dividends by the end of 1853, when shares went up to £75. The following year they went up to £100. The Rule Book now contained 150 rules in 57 pages (by 1900 there would be 200 rules in 80 pages). Brokers still had to be Freemen of the City, and many of the new candidates chose the Plasterers' Company, which was relatively cheap to enter—£80 plus broker's licence. Not until 1884 did brokers, having grumbled for many generations about the law of Edward I which still bound them to the City, actually threaten the Court of Aldermen with the draft of a Bill. Two years later this tactic worked, and they were granted freedom from licences; which was very decent of the City, since it had been making £9,000 a year out of them.

The number and variety of stocks they were dealing in was slowly increasing—mines, for example. In the 1830s and 1840s there had been a rash of tin mining companies which for some years had their own exchange at Truro, and in 1850 there was an attempt to form a separate exchange for all mining shares, if they could not have their own market in the Stock Exchange. This exchange seemed to consist of a handful of dealers trying to do business outside the House in Capel and Hercules Courts, 'to the great inconvenience of the public', and the historian of Devon and Cornish mining, Richard Tredinnick, who was both mine-owner and stockbroker, sternly advised his clients to use the established Stock Exchange. Mining shares were anyway highly speculative—how speculative we shall see when we come to the Kaffir Circus.

By the 1870s, the Stock Exchange was dealing in shares as varied as the Aerated Bread Company Ltd. (1862), the newer joint-stock banks, insurance companies, local government authorities, even (in 1872) the Channel Tunnel. And we find (in 1868) what seems to be the first unit trust, 'for enabling the public to make investments in foreign and colonial securities without encountering the risks incidental to any individual purchase', said *The Times* approvingly. Investment trusts had been going for about ten years before this.

The Channel Tunnel might not have seemed a very good risk in 1872, and perhaps it was not sold hard enough; after all, Germany had just invaded France, and as the Duke of Wellington had pointed out more than twenty years before, it would be difficult (except by flooding) to frustrate the knavish tricks of any foreign horde if we allowed our sacred 22 miles of sea to be undermined.

Honduras was a different proposition. It was a good 4,000 miles away and therefore romantic, and it would take a long memory to recall the disastrous Poyais affair of more than forty years ago. Besides, this concerned a railway, and railways were now respectable. Finance houses such as Rothschilds and Barings had never been keen on lending money to foreigners they didn't know, especially Latin-American ones; but somehow the Honduras Government had, by 1871, raised enough money in Paris and London to build half a railway between the Atlantic and the Pacific coasts. Ever since the sixteenth century men had been trying to find a way across that narrow strip of land which would save shipping 6,000 miles round Cape Horn.

Why not, some inspired lunatic, or possibly genius, thought, build fifteen parallel railways which could actually carry ships from ocean to ocean on some kind of multiple articulated truck? At any rate, the Honduras Government thought (and the London contractors Bischoffsheim & Goldschmidt seemed to agree with them), it was a splendid excuse for raising a really large sum of money—say £15 million. The prospectus, issued in May 1872, read rather like a Stock Exchange spoof—'Chinese Turnpike Bonds', or 'Universal Widgets' —and didn't even get its arithmetic right. It failed, but at least it was funny.

To the House of Commons, however, it was no laughing matter. They saw it as the last straw in a whole series of doubtful foreign loans (about 150 of them, involving a theoretical £720 million, had been launched in the past fifteen years), and they appointed a Select Committee of inquiry. They did not blame the Stock Exchange— well, not very much—but they surely had it in for certain issuing houses. They hadn't troubled to do their homework, they had drawn up woolly, over-optimistic, and downright fraudulent prospectuses, and they had often given no undertaking that the money borrowed would actually be used for the purpose stated in the prospectus. This was not to deny that very many foreign loans were good investments; but there were fears that, like Gresham's Law, the bad might harm the good. The reputation of the City of London, now the greatest money market in the world, must not be jeopardized in this way.

The Select Committee on Foreign Loans reported in 1875. Among many things it disapproved of pre-allotment dealings, which drove prices up artificially; of a certain kind of financial public relations, which caused puffs to appear in the press and make new issues excessively desirable—'apply now to avoid disappointment'; and of 'bear raids' which could have the opposite effect.

The Committee found the Stock Exchange rather apathetic about these things: had they no ideas for improving them? No, the Stock Exchange said in effect; have *you*? Well, there was the question of official quotation which 'gives to a loan a certain prestige to which it may not be entitled'. Yet how could fitness for official quotation be decided, and who should so decide? The Committee ran away from this one: 'The business of the Stock Exchange,' it said, 'is to buy and sell, not good securities only, but all securities that are dealt in, and it is hardly fair and hardly wise to entrust to it the power of suppressing those questionable proposals by which it alone, of all the public, is certain to benefit'. The great weapon in the Stock Exchange's armoury was its power to expel members: as long as it had this, it could and should remain self-governing.

Was the Select Committee a non-event? Maybe, at the time; but it exposed a certain antagonism between Parliament and the Stock Exchange. The latter, wishing to keep its own house in order, had not always, traditionally, observed the law: Sir John Barnard's Act of 1733, by which it was illegal to buy stock without paying for it, or to speculate for 'differences' (balances due to or from clients on the purchase and sale of securities during a Stock Exchange account), was repealed in 1860, but had never been taken very seriously; neither had the much more recent Leeman's Act of 1867, to prevent speculation in bank shares (which had been one of the reasons for the collapse of Overend, Gurney); and the Chairman of the Stock Exchange told the Foreign Loans Committee so very frankly.

There was a general feeling, in fact, both inside and outside the Stock Exchange, that it ought to be thoroughly examined. The general public knew astonishingly little about it; its prestige and 'image' (in twentieth-century jargon) left something to be desired. We shall see, in the next chaper, what was done about these matters; but first we will take a turn around the Floor of the Stock Exchange, trying to recapture the flavour of the early '70s. We have, at last, a Clearing House, established in 1873, still privately run, but however did we ever do without it? One humane result of it is that it gives employment to 'broken-down Members drawing pensions from the Stock Exchange Benevolent Fund' who receive a guinea a night for a bit of overtime, plus free coffee and biscuits almost ad lib., and a bite of supper at 10 p.m.

Since 1866 we have been in daily touch with the New York Stock Exchange, which is increasingly important since we are both dealing in each other's stocks. Some years before—in 1860, to be precise—there was some agitation about fixing uniform scales of commission for brokers, but it was not destined to come to anything for another fifty years.

What does our stockbroker advise, as we, Average Investor with a few hundred pounds capital inherited from a celibate uncle, face the 1870s? Gilts, of course, for prudence; railways by all means, especially the Great Western, which has just put 45 per cent on its profits, and the Midland, which is going out to get the working-class pennies by instituting a third-class fare; but not the Brighton & South Coast —there was that very expensive crash at New Cross recently. . . .

Messrs. Bischoffsheim & Goldschmidt are still at it with Egyptian 7 per cents and Japan 9 per cents (by the way, where *is* Japan?), but personally we regard them as excessively spicy and even potential wallpaper. Submarine cables not bad, if you want a flutter, but watch out for Southern Florida where a giant turtle has just bitten through it.

Mr. Disraeli has pulled a fast one on the Whigs—or should we now call them the Liberals?—by buying 40 per cent of the shares of the Suez Canal Company. Did it through his friends the Rothschilds, of course—£4 million, added to the National Debt: if we'd paid £11 million for a State telegraph, £4 million for a short route to the Far East, now that we were no longer frightened by French designs on India, was a fleabite.

The telegraph, of course, had been connected to the House as long ago as 1853. This gave quick and easy communication with Continental *bourses* and agents abroad, and we have seen how promptly the Stock Exchange took advantage of the first transatlantic cable in 1866. The tickertape, already used on Wall Street, arrived in London by courtesy of the Exchange Telegraph Co. in 1872.

Exchange Telegraph (Extel) had a special licence from the Postmaster-General 'to carry out a system of exchange by telegraph in which identical information is supplied from certain central stations to any number of subscribers'. It had special correspondents at the Stock Exchange to report share prices by ticker-tape machines which worked, a century ago, at six words a minute.

The original company, with offices in Cornhill, was founded by seven men who included Lord Borthwick, a stockbroker; a banker; a City merchant; a 'gentleman of no occupation' of whom we know nothing except that he lived at Walton-on-Thames; Sir James Anderson, an ex-Cunard sea captain who had commanded Brunel's *Great Eastern* when it was laying the Atlantic cable; and an American from Wall Street.

With all these improved communications, theoretically, rumour and fraud would gradually cease to exist. But then, as the Mother Superior of my daughter's convent school frequently observes, the Devil is always winning.

1. Garraway's—one of the eighteenth century coffee houses where dealings in stocks and shares began.

On the 16 MAY in the YEAR 1801
And the 41 of the REIGN of GEORGE III

THE *FIRST STONE* OF THIS *BUILDING*

ERECTED BY PRIVATE SUBSCRIPTION

for the TRANSACTION of BUSINESS in the PUBLIC FUNDS
―――― was laid ――――
IN THE PRESENCE OF THE PROPRIETORS
And under the Direction of

| WILLIAM HAMMOND | | ISAAC HENSLEY |
| WILLIAM STEER | | ROBERT SUTTON |
| THOMAS ROBERTS | MANAGERS | JOHN BRUCKSHAW |
| GRIFFITH JONES | | JOHN CAPEL and |
| WILLIAM GREY | | JOHN BARNES |

James Peacock, Architect

At this ÆRA
BEING THE FIRST YEAR OF THE UNION BETWEEN
*GREAT BRITAIN AND IRELAND*
THE PUBLIC FUNDED DEBT HAD ACCUMULATED IN FIVE
SUCCESSIVE REIGNS TO £552,730,924

THE INVIOLATE FAITH OF THE BRITISH NATION
AND THE PRINCIPLES OF THE CONSTITUTION
SANCTION AND SECURE THE PROPERTY EMBARKED IN THIS UNDERTAKING

MAY THE BLESSINGS OF THAT CONSTITUTION
―――― BE ――――
TRANSMITTED TO THE LATEST POSTERITY

*2a.* The Foundation Stone of the 1801 building—discovered in the vaults in 1883.

*2b.* William Hammond, Chairman 1806–7, leading spirit among the founders of the Stock Exchange in 1801.

3.  The Capel Court entrance as it was about 1820. It was demolished in 1970.

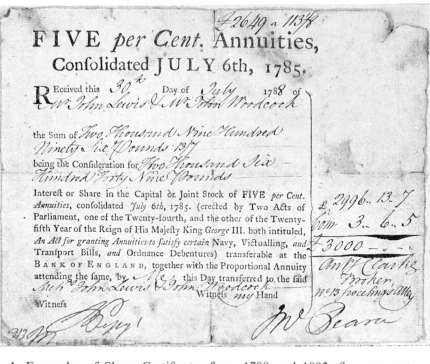

4. Examples of Share Certificates from 1788 and 1893: five per cent
annuities and Welsh Patagonian Gold Fields.

5. George Hudson, the Railway King. Today he might have been jailed; but Mr. Gladstone praised his 'courage and rich enterprise'.

6. Barney Barnato, 'ringmaster of the Kaffir Circus'.

7. Two practical jokers of the Nineties: (*left*) Charlie Clarke, leader of community singing; and (*below*) H. K. Paxton, the long distance walker.

8. 'Mafeking has been relieved' – and so is the Kaffir Market.

9. Horatio Bottomley (in the topper)—wine, women, and War Loan.

10. Lord Kylsant – a false prospectus. (The lady is his daughter.)

11a. Martin Harman—King of Lundy Island (and Lena Goldfields).

11b. Clarence Hatry — 'brilliant ideas, but over ambitious'.

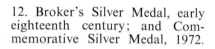

12. Broker's Silver Medal, early
eighteenth century; and Com-
memorative Silver Medal, 1972.

13*a*. The new Stock Exchange Building: the Queen Mother laying the Foundation Stone in 1967.

13*b*. H.M. the Queen opening the new building, 8 November 1972. To the left is the Lord Mayor (Sir Edward Howard, Bart.), and to the right Sir Martin Wilkinson.

14*a*. Sir Martin Wilkins
Chairman of the Stock Ex-
change, 1965–73.

14*b*. The Lord Ritchie of
Dundee, P.C., Chairman of
the Stock Exchange, 1959–65.

15*a*. The old Floor of the Stock Exchange.

15*b*. Jobbers on their pitch at the new Building.

16. The new Stock Exchange Building—26 storeys, 321 feet high.

# 10

# 'Fair Dealing and the Repression of Fraud'

'Money has a mystical quality; the markets of antiquity
were sacred places, the first banks were temples, and the
money-issuers were priests and priest-kings.'

—J. M. KEYNES

Now, gentle reader, if you really want to know what the Stock
Exchange is all about, its aims, its functions, its significance, and—
yes—its ideals, throw this book of mine out of the window, together
with all other books about the Stock Exchange, and Investment, and
Money, and get hold of a short, 20,000-word, plainly laid-out Report,
printed in 1878 by George Edward Eyre and William Spottiswoode
for the Queen's Most Excellent Majesty's Stationery Office.

It is called *Report of the Commissioners of the London Stock
Exchange Commission.* I do not know who wrote it, but it is one of
the best pieces of sustained, lucid, expository English prose in the
language. It minces no words, pulls no punches, says exactly what it
thinks in short sentences with a predominance of Anglo-Saxon words;
and it makes most other Reports of Royal Commissions look like
oratorios in praise of the *status quo,* composed and sung by prima
donnas. While much has happened to change the circumstances it
describes in the near-century since it was written, the basic principles
are all the same.

It brings out both the Stock Exchange's internal problems, and its
external—and public relations—difficulties. It indulges (though the
word did not then exist) in introspection. While jealously guarding
its right to set its own house in order (which it had been doing quietly
during 1876, with alterations to the Deed of Settlement—dividing
shares into ten parts, ruling that no proprietor could hold more than
ten, modifying the system of appointing managers, and creating a new

D 87

Committee of Consultation), it yet humbly asks for outside opinions. It hides nothing, and acquires merit. And so it should, for the Royal Commission was appointed by the Government on 20 March 1877, after a number of questions in Parliament which showed quite clearly that the public did not understand it, and what the public does not understand, it generally distrusts. The Stock Exchange, rather like Bill the Lizard in *Alice in Wonderland*, was on trial for—it knew not what.

The Commission began on 9 June 'to inquire into the origin, objects, present constitution, customs and usages of the London Stock Exchange, and the mode of transacting business in, and in connection with, that institution, and whether such existing rules, customs and mode of conducting business were in accordance with the law and with the requirements of public policy, and if not, to advise in what respect they might be beneficially altered'.

The Committee, chaired by Lord Penzance, was a strong one, nicely balanced between Parliament and City—Lord Blackburn, Spencer H. Walpole, M.P., E. Pleydell Bouverie, the Hon. Edward Stanhope, M.P., Sir Nathaniel M. de Rothschild, Bart., M.P., H. Hucks Gibbs, M. Buck Greene, John Hollams, Coleridge J. Kennard, Septimus R. Scott, and Reginald Yorke, M.P. The Secretary was R. G. C. Mowbray.

They sat for over a year, examined more than fifty witnesses, including the Town Clerk of the City of London, accountants, officials of the Liverpool, Manchester and Glasgow as well as the London Stock Exchanges, brokers, jobbers, clerks. These witnesses answered between them 8,831 questions, and the minutes of evidence ran to nearly 750,000 words, which is *War & Peace* plus *Ulysses* plus *Gone With the Wind*. (And the anonymous author of the final Report was able to boil it all down to less than 3 per cent.)

The Report is usually described as a 'complete vindication' of the Stock Exchange and its methods, as if its main purpose was to justify the *status quo*. But it was considerably more than that, and, for anyone who reads the actual text, and between the lines, points some of the way ahead. Some of the recommendations were drastic, but were not unanimously agreed. Eight members of the Commission signed the whole Report, and four (Messrs. Walpole, Stanhope, Greene, and Scott) had reservations which they expressed in separate Reports at the end.

The Commission 'recognized a great public advantage in the fact that those who bought and sold for the public in a market of such enormous magnitude in point of value, should be bound in their dealings by rules for the enforcement of fair dealing and the repression of fraud, capable of affording relief and exercising restraint far more prompt and often more satisfactory than any within reach of the courts of law'. In the administration of its own laws, the Committee for General Purposes had 'acted uprightly, honestly, and with a desire to do justice'.

*Dictum meum pactum*, 'my word is my bond', the 'honour' system peculiar to the London Stock Exchange, by which jobbers and brokers agree a transaction with nothing on paper but a scribble in a notebook, was much praised: 'The want of a written Contract between Members had in practice no evil results, and that out of the millions of contracts made on the Stock Exchange, such a thing was hardly known as a dispute as to the existence of a contract or as to its terms'.

The Commission disliked 'dual control'—government of the Stock Exchange by *two* bodies, the Trustees & Managers and the General Purposes Committee. (We have seen cases of friction between them, dating back to 1802 and even earlier, though they seemed to have settled into an uneasy harmony by 1878.) The Trustees represented the 502 proprietors, and were responsible for managing the building and fixing the subscription. The Committee was responsible for admissions and rules, and represented over 2,000 subscribers. They should amalgamate into one governing body—and indeed 'the provisions of the new deed of settlement of 1876 seem to have been framed with a view to the ultimate amalgamation of the two bodies', and had at least got as far as a joint sub-committee to discuss matters of general interest. But this was the limit of rapprochement for the next sixty-seven years: dual control was not finally abolished until 1945.

The jobbing system had been under desultory discussion for years. The jobber is today a kind of 'wholesaler' or specialist in certain kinds of stock—say, mining shares, or industrials, or textiles—and is not allowed to deal with the public, but only to make prices in various securities to fellow-Members. He makes in fact a buying price and a selling price, and theoretically does not know whether the broker with whom he is about to deal is a buyer or a seller. Out of the difference between the two prices must come the jobber's profits, but he can just as easily make a loss.

In 1878 things were still not quite so cut and dried. Although the Government Broker told the Commission that 'I look upon a broker and a jobber as totally distinct' (and this was certainly true in his own Consols market), there were occasional, rather frowned-on, border-line cases of 'jobbing brokers', often dealing in American securities. The Commission almost invariably referred to jobbers as 'dealers', possibly reflecting a Victorian, if not traditional, elegance about nomenclature. 'The dealers constitute a class which is a distinctive feature of the London Stock Exchange; it has no parallel on the foreign Bourses or on any of the provincial Stock Exchanges, but we have no hesitation in affirming that it is one of extreme value to the public. . . . The buyer or seller can make his bargain at once without seeking out someone else who wants to buy what he has to sell, or who wants to part with what he wants to buy. So great is the accom-modation provided by the system that purchases required on the provincial Exchanges or the foreign Bourses are constantly sent to London to be made on the Stock Exchange there.'

Excellent, excellent. But it is time to inspect one or two skeletons in the cupboard. The section, for example, on 'New Companies and Foreign Loans'. The last twenty or thirty years, despite Dual Con-trol's best endeavours and Company Acts and Limited Liability and all, had seen, in every ten-year boom, and in between as well, a shaming number of unsound investments. These were due partly to greedy investors chasing high rates of interest, and partly to dis-honest promoters artificially inflating prices. Could the Stock Exchange do anything to stop this, and if so, what? Still more basically, was the Stock Exchange ultimately responsible for the soundness of the stocks it dealt in?

The Commission considered a number of case histories. There was the Australian and Eastern Steam Navigation Co. of 1864, whose prospectus had failed to mention certain reserved shares, and whose application for settlement (in March, when the premium was at its highest) had been refused for this reason, and also because 'large purchases made by the directors before allotment practically gave them the whole control of the market'. The Marseilles Land Co. (1866) had also been a case of 'shares bought before allotment in order to create a premium'. The City of Moscow Gas Co., brought out in

1865 and liquidated four years later, had been promoted by the company's brokers, involved a 'fictitious contract' and had 'starved for want of capital'. Another Gas Company, the Eupion (1874), had been a straight conspiracy 'to defraud the brokers' and 'to deceive the Committee of the Stock Exchange with intent to defraud the public'. On this occasion, the Stock Exchange maintained, 'their rules, though powerless to prevent the fraud originally, led ultimately to the detection and punishment of the offenders'.

In the two remaining case histories, Charles Laffitte & Co. and Peruvian Railways Co. (1865—both liquidated within two years) 'the machinery of the Stock Exchange was made use of to float companies which never seem to have had any real existence, but to have been simply created for the purposes of speculation'.

Could, or should, the Committee have done more than it did to protect the public? The average investor had nothing to guide him, as to the soundness of an investment, but the promises of a prospectus. Yet it was not usually this that tempted him: it was more often 'the statement which he reads in the newspapers, that the shares of the company, not yet allotted, are already being sold in the market . . . at a premium'. The Committee had tried to prevent dealings before allotment by a new rule in 1864, but it had not worked: should it not now be made to work, and was not legislation the only answer?

Even the fact that a company was quoted on the Stock Exchange was liable to give it 'a sort of spurious stamp of genuineness or soundness' for which the Committee could not be responsible. The Commission criticized the Committee's methods of vetting new issues—not because they lacked thoroughness, but because they even sometimes went too far, and gave investors the impression that listing and recommendation were practically synonymous. The Committee did not feel competent to do any more than it was doing, and said that if the soundness of a stock was questionable, inquiries should be undertaken 'by some public functionary and enforced by law'.

Yes, but *what* public functionary? Mr. Stanhope was one of the objectors to this idea. No outside 'functionary' would ever know the market well enough to decide what securities were sound; and failure would simply bring discredit on the Stock Exchange.

One traditional criticism of the Stock Exchange was that it encouraged gambling. The Commission examined this charge minutely in its section on 'Speculation', which is almost a manual on 'evil practices' some of which were to take many years to stamp out. The type of gambling peculiar to the Stock Exchange was defined as 'pretending to buy and sell, but in reality doing nothing more than agreeing to pay or receive the difference between the market price on the day of the agreement and that on the account day'. The Committee could not hope to control the motives of investors, but it could award stiffer penalties to members who indulged in 'extravagant speculation' themselves, and this was recommended. There *was* gambling, but it could not be said that the Stock Exchange encouraged it.

Was the Stock Exchange a monopoly? It had tried to open its doors as widely as possible to admit members, but the public regarded membership as a guarantee of respectability, and the Stock Exchange would only 'bring odium upon itself' if it made admission too easy. The Commission recommended a sub-committee on admission, which would inquire more closely into the character of prospective new members. This led naturally to the question of defaulters: there had been no fewer than 265 in the decade 1866-76, of whom 116 had applied for readmission and 105 had got it. This was too many, and the system needed tightening up. It was not enough to post defaulters' names in the House: there were bad cases whose names should be publicized in the press.

The Commission's most revolutionary recommendation was that the Stock Exchange should be incorporated either by Royal Charter or by Act of Parliament. It would have 'bye-laws' which could only be altered by 'the President of the Board of Trade or some other public authority'. It was hoped that any such external control 'should be exercised with a sparing hand'. Three of the four dissenting reports strongly objected to this: it would make the Stock Exchange 'state-regulated', whereas it would command far more public confidence if it remained a voluntary association; and if anyone complained that it already had a tendency towards monopoly, this was the certain way to make it so. Was the Commission serious, or was this a self-protective piece of buck-passing? Anyway, it never came to pass.

The Commission decided that it was unnecessary to fix brokers' commissions or the manner of sharing them: the subject seems to have been rather distasteful to them. They definitely recommended a Committee on the Official List, which 'should be made as perfect as possible for the dissipation of unjust suspicions and the preservation of the confidence of clients in their brokers'. It was strongly urged, too, that bargain-marking should be compulsory.

One more recommendation claims our attention. Some people were mystified by, or suspicious of, what went on in the Stock Exchange. Could it not be open to public inspection? It was not envisaged that the investor should actually *watch* his broker buying or selling his shares for him, but it would show him that everything was above board. This idea foundered for want of space: the House, at its 1878 size, could only just accommodate its 2,000 members. It was postponed for seventy-five years—for it was not until 1953 that the Stock Exchange got its Visitors' Gallery.

# 11

# Gorgonzola Hall

---

'The way to make money on the Exchange is to sell too soon'

—NATHAN ROTHSCHILD

The year 1878 was celebrated for many things besides the Report of the Royal Commission on the Stock Exchange—for the first performance of *H.M.S. Pinafore*, for Mr. Disraeli's 'Peace with Honour' at the Congress of Berlin, for the arrival of Cleopatra's Needle, for the foundation of Lady Margaret Hall, the establishment of the C.I.D., for the outbreak of phylloxera in French vineyards—and for the collapse of the City of Glasgow Bank in October.

This failure revealed an appalling hole in company law about banks. There were, at this time, well over one hundred joint-stock banks in England and Wales, though barely more than two dozen were quoted in London. By law, dating back fifty years or more, all members of a banking company were supposed to have unlimited liability, so that banks, whether private or joint-stock, could not be limited either by charter or by letters patent. This seemed to work satisfactorily, and many famous banks—Midland, National Provincial, Westminster, Lloyds—were developing soundly. Since the Limited Liability Acts, it was thought, the small investor had come into his own. But how much protection had he really? For middle-class investors were also bank depositors, and banks were not yet all limited; so that, when the City of Glasgow Bank failed, 'two hundred spinsters—holding an average of £240 apiece in shares—were each called upon to stump up £6,610'.

The City reacted strongly, and the crisis seems to have become intermingled with the fear of Russian designs on the Balkans after the

94

Russo-Turkish War (members of the Stock Exchange actually staged an anti-Russian demonstration). Immediately after the Glasgow Bank failure, Bank Rate rose from 5 to 6 per cent; and Consols touched their second lowest point of the century at 93⅝.

The law was speedily amended, by the 1879 Companies Act, and henceforth the word 'Ltd.' appeared after the names of most joint-stock banks.

We saw, in the Royal Commission's Report, that brokers some-times acted as company promoters: thus were born, through the midwifery of Messrs. Foster & Braithwaite (whose senior partner, Sir John Braithwaite, was Chairman of the Stock Exchange Council 1949-1959), the Anglo-American Brush Electric Lighting Corpora-tion (1880), the Australian Electric Light & Traction Co., and others. They had moved fast—the Ediswan carbon filament lamp had only been patented in—*annus mirabilis!*—1878. Railways (home and foreign) and steam tramways boomed; chemicals, Cunard shipping, Claridges Hotel, breweries like Bass, Ind Coope, Meux, local authori-ties like Birmingham, Leeds and Leicester, and numerous waterworks, all were coming to market.

It was becoming easier for shrewd students of new issues to sort out good and bad promoters. At one end of the scale was Osborne O'Hagan, who would nowadays be called a whizz-kid: before his thirtieth year he had given trams to London, Birmingham, Man-chester, and the Potteries. He was a true professional, did his home-work, drove a hard but fair bargain, chose his directors well, and arranged most of his underwriting through Panmure Gordon & Co. He was afterwards to found American railways and meat-packing companies, Trinidad Lake Asphalt, tobacco concerns and breweries (which, however, he regarded as speculative 'because the Temperance Movement was so strong').

At the other end were men like Horatio Bottomley, whom we shall meet again later in this narrative. For the moment it will suffice to say that he did most of the things the 1878 Royal Commission said people shouldn't do, went bankrupt more times than any other man on record, and by a lucky fluke was instrumental in starting *The Financial Times*. In 1886 he went to O'Hagan for financial backing to form McRae, Curtice, a small printing and publishing concern with a handful of trade papers, including the *Drapers' Record* and the then ailing *Financial Times* (previously known as the *London Financial*

*Guide*), which was competing with the *Financial World* (established two years before). O'Hagan, who never made the same mistake twice, financed no more Bottomley companies. Fortunately, Mr. Bottomley's influence on the F.T. was very short, and he turned his attention to the fifty other companies he promoted within ten years, with a total capital of over £20 million. These included the Joint Stock Trust Institute (whatever that was), and, when the Kaffir Boom came, Associated Gold Mines of West Australia, Great Boulders Proprietory Gold Mines, and the incredibly-named Nil Desperandum Mines Co. Few of these ever paid any dividends, and their author, some twenty-five years later, went to prison for fraud.

Meanwhile, 'How are Consols?' as Timothy Forsyte asked in the television version of *The Forsyte Saga* (but not in the book). Consols still stood unrivalled, above many a security yielding higher interest. The Victorians believed in them as they believed in God, the Queen, and the Empire. And with good reason: banks and insurance companies loved them and bought them, and, wrote an authority on country banking, they had 'the supreme quality of convertibility. They are the one security which you can, with absolute certainty, turn into cash at any hour of any business day, even in the worst throes of panic'. Sir Stafford Northcote, in 1875, had introduced a *New* Sinking Fund; and in 1888 came Chancellor Goschen's conversion of the National Debt. It must have seemed to many a small stockholder that the end of the world was at hand. Was it not Mr. Gladstone who had said that democracy was a costly mistress? Here was Goschen, 'converting £892,000,000 of good 3 per cent stocks into a new issue of Consols, the rate of interest on which was to fall to 2¾ per cent in the following year and to 2½ per cent in five years' time'. 2½ per cents quickly became known as 'Goschens'.

The Forsytes were never exactly 'average' or even 'typical' investors, but the *Saga* opens in 1886 and we may as well glance at what they thought of the Stock Exchange and all its works. They weren't actually on dining terms with their brokers. 'They had shares in all sorts of things, not as yet—with the exception of Timothy—in Consols, for they had no dread in life like that of 3 per cent for their money'. (How they must have hated Goschen!)

It will be recalled that Old Jolyon had failed to get elected to the Hotch Potch Club because he was 'in trade'—a tea merchant. So he joined the Disunion—'he naturally despised the club that *did* take him. The members were a poor lot, many of them in the City—stock-brokers, solicitors, auctioneers, what not!' When Kaffirs began to look promising, he joined the board of Globular Gold Concessions. And when Young Jolyon made an unsuitable marriage, Old Jolyon sent his son £500, which was proudly returned; so old Jolyon invested it for his grandson at 5 per cent, adding £100 every year. No Consols for *him*.

The Royal Commission had noted the smallness of the Stock Exchange building for its 2,000 members. Mabey's restaurant had been turned into a settling room in 1872, but there still was not enough room on the floor for the many new members. So in 1881, Mr. J. J. Cole, architect to the Trustees, designed a splendid new building fit for a cathedral of commerce. It was to occupy 10,000 square feet, and it was to be 'in the Italian style'. Mr. Cole loved veined marble, which came from old Roman quarries at Carthage, and not only were the walls of the New House to be faced with it, but so were the plaster walls of what would henceforth be known as the Old House. The New House had an octagonal hall, and a dome seventy feet across and one hundred feet above the floor, which was of teak, because members' feet wore out oak too quickly (at an estimated rate of $1\frac{3}{4}$ inches per decade). It was opened in 1884, *not* by the Prince of Wales, who wished to inspect it *incognito*, and did so under certain precautions, lest any member should fail to recognize him and subject him to the usual horseplay meted out to strangers. Members lost no time in christening the New House 'Gorgonzola Hall'.

While the New House was a-building, the Stock Exchange got its first encyclopaedia or year-book, *Burdett's Official Intelligence*, first compiled in 1882 by the secretary of the Share and Loan Department, Sir Henry Burdett; and four years later broker-members finally got rid of the necessity of paying 'rents' to the Corporation of London through the Court of Aldermen.

Members were beginning to get used to the new-fangled telegraph and telephone, which would soon bring a new inrush of business with Paris, New York, Johannesburg (where gold had been found just as the New House was being completed). It was not until April 1891 that the House installed two lines to Paris, and for some reason it, three years later, had a line to Brighton, which was used no fewer than eleven times between its installation on 1 August 1894 and 31 December.

Provincial stock exchanges were becoming more important and drawing closer to London. They tended to specialize—Manchester in cotton, Glasgow in shipping, Cardiff in coal, Liverpool in insurance shares. Three of them had given evidence to the Royal Commission and all were in telephone contact with London jobbers. Liverpool took the lead, in 1890, in forming the Council of Associated Stock Exchanges, whose backing was valuable in bringing about the Forged Transfers Act of the following year.

It was the 'Barton forgeries' on transfers of London & North Western Railway shares that had shown the injustice of a law by which the purchaser had not only to hand back the stock he thought he had bought, but also refund all his dividends. On 20 February 1891, there was a meeting in the Library of the Stock Exchange to discuss it. Through no fault of their own Edward Rae, Chairman of both the Liverpool Stock Exchange and the Association of Provincial Stock Exchanges, and his colleagues from other cities were a little late, having been treated as 'strangers' and thrown out by members who did not recognize them; but they took it in good part, and the Bill was drafted.

Advertising had for long been an ethical problem: how far might members go in self-promotion? In the early decades of the century brokers had sent out circulars and taken paid insertions in the press; and around 1820 one John Ashby, of 3 Bartholomew Lane, a member from 1814 until 1834, had presented pretty little medals to prospective clients with a bull on one side, a bear on the other, Mr. Ashby's address and office hours (10 till 3), and a list of the thirty-two holidays a year when his office was shut. It must have been like getting the Lord's Prayer on to a sixpence. The trouble was that outside brokers were always advertising, and members, tempted to retaliate, were periodically reprimanded by the Committee for going too far. But how far was too far? It had never been defined.

Deeply imbedded in Stock Exchange lore, but unconfirmed by name or date, is the irresistibly quotable story of a broker of great charm who specialized in investing for maiden ladies. He was deacon of a chapel in Islington, and in ushering worshippers to their pews, handed them hymn-books stamped with his name and business address—'British and Foreign Stock and Share Broker, Capel Court, Bartholomew Lane, London'.

It seems almost cruel to discourage such enterprise, but in 1885 a new rule banning all publicity of any kind was formulated by the Committee and publicly announced in the press. This same year yields the first hint that some members actually went in for cultural activities, such as playing musical instruments; for it was in 1885 that the Stock Exchange Orchestral Society was founded, a Male Voice Choir being added shortly afterwards.

Perhaps the story of the Islington deacon was just another Stock Exchange practical joke. The most notorious practical joker whose name has come down to us was Dick Cohen, who went far beyond the usual japes of inventing fictitious companies, setting fire to people's newspapers while they were reading them, and emptying bags of sawdust on silk-hatted heads from the gallery. He is credited with having organized an elaborate party for a rather untidy and unpopular member at which the victim was to receive 'a token of his fellow-members' regard', which turned out to be a bar of soap and a towel. It is not clear whether Dick Cohen was the organizer or the victim of a Christmas turkey raffle in which a Jewish member won, not a turkey, but a pound of pork sausages.

We must turn to more serious matters. Wars are good for Gilts but bad for foreign investment, and it was several years since we had had a full-scale military conflict. Such a period makes for boom conditions, which characterized the years immediately before 1890—but it was in this year that the City came within a hair's breadth of the biggest financial crisis since August 1825, when the Bank of England had almost run out of gold in an effort to cope with bubble companies with names like London Genuine Snuff, Dover to Calais Railway, Economic Funeral, and British Personal Palladium.

The old, large and highly respectable merchant banking firm of Barings, still a private company, whose main business was in foreign loans, had been diversifying lately—into banks, railways, waterworks, and other major projects. Unfortunately they had been doing this in South America; not only too many eggs in one basket, but too many eggs altogether—and all without arranging guaranteed underwriting. Rothschilds were doing the same sort of thing, but—characteristically—with more caution. It is easy to blame Barings for breaking one of the first rules of company promotion (especially one which had been heavily stressed by the Royal Commission), but it is difficult to see what any merchant bank could do about a country—

it happened to be Argentina—which defaults on bond payments leaving you with liabilities of £21 million, and no reserves.

In this case Rothschilds, impassively and graciously, together with all the other leading clearing and merchant banks in the City, passed the hat round to rescue their stricken brother. They had to, because they were all involved. But the real leadership came from the Governor of the Bank of England, William Lidderdale, who having raised Bank Rate to 6 per cent, took the initiative of rallying the whole City to lend Barings enough money to carry on as a limited company. It took four years to sort out Barings' affairs, but the company survived, and, half a century later, was entrusted with the liquidation of British assets in America during the Second World War.

The Stock Exchange played no direct part in the Barings crisis ('crash', the dramatic word so often used to describe it, is not quite appropriate), and indeed showed surprisingly little reaction to it. The Bank of England had acted so swiftly that most of the remedial action had been taken before the news got out. Consols fell to 93¾ (the lowest point since the City of Glasgow Bank crisis), Argentine securities fell 13 points in five days, and there were a number of 'hammerings' (the custom by which waiters strike three heavy blows on their rostrums when announcing that partners of a defaulting firm 'cannot comply with their bargains'). However, the Stock Exchange was mightily relieved, and sent a deputation consisting of the Chairman, Hall Rokeby Price, Deputy-Chairman Underhill and Secretary Francis Levien, with a (presumably illuminated) address thanking the Governor for 'the firm and decisive manner' in which his 'great influence' had been 'so wisely and courageously exercised'.

Governor Lidderdale replied, with no little pomp, 'I shall always remember with pride and satisfaction that, in the opinion of such a body as yours, in a moment of danger I was able to do my duty'.

For the other great talking-point of these years, let us turn up *The Economist* of 25 September 1886. 'There seems to be no doubt that goldfields of considerable productive capacity have been discovered in South Africa,' it said warily. But it shared the general opinion of the Stock Exchange that gold was strictly speculative, and 'no prudent man who is dependent for his living upon the return of his capital would feel warranted in touching them'.

In a few years' time nearly everybody would be touching them like mad, but for the present the Stock Exchange tended to look pretty hard at *all* mining shares. Some of them were still dealt in on the old Royal Exchange, and in 1889 there was an attempt by about eighty brokers to form a separate Mining Exchange, whose secretary, a jobber named Martin, was not actually a member of the Stock Exchange. It quickly vanished, and in Gorgonzola Hall the sound of distant tom-toms drew inexorably nearer until the noise was deafening.

The Kaffir Circus was coming to town.

# 12

# All That Glitters

'They wonder much to hear that gold, which in itself is so useless a thing, should be everywhere so much esteemed, that even men for whom it was made, and by whom it has its value, should yet be thought of less than *it* is.'
— SIR THOMAS MORE, *Utopia*

To discover what was happening in South Africa, it is instructive to see it through the eyes of one man. We first meet him at the age of 21 in 1873—hitch-hiking nearly six hundred miles from the Cape to Kimberley by ox-cart with £30 capital and forty boxes of cigars as his main luggage. Born in the slums off Petticoat Lane, where his parents ran a secondhand clothes stall, he had tried his hand at boxing and music-hall juggling before being seized with a vision of South Africa as a promised land of diamonds and gold. His name at this time was Barney Isaacs: twenty years later he would be world-famous as Barney Barnato with a reputed income of £5 a minute.

Something like the world he was entering had been seen twenty-five years before, in California, when, with almost indecent haste after Mexico had ceded the state to America, gold was discovered at Sutter's Mill, and (says Professor Chapman, sometime Professor of History at the University of California, Berkeley) 'homes, farms were abandoned. Ships deserted by their sailors crowded the bay at San Francisco . . . soldiers deserted wholesale, churches were emptied, town councils ceased to sit, merchants, clerks, lawyers and judges and criminals, everybody in fact, flocked to the foothills'; and the landscape began to be transformed from one of peaceful Spanish mission houses to the world of freeways and Hollywood and Los Angeles smog we know today. It was happening on a smaller scale in Australia, at Bendigo and Ballarat, where one gold nugget, the Welcome Stranger, weighed 2,520 ounces; it would happen again at Juneau, in Alaska, and, still later, in the Klondike.

Barney was well-informed. He knew that South Africa was yielding more diamonds of gem, as opposed to industrial, quality than any other country. He had heard of the Star of South Africa, the first diamond found on the bank of the Orange River in 1867, which had been bought by the Earl of Dudley for £25,000. But he was not exactly in the vanguard of the rush: by 1870 there were already about 10,000 people combing the gravels of the Orange and Vaal Rivers for sparklers. There had been important finds at Jagersfontein, Dutoitspan and Bultfontein, and in 1871 at what became known as the Kimberley mine.

Kimberley, seventeen miles from the Vaal River, was just three years old when Barney first saw it, and it had only just got its name—from the Earl of Kimberley, Colonial Secretary, who had 'taken the mines under British protection'. It had been founded by diggers who had found diamonds on farms. This was an important discovery, because hitherto they had expected the richest sources to be alluvial. Not so: the best diamonds in this area were in oval 'pipes' that ran deep into the earth, and they must be dug for. So the farmers were bought out, and the claims—each 31 feet square—were staked out. There were three main camps, Dutoitspan, De Beers (named after the farmer whose land it was, and also known as De Beers Rush or Old De Beers), and Colesberg Kopje (known as De Beers New Rush). It was this last camp that became the town of Kimberley.

The other element of the coming Rand boom, gold, came eleven years later, when the Barber brothers found large deposits of gold-bearing quartz at what is now known as Barberton. There was the expected gold rush, with shops and hotels going up overnight, house property soaring, banks open all day, bubble companies, and inflated stock. But Barberton collapsed, as an investment prospect, in one day when Gardner Williams, an American mining expert, put in an adverse report on it. (He eventually became Chief Engineer and General Manager of De Beers.)

The scene changed to Langlaagte. where two former Kimberley diggers found ore in an outcrop of rock on a farm. This, it took some time to realize, was the Main Reef. In September 1886 the Rand was officially proclaimed a goldfield, and by Christmas 3,000 miners, some arriving in carts, some walking, were at work on 30 miles of reef. They lived in tents and reed huts, had offices made of old sheets of tinplate, and huddled round camp fires in the evening by oil lamps.

Soon there was a corrugated iron shack called the Grand Hotel. In the summer rains the whole place was a sea of reddish mud, there were no drains or doctors, and many died of pneumonia. Food was sometimes so scarce that potatoes were fetching five shillings a bucket. One of the camps on a farm where a prospector named George Harrison had struck the Main Reef, was already known as Johannesburg.

When Barney Barnato arrived in Kimberley in 1873, he just missed meeting a man, a year younger than himself, with whom he would one day divide an empire. Cecil Rhodes had come to South Africa in the hope that the climate would be better for his TB than England was. He had tried to grow cotton in Natal with his brother, had managed some of his brother's claims at Kimberley, in 1872, and was now on his way to Oriel College, Oxford. But his health again deteriorated, and for the next eight years he commuted between Oxford and Kimberley, taking his degree in 1881. He had been given six months to live; sustained by 'patriotism plus five per cent' he was to live another twenty-one years.

The baffling contrast between these two men was felt on the London Stock Exchange. Rhodes was a man of vision, educated, a gentleman: it was easier to trust his companies, with their official backing, than it was to trust Barnato's, of which, for a long time, the City was suspicious. What could one make of a man who had his visiting cards overprinted: 'I'll stand any man a drink, but I won't lend him a fiver'?

Soon about 300 mining companies were registered in South Africa. No wonder Paul Kruger called Johannesburg 'the Devil's City'. Some of those companies were Barney's, and the biggest was Johannesburg Consolidated Investment Co., of which he was both founder and chairman, which embraced development, gold mines, breweries, newspapers. Yearning for respectability, the sort of respectability the Rothschilds enjoyed, he dreamt of a Barnato Bank.

But the Rothschilds were putting their money—£1 million of it— on Rhodes. In 1880 he founded the De Beers Mining Co.—and began buying up Barnato shares. He also (in 1887) founded his own Gold Fields of South Africa Co.

By 1887, it was clear that two things were badly needed in Johannesburg—a synagogue and a stock exchange. The first was founded by the Witwatersrand Goldfields Jewish Association, who had to get the land from Kruger. He would allow them only two plots—'because your people only believe in half the Bible. If you change, I'll give you two more'.

Share gambling in street and saloon was getting out of hand, and so on 8 November 1887, Benjamin Woollan, a Londoner, founded the Johannesburg Exchange & Chambers Co. Ltd. It was a single-storey building on the corner of Simmonds and Commissioner Streets. Street trading was usually done in a section closed to traffic by stretching chains across it—so that 'between the chains' became synonymous with the Stock Exchange. Barney bought huge blocks of shares. William St. John Carr, a clerk who became first Mayor of Johannesburg, made £20,000 in one day. There was a lunatic time when the nominal value of gold shares exceeded £100 million, although the Rand's gold output was calculated at less than 3 per cent of this value. A rumour that the Main Reef was giving out, despite geological advice to the contrary, could cause panic selling: once it was so bad that £1 shares fetched only 3*d*. each and three banks had to close.

Mr. Woollan did his best to run the Exchange soundly. There was no time for a jobbing system; it was more like a cattle auction. Stock issues were called out daily in alphabetical order, and trading was a matter of shouting. In 1890 a new and bigger building was opened on the same site, but unofficial trading still went on 'between the chains' as brokers, financiers, gamblers, and miners went on shouting from 6.30 p.m. until past midnight.

Every day brokers asked: 'What's Barney buying?' before making their starting prices. There were no rules about dress: share-pushers seemed to prefer breeches and riding boots, Barney himself was generally in shirtsleeves and braces, and the others wore solar topees, cricket caps, deerstalkers, anything. There was once an attempt to discipline Barney: a German, Artur Lilienfeld, called him 'a cheap little Yid who ought to go back to Whitechapel where he belonged'. Barney, a trained boxer, knocked him flat. They were both told by Ben Woollan to sign mutual letters of apology, or to resign. Barney signed under protest: 'How can I resign? I *own* the bloody place.'

What might have been a crisis for Barney turned into a triumph when, on 13 March 1888, De Beers Consolidated Mines was formed by Cecil Rhodes with the help of a financial wizard, Sir Alfred Beit; and Barney was made a Life Governor. The interests of Barnato and Rhodes were amalgamated, and the Kimberley mine was bought for £5,338,650. The group now controlled 95 per cent of the world's diamond output and nearly half of the world's gold. Barney was respectable at last, and not only because he earned £250,000 a year.

In London the word 'Kaffir' was acquiring a new meaning. 'If there is anyone who does not own some scrip in a gold mine,' said the *Financial News*, 'he is considered not quite right in the head'. The City, which had hitherto clung to Rhodes's British South African Co. as 'a financial Gibraltar' because it had a Royal Charter and an aura of dividends as well as of glamour, became warily interested in De Beers when at last it was officially quoted. Meanwhile Barney, whenever he visited London, gave dinners for stockbrokers, diamond merchants and their wives, and in his London office the portrait of Cecil Rhodes, now Prime Minister of Cape Colony, further testified to his reliability.

What really confirmed City confidence in gold mines was the cyanide process for preparing gold from crude ore. Ridiculed in 1887 when it was first proposed, its industrial possibilities were recognized in 1890. It was about this time that Lord Randolph Churchill came out to Johannesburg and bought gold shares; and it was no coincidence that Barney happened to be on the same boat returning to England.

Rhodes entered London in triumph, and was invited to Windsor. Barney's triumph was different, yet in some ways greater. The City not only took Kaffirs seriously, but went mad on them. Barney was called 'ringmaster of the Kaffir Circus', and South African mining shares became known as Johnnies and Barneys. At the Empire music-hall, Ada Blanche sang a song in his honour, 'Golden Africa'. The Lord Mayor, Sir Joseph Renals, gave him a banquet. In September 1895 Barney's ultimate dream came true; the Barnato Bank was opened.

Disaster followed, and it had a political cause. Rhodes, whose greatest obstacle all along had been President Kruger, tried to use force to overthrow the Transvaal Government. A futile eleventh-hour effort was made to stop his friend Dr. Jameson from carrying out his raid, on 29 December 1895. Cecil Rhodes's reputation never recovered from this blunder. In London, Paris, and Johannesburg the Kaffir market crashed. Barney bought £3 million of gold shares in an attempt to save the market, and it may have been for this gesture that the next Lord Mayor made him a Lieutenant of the City of London. But the Jameson Raid developed into the Transvaal War, and Kaffirs were never quite the same again: leading shares fell by 10 to 25 per cent. Some members of the Stock Exchange seem to have had inside news about the Jameson Raid, and acted in time to avoid losses, but others were less fortunate.

As for Barney Barnato, he bought a site in Park Lane from the Duke of Westminster and built thereon a kind of palace, in a style which, thirty years later, might have been called Early Metro-Goldwyn-Mayer. But he never had time to live in it. On 14 June 1897, he was sailing home to England on board the *Scot*, just off Madeira, when there was a cry of 'Man overboard'. The man was Barney. It has generally been assumed that he committed suicide: but no clear reason has ever been given. A year later his relative Woolf Joel was shot dead in his office in Johannesburg. Perhaps Paul Kruger had been right about the 'Devil's City'.

The Kaffir boom highlighted two points of Stock Exchange organization. Fourteen years before, the London Stock Exchange had agreed with the Board of Inland Revenue a simplified procedure by which the Share and Loan Department took over the stamping of transfers. In the old days unstamped executed transfers had been taken by hand all the way to Somerset House to be stamped. Spoilt or damaged stamps had to be 'sworn off' at the city office of the Inland Revenue. No doubt it created employment, but it was maddeningly slow. It was reckoned that the new system made it possible to do business five times as quickly, and the proof of it was given during the Kaffir boom in October 1895, when more than 4,000 foreign transfers were stamped in a single day.

The second point of organization concerned settlements of mining share transactions, and there was strong criticism of the Clearing House. The Settlement Department was actually extended in 1894, but it simply could not cope with the volume of traffic in 1895. This was one of several matters which particularly exercised younger members, some of whom were saying openly that the Committee was fossilized. The annual election of 20 March 1896 was one of the most vigorous on record: more than two-thirds of the 3,600 members used their votes, and got at least one thing they wanted: a younger Committee.

# 13

# The Roaring Nineties

'Lupin was riveted to the *Financial News* . . . "I give you
the tip, Guv.—Chalk Pits are as safe as Consols, and
pay 6 per cent at par!" '

*—The Diary of a Nobody*
GEORGE AND WEEDON GROSSMITH

The enormous increase of business during the Kaffir Boom led to
the election of many new members, and the engagement of more
staff. There had been so many alterations to the Stock Exchange
building, in spite of the architects' grand designs, that a contemporary observer said despairingly: 'The shape of the Stock Exchange
is shapeless'. The Settling Room had been extended, so that there
was even more scope for the high spirits of the clerks: 'Let a young
gentleman have the temerity to enter with any peculiarity of dress,
and the room rises as one man. Rows of fellows stand on the desks
and yell at the wearer: 'Take it off!'

In 1888 the new 'east end' had been finished, and the new electric
lighting system installed there: 'the current generated is stored in
accumulators placed on the roof'. The House was illuminated by
arc-lights, and now had electric lifts. Seven years later the premises
at 22 Throgmorton Street were rebuilt to provide more offices and
lavatories, and it was calculated that 'the Stock Exchange consumes
no less than fifteen million gallons of water and uses about one
million towels annually'. The central heating system installed in the
New House in 1885, which worked by 'pumping warm air', did not
in fact work very well, and members, forced to wear their overcoats
all day in winter, longed for the old open fires.

There was also an air-cooling system for the summer, but despite
its 'engine-driven fans', we are told, 'it is not so very unusual for a
member to drop in a dead faint', so great was the heat. This led to

an outbreak of straw and panama hats, and members 'even appeared in flannel suits' without being attacked. Even the rule against smoking before 4 p.m. broke down in 1889, when a peculiar smell was noticed in the House. There was a plague of enteric fever at the time, and members felt that tobacco was both a deodorant and a prophylactic. An inquiry by the Medical Officer of Health and Public Analyst for the City of London, Dr. Sedgwick Saunders, exonerated the House sanitation and blamed the drains in Throgmorton Street; and the no-smoking rule was re-enforced.

The 'speculative fever' of the 1890s found other outlets than the House itself. There were, within three hundred yards of the House, several illegal gambling clubs, notably the Copthall Club which was eventually raided by the police, though we do not hear that any member was arrested: 'it is perhaps the clerk with his £150 a year,' we are smugly told, 'who is the mainstay of most of these places'. In slack moments—and there seem to have been many of them—the Settling Room had its own casino, where people gambled in American Rails, 'paying their differences in pennies instead of pounds'.

The Orchestral and Choral Society gave three subscription concerts a year at the Queen's Hall, and several of them were attended by the Prince of Wales, who liked to tap his foot to a Sullivan tune. The orchestra, 110 strong, had a weekly $2\frac{1}{2}$-hour rehearsal, and the choir's 65 members rehearsed every Monday evening for an hour and a half, and occasionally performed members' own compositions.

Moore & Burgess's Ministrels had set a fashion for Nigger Troups, and the Stock Exchange had one which gave charity concerts complete with 'corner men, bones and interlocutor'. Charity, however, was not the object of the 1886 'handsomest member' contest, which ran for five weeks and was won by a Mr. H. Maas with a dozen bottles of champagne. As the century drew to a close, the Stock Exchange Art Society was formed and gave exhibitions of members' painting and photography: it was hoped that this would give them an outlet for the creativity already expressed in rude caricatures on the white walls of the House.

The Stock Exchange has produced—and no doubt deliberately recruited—many sportsmen, and these turn-of-the-century years are rich in names such as Stoddart and Leveson-Gower (cricket), Maclagan, MacGregor, and Wauchope (rugby), Christopherson and Kitcat (hockey), Guy Nickalls (rowing), several de Zoetes (golf), and Chinnerys (athletics). As for the famous Brighton Walk, which most writers on the Stock Exchange allot to the year 1903, there is evidence that there was some kind of Brighton Walk as early as 1891, and that it included a certain H. K. Paxton, a 19-stone jobber celebrated for his uproarious humour, who was given 23 minutes' start. And as for that humour, there was an outbreak of indoor fireworks in 1896 severe enough to call for a Committee reprimand: and an increasing number of light-hearted books, usually sold for charity, by Stock Exchange members, including several books of cartoons and a collection of 'Stock Exchange Ditties' by M. E. Greville, set to music by Frederic Norton, the future composer of *Chu Chin Chow*.

Towards charities, members and clerks were generous to a fault: they also looked after their own. 'The Decayed Members Fund' took on the happier title of Benevolent Fund some time during the 1880s. Some members felt that it did not do its job properly, and a Mr. M. O. Craven called it 'a model to misers'. The Fund had £167,000 at the time, and it was earning £5,800 per annum interest. In one year, the stewards had collected £11,000, yet only £7,535 had been paid out in annuities. The Committee, to whom Mr. Craven must have appeared a dangerous Radical, mildly observed that the number of annuities had quadrupled in the past twenty-five years, and that the Fund's income ebbed and flowed. By the end of the century its capital exceeded £220,000, and 'distressed members' were receiving up to £80 a year.

The twentieth century is only a few years away, and readers of *Punch* in 1891 may have felt it coming in the person of Lupin Pooter, the dreadful 19-year-old son of Charles and Carrie Pooter in *The Diary of a Nobody*. Lupin hires a pony-and-trap out of the £200 he makes in one day because of 'Job Cleanands putting me on to Chlorates'. This annihilates his poor father, who has just been given £100 rise after twenty-one years' faithful service. 'My dear Guv.,' Lupin explains, 'I promise faithfully that I will never speculate with what I have not got. I shall only go on Job Cleanands' tips, and as he is "in the know" it is pretty safe sailing.' Lupin works for Mr. Murray Posh, of Posh's Three-Shilling Hats, who has in fact *lost* £600 over Lupin's advice about Parachikka Chlorates, but still thinks him a very bright young man. Lupin persuades all his family and friends to invest in Chlorates, until Pooter Senior is stunned to read in the

110

*Standard*: 'Great Failure of Stock and Share Dealers! Mr. Job Cleanands Absconded!' This does not in the least surprise Lupin: for him it is all part of 'good old biz'.

So the Stock Exchange appeared, in the last decade of the nineteenth century, to Brickfield Terrace, N., and to the brothers Grossmith. Inside the House, there were certain dissensions as the Kaffir Boom moved on towards its climax and anticlimax. Some members tried to form a rival Stock Exchange, with lower subscriptions, and more flexible rules of admission: they even found premises in Leadenhall Street. Like so many schemes, it fizzled out; but it seems probable that its instigators were again mainly dealers in mining shares. The Mining Market was not clearly defined until July 1897, when it was divided into three—Miscellaneous, South African, and West Australian. To these, West African (hitherto known as the Jungle Market) was added three years later.

The 'Westralian' market had suffered from the promotions of Horatio Bottomley, and there were several failures. Bottomley's standard procedure has been summarized as: 'Subscription; Stock Exchange quotation, with price artificially pushed up for a short time; issue of a 20 per cent dividend; slow or speedy decline of the stock; liquidation or reconstruction'. And, it might have been added, a wonderful vagueness about detail in subsequent inquiries. However, all this went wrong in the case of the Waitekauri Gold Mining Co., floated by Bottomley in 1896. Jobbers and brokers sold shares at a premium (before allotment, of course) and forced him to buy up his own shares to maintain the price. The issue went badly, speculators realized something was wrong, and the Lord Mayor was asked (but refused) to issue a summons against Bottomley for conspiracy. The Stock Exchange had at last got the message: Bottomley was too hot to handle. One dealer, whose hammering was entirely due to the collapse of some Bottomley shares, was readmitted to membership after a petition from his creditors to the Committee.

There was also, in 1897, a test case which showed that broking and jobbing were still in need of official separation. A jobber complained that a broker had been making prices in the Kaffir Market. This blew up into a general row, in which brokers complained that jobbers were *always* invading their territory, especially in accepting commission orders from provincial brokers. The Committee issued a few mild scoldings, and nobody was satisfied.

111

We have heard rumblings about 'a younger Committee', and a symptom of this was a stiff memorandum in 1894 to the Committee and Managers jointly, reminding them of the 1878 desire for incorporation, which would of course mean the end of dual control. Duality was never more single-minded than in the reply, which rested mainly on the assertion that this constitutional change would 'expose the affairs of the Stock Exchange to public inspection and bring it under the control of the Board of Trade'. This had been made abundantly clear in the 1878 Report, and the astonishment of the petitioners suggests that they had not done their homework.

Meanwhile, 'how are Consols?' Several Australian banks had crashed in 1893, and Consols fluctuated between $99\frac{5}{8}$ and 97, showing, perhaps, like a seismograph, how international finance was becoming. They touched their highest-ever point, $113\frac{7}{8}$, in 1896 (although, if we go by Galsworthy, they were once at 116, causing James Forsyte, aged 91 just before the Boer War, to shake his head and get in 'a fantod' at the prospect of becoming a limited company). The Boer War was a week away when, on 3 October 1899, Bank Rate rose from $3\frac{1}{2}$ to $4\frac{1}{2}$ per cent, and Consols fell by $1\frac{3}{8}$ to $102\frac{5}{8}$, lower than they had been for five years. On 5 October Bank Rate jumped again to 5 per cent, and Consols fell again to $101\frac{3}{4}$.

Consols were getting quite a lot of competition in this last decade of the century. To the gambling fever was added the investor's desire ('good old biz!') to get a little more for his money; prices were rising, and would go on rising until 1914. There were mergers in basic industries such as cotton, brewing, steel, chemicals, food and catering (Lyons, Liptons, Home & Colonial Stores, all date from this time); and most of them sought quotations in London. Provincial banks, too, merged and came to the City. There were more sound equities to choose from, and usually they were established companies coming to the market for the first time. Unhappily, some of them were not, some barely existed outside the imaginations of their promoters; and here the name of Bottomley appears again, and also E. T. Hooley, who made £5 million profit out of twenty-six companies, and somehow managed to go bankrupt after three years, but not before he had pulled off his single claim to fame—the flotation of the Dunlop Rubber Company.

The Battle of Throgmorton Street, some months before the height of the Kaffir Boom, was only indirectly related to business, except insofar as it demonstrated the tightness of accommodation in the House. Some members were in the habit of slipping back into the Stock Exchange after official closing time, on the pretext of having forgotten something, and, against the rules, dealing went on. One trouble was the difference in clock-time between London and New York. Wall Street opened just as London was closing, and dealers in American shares gathered in Shorter's Court (a custom which persisted for many years afterwards). All this (in police terms) 'caused an obstruction' in the narrow streets around the Stock Exchange, and the City of London Police decided on a test raid (19 March 1895).

Members of the Stock Exchange, some of whom (such as H. K. Paxton) were somewhat larger than the police officers, had a bantering relationship with them at this time. When, therefore, police ordered members to 'move on', the usual horseplay turned suddenly into a scuffle, and a Mr. Macbrair was actually arrested. Three members went to his aid and they were joined by other members and spectators until the crowd could be deemed a demonstration if not an insurrection.

Next day the four members appeared before Alderman Faudel-Phillips at Guildhall. There was uproar when the police alleged assault and intoxication. Brokers, the Alderman said, must not regard the streets as their property; and Mr. Macbrair was fined £10 and the other three lesser sums.

Meanwhile the police had organized a number of hansom cabs which, empty, drove up and down Throgmorton Street 'to keep it clear'. As the fined members, at the head of a swelling crowd, made their way back to the House, they saw that one of the cabs contained, to its peril, Mr. H. K. Paxton, who acknowledged the cheers of the public as if he were royalty, and he too was arrested and fined. Everyone looked to the Committee for some major disciplinary measure. but all that happened was the posting of a notice reminding members that 'street trading was forbidden'.

There were two important changes of personnel towards the end of the decade. In 1896 Edward Satterthwaite succeeded Francis Levien as Secretary (at an 'emolument' of £1,500 a year); and in 1897 Sir Henry Burdett resigned as Secretary of the Share and Loan Department after seventeen years' distinguished service. He had been knighted for his hospital charity work, he was still only 49. and it was assumed that his private means were more than adequate.

The Trustees and Managers therefore handed him a cheque for a thousand guineas with their heartfelt thanks.

To their consternation, Sir Henry asked: 'What about my pension?' Sorry, said the Managers; there wasn't one. But, Sir Henry protested, 'I added £3,800 a year to your resources by reorganizing the Stamp Department,' and this had resulted in the abolition of his £800 a year pension. Besides, he had lost £30,000 by giving them the copyright of *Burdett's Official Intelligence*. Unfortunately he had saved nothing out of his £4,500 a year salary (which had included profits from both stamps and the *Official Intelligence*). Sorry, said the Managers, but that was none of their business; as Sir Henry had recently accepted a number of lucrative chairmanships in the City, he surely would not starve. Sir Henry sent back the cheque in disgust. His successor, Mr. Torres-Johnson, was paid only £1,500 a year, and his contract stipulated sharply that he was to be in his office by 10.30 every morning.

Two years later, the *Official Intelligence* was rechristened *The Stock Exchange Official Intelligence*. When Burdett had started his publication in 1881, succeeding Mihil Slaughter as editor, the securities quoted totalled £3,586 million. Now, in 1899, they were £5,411 million and the book had three times as many pages as in Slaughter's time. It was in 1899, too, that the *Official List*, published by the Committee, was also enlarged (to twelve pages instead of eight) and changed its name from the *London Daily Stock and Share List* to the *Stock Exchange Daily Official List*.

But now the century was about to close in a fever of emotion which is difficult to imagine today. We have seen that Members were prone, at the drop of a silk hat, to demonstrate their patriotism even to the neglect of business. They had done it in 1893, forming fours and marching to Guildhall to protest against Home Rule and sing patriotic songs to the Lord Mayor. The country had been perilously near war with France in 1898 with the Fashoda Incident: anyone saying anything nice about the French was liable to be debagged, until the Chairman of the Stock Exchange smoothed things over by sending a message of sympathy to the Paris Bourse on the death of President Fauré.

The Boer War, then generally called the Transvaal War, gave members an emotional outlet which they seemed to have been needing for several years. On the day it began (11 October 1899), the

Rhodesian Market unfurled a huge Union Jack, and Charlie Clarke, one of those licensed-buffoons-with-a-heart-of-gold who have always been popular on the Floor, conducted the entire House in the singing of the National Anthem, with special emphasis on the verse containing the line 'frustrate their knavish tricks'. He then symbolically 'hammered' President Kruger for having 'failed to comply with his bargains'. Kruger was then hanged in effigy, and burnt. About a thousand members then marched to Guildhall to assure the Lord Mayor that they supported Government policy. The Lord Mayor, for his part, had started a Transvaal Refugees' Fund, to which the Stock Exchange within a month contributed £22,268.

The Stock Exchange, especially the South African Market, had an interest to declare, as well as the natural overflowing of its warm heart. 'The war', a contemporary observer wrote, 'is peculiarly connected with the Stock Exchange. It has been undertaken on behalf of the Uitlanders, practically without exception engaged in the mining industry; its effects, it is trusted, will be . . . to bring more prosperity to the Rand mining companies.' There was no panic, but Consols were down below par, there would be a large increase of the National Debt, 'the Kaffir Market is in a state of nervous anxiety', and although some gold had been seized by the enemy, the mines themselves had not been destroyed. True, there would be 'some postponement of dividends'.

There was a Horse Fund, to which members gave thirty-eight of their own horses and £2,884 in cash, enough to buy at least one hundred animals. Charlie Clarke made history again by bringing a pony into the House with a collecting box on its back, the proceeds to buy tobacco for the Royal Dublin Fusiliers who were defending Laing's Nek. Rudyard Kipling supplied the title for the 'Absent-Minded Beggar Fund' for comforts for the troops.

One or two cads made small killings by the old 'Death of Napoleon' method; only this time it was Ladysmith that kept on being falsely relieved. The House sang 'Soldiers of the Queen' whether they thought it was true or not, and woe betide anyone who wasn't wearing red, white and blue—he must be a pro-Boer, so knock his hat off.

When Ladysmith finally *was* relieved, the news came through at five to ten in the morning, and we are told that 'members did not trouble to go to their offices'. Charlie Clarke, the National Anthem, cheers for Generals Buller and White; and one member 'tried to play

115

"Soldiers of the Queen" on a post-horn'. And yet—'the Kaffir Market hardly moved'. The Kaffir Market, to judge from euphemisms used by contemporary members, was too drunk to move.

The news of the relief of Mafeking, several months later, was heard on a Friday night. Saturday morning business began at 10.15 and lasted precisely fifteen minutes. Then Charlie Clarke, National Anthem, flags, post-horn, cheers—special cheers this time for Colonel Baden-Powell, who, it was remembered, was an Old Carthusian, which caused his school-fellows to wear their ties round their hats.

About forty members and eighty clerks had volunteered for South Africa, most of them joining the City Imperial Yeomanry. It went without saying that subscriptions and other fees were waived, and their jobs would be kept open for them until their return. This last provision was not universally observed, and gave rise to an 'ugly incident'. A partner in one firm, which was said to have refused to guarantee a clerk's job, was 'roughly handled' on 15 January 1900. The victim denied the allegation, and complained to the Committee for General Purposes about 'a violent personal attack'. The Committee, however, could not enforce Rule 117 because the member was unable to identify his attackers.

It is not clear whether he complained to his M.P. or to the press; but soon a question was asked in the House of Commons by someone who had no love for the Stock Exchange. It was now said that the member had been 'kicked until he fainted' by 'a crowd of stockjobbers interested in the Transvaal War'. There was in this an unpleasant implication that 'stockjobbers' (note the rhetorical effect of the contemptuous old word) were only interested in protecting their mining interests. Could nothing be done, the Home Secretary, Sir Matthew Ridley, was asked, to prevent the riotous behaviour for which the Stock Exchange was so notorious? The Home Secretary was sorry: no action could be taken, since 'the Stock Exchange is a private place'.

However, the House could console itself that it had a V.C., awarded to Lieut. A. C. Doxat for rescuing a patrol on horseback under fire.

Looking back on the last quarter of the century, the Stock Exchange historian of the day, Charles Duguid, normally an ebullient chronicler whose tongue was frequently in his cheek, turns suddenly a little sour. Thinking of the great ideals of the Royal Commission's

116

1878 report, as he writes in 1901, he regrets that 'the main part of the Report has not been carried out ... The public are not admitted; there is no real register of neglected securities, despite the slighted board hanging in the Railway Market; dealing before allotment is as rampant as ever; the Stock Exchange committee still imparts prestige to a security, however unwittingly, by granting it quotation; it does not license outside brokers and their bucket shops; there is no Public Functionary to control the business of the House; and the Stock Exchange has received no Royal Charter.'

The old Queen died on 22 January 1901. 'The House, emotional to excess in other directions, never weeps,' Duguid says. A few price lists were to be seen, but nobody dealt. Somebody had forgotten to switch off the ticker-tape, which was almost the only sound to be heard. This was no occasion for Charlie Clarke to conduct patriotic songs, as he had done twenty months before on the Queen's eightieth birthday. It was noted that Consols were 96¼ the night before she died, and 96½ the day after. This was taken as incontrovertible evidence of national stability.

# 14

# The Edwardians

'What's the market gonna do, sir?'
'Fluctuate, my boy; just fluctuate.'
　　　　　—alleged conversation between J. Pierpont
　　　　　Morgan and an elevator boy

Edward VII—'Bertie' to the family, 'good old Teddy' to the masses
—was the first British monarch who had any real idea of what the
world of finance was about. He had been at Trinity College, Cambridge, with Nathan, Leo, and Alfred Rothschild, who remained
his lifelong friends, and who knew him as either 'Bertie' or 'Wales'.
Victoria did not quite approve, perhaps because, like other people
at Court, she feared that State or family secrets might be leaked to
the City after the extra glass of champagne; but her friendship with
Disraeli drew her closer to Jewry, she had raised one of the Rothschilds to the peerage, and it is said that she sometimes used the
Rothschilds' private courier system for exceptionally confidential
correspondence.

Edward, as Prince of Wales, had often stayed with Lord Rothschild at Tring Manor, shot with Leopold at Leighton Buzzard, sailed
with Ferdinand in Pegwell Bay. Rothschild invitation cards tended
to read: '. . . to have the honour of meeting their Royal Highnesses';
and after Edward's difficult appearance in the witness box at a Society
divorce hearing, it is said that Alfred soothed his nerves by playing
the piano to him. There was also a Rothschild house in Hamilton
Place, many years later converted into a nightclub and restaurant,
where people used to point out the banisters H.R.H. loved to slide
down.

Edward had travelled more than any other Hanoverian king, saw
himself as a man of the world with a diplomatic, almost a business

duty to cultivate good relationships with other countries. (At top level, of course.) He liked financiers, enjoyed picking their brains, revelled in the stock market tips he got from Sir Ernest Cassel. Financiers were men who had done things, and Edward admired them. Cassel, who came from a German banking family, had financed the Asswan Dam in 1898, helped to create the National Bank of Egypt, irrigated a tract of the Sahara and founded an Agricultural Bank and a cotton-growing company. His grand-daughter Edwina would one day marry Lord Louis Mountbatten.

All the great financiers of the day went racing, some of them to watch their own horses running; and Edward went with them. It is probable that he never forgot his visit to the new Stock Exchange building in 1885, where the jobbers at their pitches must have reminded him of bookies shouting the odds. When Edward went racing, he talked business as well as horseflesh. He probably chuckled at many a Jewish joke, especially jokes from the Berlin Stock Exchange which were said to be specially collected for him by the German diplomat, Baron von Eckhardstein.

Sir Osbert Sitwell, in *The Scarlet Tree*, pinpoints 1909 as 'the year of the Stock Exchange', but gives no reason. It was certainly eventful, as we shall see; but the landed aristocrat is probably turning up his nose at what seemed to him the materialism and extravagance of the decade, the middle-class cheerfulness, and *The Merry Widow*.

The twentieth century had not begun well for the Stock Exchange. As Edward VII was crowned, they were still clearing up the mess left by the collapse of the London & Globe Finance Corporation, whose chairman was the Marquis of Dufferin and Ava. This was the brain-child of Whitaker Wright, a financier who perhaps falls into the category of over-ambitious rather than crooked promoters, but was guilty enough to commit suicide rather than face imprisonment. The crash caused the failure of thirteen stockbroking firms and twenty-nine members of the Stock Exchange, one of whom had been a member for fifty years. Another was on his honeymoon at the time, and another was commanding a battalion in South Africa.

The Globe group embraced a number of subsidiaries, among them Lake View, the British America Corporation, Standard Exploration, Kootenay, Rossland Great Western, and Le Roi. One of them, known as Le Roi No. 2, was definitely suspected of a rigging operation. Its £5 shares stood at 23, and to the uninitiated all seemed well until

E                                    119

Friday 28 December 1900. Suddenly everyone wanted their cash back, in banknotes, please, to pay for transfers. Why? Because London & Globe's cheques were bouncing. Not only were Le Roi No. 2 shares suddenly halved in value—that might have been expected—but the same thing was happening all through the group. Le Roi's were worst of all—overnight they fell from 23 to 3.

New Year's Eve 1900 was the gloomiest on record: 'the very hand of Barker, the waiter, shook like an aspen leaf as, amid death-like silence, he announced failure after failure'. It was an old story: loans had been called in, and Wright had been panicked into buying his own shares (with money he had not got). He owed money to the jobbers, the jobbers owed money to the brokers, the brokers owed money to their clients, and so the wretched chain reaction went on.

What was the Committee to do? It would be technically within its rights if it decided not to fix special settlements. There was a feeling that if accounts were payable before 11 a.m. on settlement day, members would at least have 'time to turn round' after a default. Was a new rule needed? There was simply no time to discuss it: the honour of the House was at stake; it had endured a good deal of criticism in recent years, and now was the chance to show its public spirit. Every investor involved in the crash must be paid; and so they they were.

There had been one or two new rules lately, of a domestic character. Since 25 March 1899, new members' subscriptions had been 40 instead of 30 guineas, and on Lady Day 1900 it was decreed that this should also be paid by clerks after four years' apprenticeship: they also had a stiff increase in their entrance fee (from 150 to 250 guineas), while members who had not been apprenticed as clerks had to pay 500 guineas entrance fee and provide three sureties.

Another attempt, by a member named H. H. Pain, to revolutionize the Deed of Settlement in 1901 once again urged the abolition of Dual Control, but went much further: every member was to become a shareholder in a new Stock Exchange Company with ten times its present capital; and there was to be an annuity scheme 'to induce members no longer actively engaged in business to retire'. A young man's scheme, obviously; but the new younger Committee was not in a mood for quite so much new blood. As an example of longevity in the Stock Exchange, there was still living in 1901 a jobber in the Railway Market named William Baines, who had been a member since 1836; and *he* could remember another 'Father of the House', still alive thirteen years before, who had been in the French Army when Napoleon retreated from Moscow.

'Inducing members to retire' was one way of keeping numbers down in an overcrowded House; but the Managers and Committee had another scheme based on restricted membership. It was eventually ruled that, to qualify for election to membership, everyone must have served as a clerk for two years, one of which must have been on the Floor of the House itself. No firm might send more than five clerks into the House, but one clerk should have access to the Settling Room.

But members wanted more restriction than this. Three thousand of them petitioned for a sub-committee on the subject, and in 1904 the 'nomination' system, destined to last for more than sixty years, was instituted. Henceforth would-be members must buy a nomination from a retiring member or from the estate of a dead member. Clerks with four or more years' service, however, could put their names on a waiting list, with a reasonable hope of some day being elected without nomination, and they were required to buy one share in the Stock Exchange, while all other members had to buy three.

Obviously it was getting much more expensive to become a member, and it seemed to some that, however costly a mistress democracy was, the trend towards a closed shop was even costlier. But the new rules at least realized one of Mr. H. H. Pain's principles: all members would eventually become proprietors, and Managers and Committee were bound some day to merge. Nobody, however, fixed a sum for the cost of a nomination, and the result was sometimes not so much an auction, more a ransom. In the early 1900s a clerk had to have about £450 handy to get elected (multiply by ten for an equivalent 1973 figure) plus a share of about £175; and a nominated member well over £1,100. H. Withers, the American historian of English banking, observed (in 1910) that British brokers and jobbers were far better off than their American or French colleagues, who might have to pay the dollar and franc equivalents of £16,000 and £92,000 respectively.

Another set of new rules was on the way, and came to fruition in 1908. Custom and unwritten law was not enough to define the separateness of jobbing and broking; in future, jobbers must only job, and brokers must only broke, and if they wanted to change sides they must have the Committee's permission to do so. Brokers might deal with non-members if they could genuinely get better terms, but jobbers were forbidden to do this. The only exception to this rule was in the case of 'arbitrageurs' (firms transacting business with foreign brokers, especially with Wall Street) whether brokers or jobbers. An American broker named van Antwerp, who visited London just before the First World War, was unable to see much advantage in the British jobbing system, except that it got through an enormous volume of business in a short time. He also thought that London had simply no idea how to use the Exchange Telegraph service: very few firms had Extel machines, only a few price lists were transmitted every day, and 'almost nobody looks at them'. Why, in New York, the machine never stopped ticking all day long! The British didn't know how to use the telephone, either—British telephones were terrible anyway—no wonder London brokers had to waste so much time in their offices reading hundreds of letters and telegrams.

It is recorded that one firm of stockbrokers kept their telephone in the partners' lavatory, for fear that the clerks would use it to ring up their girl friends. Besides, telephones were felt to be detrimental in dignity and good manners. Principals either wrote letters or went to see each other. Walter de Zoete, who retired from de Zoete & Gorton in 1909, never used the telephone at all, although the firm had had one since 1895 (at a cost of £10 a year irrespective of the number of calls), and thought his clerk Pericles Freme (an Egyptian Greek who had changed his name from Nassif) 'a somewhat pushing young particle' for wanting to extend its use. Immediately after Walter's retirement, his firm's switchboard acquired seven extensions and two dozen private lines to important clients—one of them was Sir Ernest Cassel, who got on well with young Pericles—and de Zoete's had its own, its very own, Extel tape machine: like other progressive firms, it also used typewriters (in 1897 it had had only one).

Early typewriters (usually called typewriting-machines, because typewriter originally meant the man or girl who used it) were noisy and cumbersome, and in many stockbroking firms good copperplate handwriting was still one of the qualifications of a junior clerk, who, since few partners dictated letters until the early 1900s, preferring to draft them in pencil, had to make file copies by hand.

But things were stirring in the reign of 'good old Teddy'. London was electrifying its trams, had its own united Metropolitan Water

Board (at last taking over the New River company of 1619); the first submarine was laid down at Barrow-in-Furness, just before Krupps took over the shipbuilding yards at Kiel in 1902; in America Henry Ford founded his motor company, two years before Herbert Austin, and three years before Rolls-Royce was founded in 1906; country bus services were started (usually by railway companies, to bring passengers to their stations); the Bakerloo and Piccadilly Tubes were opened (the 'Drain', from Mansion House to Waterloo, had been electrified in 1898, and the Central London in 1900).

Invention, innovation, 'progress', were in the air; and yet the number of companies coming to the market was not as great as might have been expected. Many new enterprises were undertaken by local authorities, and thus joined the Gilts market. By 1907 all old tramways, and more than a thousand miles of new ones, were electrified, and some of these were built by the British Electric Traction group. Chemicals, cotton, big stores like Harrods, were quoted. Lever Brothers were on the take-over trail to consolidate a dominating position in the soap trade; artificial silk (rayon) was being exploited by Courtaulds who 'went public' in 1913; banks were conglomerating into formations which, thirty years later, would become the Big Five. Often the banks would seek the advice of a stockbroking firm in arranging a merger; but that was all. Brokers, however, were more and more asked, by existing companies other than banks, to arrange underwriting for new issues, and some even undertook promotions themselves. Levy & Cohen, Foster & Braithwaite, Greenwell, Panmure Gordon, are names that spring to mind.

In general, the more conservative brokers of these years were still wary of industrials, and even Electric Supply Company shares were felt to be too speculative. Foreign stocks were regarded as much safer, especially railways. A young broker was sometimes sent to Kennedy & Robertson, a leading firm of Foreign Railway jobbers, to get his investment training.

It was no bad thing to be in tea. All commodities are subject to fluctuation according to the crop and the uncertainty of matching supply and demand, but the Indian and Ceylon growers had a good record for regular dividends. In the first few years of the twentieth century, however, tea had been over-produced, and had Old Jolyon Forsyte still been alive, he might have been tempted to sell. Those who hung on until Lloyd George's Old Age Pensions Bill came, giving pensioners 10*s*. a week, did not regret it; for old people drink large quantities of tea, and the new concept of tea as a necessity rather than a luxury, encouraged by Lyons and Liptons and Twinings who were packaging cheap blends, had come to stay. One broking firm finds in its records the case of a man who bought 1,000 Consolidated Tea & Lands Ordinary shares at 30*s*. in 1904; they were able to inform his widow, twenty years later, that the shares were worth £82,000.

R. P. Wilkinson, father of Sir Martin Wilkinson, Chairman of the Stock Exchange 1965–73, was specializing in tea shares for de Zoete & Gorton at this time, and in 1910 published the first *Tea Share Manual* which appeared annually and became the standard work of reference on the industry. Later, supplementary monthly and weekly lists were issued.

At the time, this was regarded as dangerously near to advertising. However, by 1911 one or two broking firms were sending their clients ('for private circulation only') Circulars offering 'a short monthly review of the Stock Markets' and recommending sound purchases: 'speculative securities will not be dealt with'. The list generally began by regretting 'the unfortunate depreciation during the last ten or fifteen years of first-class securities'. One shouldn't really be looking for high yields in times like these: stability was the thing to go for. We were all hoping for the rehabilitation of Consols; but meanwhile what was wrong with Corporation and Colonial Government loans? Cape 3%, New South Wales 3%, West Ham 3%, Middlesex County 3% all showed an upward trend and were particularly suitable for trust investments. The Banks and Insurance Companies were buying South Nigerian Government 4% 5-year Bonds at 99½: wouldn't Average Investor like to follow their example?

Foreign Government Securities, Canadian Railways, Foreign Railways were all recommended; and it is unfair, with the wisdom of hindsight, to smile at the fact that City of Baku 5% Gold Bonds at 96¼ were rated above Associated Portland Cement 5% Debenture Stock at 92½. Cement was still rather speculative, 'but the demand is increasing and the outlook appears satisfactory'.

Other popular shares of the time are to be found in a book of cartoons, published in a limited edition, and edited by W. Eden Cooper, whose faintly risqué captions inform us that Virginia New Funded Bonds were known as 'Virgins' and Buenos Aires Waterworks stock as 'Baby Wee-wee'.

By 1913, Convertible Bonds were the latest thing: you could convert to Common Shares whenever you liked. Also in the shop window were Brazilian Traction 6% Convertible Preference Shares, and Mexican Eagle 6% First Mortgage Bonds. Cities like Bergen, Budapest, Moscow, enterprises such as Greek Railways and Greek Currants were offered. Very little information was given—indeed, not much was available: in the case of cities requiring loans, sometimes only the population was given. For where could one get information? Many brokers did their best, but statisticians had little to go on but prospectuses, their own experience and hunches, annual reports (in which chairmen were apt to say nothing, and say it very elegantly), cuttings from the financial press, current news about crops and mines, and of course the Stock Exchange's own *Official Intelligence*.

After tea, rubber came into the news. Rubber had suddenly caused a city named Manaos to be established on the river Negro in Brazil, 900 miles from the mouth of the Amazon; complete with an ornate opera-house where Caruso once sang, and every kind of civilized luxury. Today it is half-choked by the encroaching jungle. In 1909, at the time of the great Rubber Boom, the Mincing Lane Tea and Rubber Sharebrokers' Association Ltd. was formed, becoming incorporated three years later. It aimed to provide a service to investors in tea, rubber and other plantation or commodity shares, and had some thirty members under the control of a committee. Today it has only five member firms.

The year 1909 must have been a tremendous one to live through. Lloyd George's People's Budget, defying the House of Lords, began a revolutionary redistribution of income which would have been called Socialist if it had not been Liberal. Galsworthy, showing that there was one law for the rich, another for the poor; Wells showing the New Woman in *Ann Veronica*, with the Suffragettes turning militant; Blériot flying the Channel; and Horatio Bottomley charged with fraud at Guildhall, defending himself with that rhetorical skill which none of his advocates could equal, and by which Horace Avory and Richard Muir, for the Crown, were baffled.

He was Liberal M.P. for Hackney, and not at the moment bankrupt; but shareholders of his Joint Stock Trust, floated in 1907, were petitioning for liquidation. Nearly ten million shares in excess of the Trust's stated capital had been issued. It had taken eighteen months to examine his books, the more important of which were missing; yet somehow he got himself acquitted. He had now founded *John Bull* with £96,000 (most of it supplied by, of all people, E. T. Hooley), with Julius Salter Elias (afterwards Lord Southwood of Odhams Press) as his business director, and Frank Harris as his literary and dramatic critic.

Of interest to the Stock Exchange, who seem never to have found a way of preventing Bottomley from debasing their coinage, was the fact that readers of *John Bull* could take advantage of the John Bull Investment Trust (registered in Guernsey), in Bottomley's pious words, 'to keep them out of the hands of bucket-shop keepers'. For once, the Trust seems to have proceeded normally: Horatio was not yet at the Victory Bond stage of over-confidence.

The words 'Investment Trust' had acquired a certain prestige in recent years. These trusts dated back to the 1860s, had been promoted with some vigour in the penultimate decade of the last century, and although they contained few Government securities offered attractive packages of foreign loans, home and foreign railways, and public utilities such as electricity, gas, and water, most of which were 'fixed interest' stocks. Investment trusts were a good way of spreading risk by putting one's money into the hands of expert investment managers. A small investor could thus feel safe, and all the safer for knowing that insurance companies were doing the same as he was. Unit trusts, though more strictly limited by deed to a certain range of securities, had similar attractions, and the first one can be precisely dated at 1868, but unit trusts as we know them today were not destined to develop until the 1930s.

So there was ample scope for the Bottomleys who promised the small investor all the advantages implied in the word 'trust', and against whom respectable brokers warned their clients in vain. But in 1909 there were more dramatic events to distract the attention of people who did not happen to be readers of *John Bull*. Several years of depressed markets and boring inactivity were bound to end in a boom, if only for the emotional release.

The comfort of motoring had been greatly increased by rubber tyres, first solid, then inflated. The first of fifteen million model T Ford cars had come off the assembly line in 1908. Gum boots had been made in America for more than eighty years, it was seventy-five years since Goodyear and Hancock had discovered vulcanization, and more than four hundred years since Columbus, on his second visit to South America, had observed Indians playing a kind of rugger with a black, heavy ball made from a vegetable gum. Now seeds of the tree had been sent from the Amazon to Ceylon and Malaya, and 11,000 tons of the end product were about to be offered on the London market.

Rubber plantations, it seemed, were going to be big business; and on Christmas Eve 1909 members and clerks of the Stock Exchange were prevented from joining their families round the Christmas tree by an abnormal outburst of dealings (especially for Glasgow brokers) which went on until 7 p.m., long after official closing time. In the early months of 1910, rubber was fetching 12s. 9d. a pound, and it was said that dealing—or at least documentation—frequently went on all night. Much of the business was done on the Mincing Lane Exchange, but the Stock Exchange reflected the chaotic conditions of these months. One observer who is still living can remember 'a tight pack of dealers, covered in dust, all trying to reach the wanted jobber. Prices moved rapidly and shares bought in 1909 were sold a year later at twenty to forty times the purchase price.'

Some purchasers were Chinese merchants in Peking and Hong Kong, who, besides being close to the plantations themselves, were skilful speculators. But woe betide anybody who bought or sold too late, for great were their losses. One man in London who did well out of rubber shares was the secretary of a London agency house, who, we are told in the company history of a famous firm of stock-brokers, 'was in the habit of adding 25% for himself in transacting orders, financing his purchases with the company's money. Detected in this at the height of the boom, he was summarily dismissed but managed to leave with a profit of over £30,000.' He then sold his investments in good time and reinvested the money in ten companies managed by his late firm, 'and derived great pleasure from attending meetings to propose votes of thanks to the directors'.

It was in 1909 that the old argument about brokers' commissions again came up, stimulated it seems by the new rules separating the functions of brokers and jobbers. A sub-committee studied the question, and reported in favour of a fixed scale. The Council of Associated Stock Exchanges in the provinces was also thinking along these lines, and Glasgow had already worked out a scale of minimum commissions. Discussions went on for two more years:

127

one big difficulty was that the rule against dealers dealing with non-members could not be enforced if a broker was employed 'at a nominal remuneration to pass his bargains through'. At last, in March 1912, by a majority of only 119 votes, a scale was adopted—2s. 6d. per cent on stock, and varying commissions (1½d. to 2s. 6d. per share) according to size.

Meanwhile, how were jobbers faring? London was, in these pre-1914 years, the undisputed financial centre of the world, and its business was pre-eminently international. Jobbers needed very much more capital than brokers in order to 'carry substantial positions', and they had various ways of borrowing it—from banks, or 'money brokers'—and in July 1914 it was calculated that all Stock Exchange firms together had loans totalling over £80 million.

Neither broker nor jobber made much money on gilt-edged securities, which were now declining in volume. They formed only about 10 per cent of all quoted stocks, of which half went to finance the National Debt. But their importance and stability would always be needed, even though Industrials were knocking at the door. Soames Forsyte, at about this time, had £250,000 'very diversely invested', yielding an income of £4,000 a year. Galsworthy never tells us in what Soames's money was invested (other than property—and he *did* give too much for that house in Montpelier Square). Indeed, he may have done his sums wrong, since it was not, by Forsyte standards, a good return for the money. But poor Soames had never been quite the same since the 1909 Budget; super-tax had hit him hard, and he lived in terror of a capital levy.

# 15

# A Clean Puddle

---

'I consider this man quite as able as I am myself.'
—F. E. Smith, introducing
Godfrey Isaacs to his wife

'It was during the agitations upon that affair,' wrote G. K. Chesterton in his autobiography in 1936, 'that the ordinary English citizen lost his invincible ignorance; or, in ordinary language, his innocence . . . It will be seen as one of the turning-points in the whole history of England and the world.'

Well, it wasn't. How many history books today bother even to mention the Marconi Scandal? (It was Chesterton who gave it that name.) It was an eighteen months' wonder in 1912 and 1913, and shocked the general public in much the same way that the Ward–Profumo case did in 1963. The average newspaper reader had been given a glimpse of possible corruption in the Establishment. Things normally hushed up had been brought out into the open. The story is worth retelling if only because it compelled the Stock Exchange to take severe disciplinary action against some of its members.

'Wireless telegraphy', as it was then called, was fresh in the public mind. It had enabled Dr. Crippen to be arrested in mid-Atlantic. It had enabled a number of passengers to be saved from the *Titanic*. There was national defence to be considered: Germany was believed to be building wireless stations in all her colonies (she was, too: on 4 August 1914 all German merchant ships were ordered by radio to 'make for neutral ports'. Britain, on the outbreak of war, had only two stations—one in England and one in Egypt.)

In 1908, Marconi, having during the past thirteen years demonstrated that wireless telegraphy was possible over long distances, had spent £500,000 on research with no sign of a dividend or a worth-while contract. By 1912, he would have companies in Russia, Spain, Argentina, Canada, and the USA, most of them run from London. But first, through his brother-in-law, he was to meet a 40-year-old promoter named Godfrey Isaacs, clever, energetic, multilingual, and acquainted with European finance houses. There was nothing wrong with wireless, Isaacs said; it had a tremendous future; it just needed promotion. Godfrey Isaacs became Managing Director of Marconi.

Isaacs submitted a plan to the Colonial Office, in 1910, to link the Empire by a network of eighteen wireless stations. A Standing Committee, formed to investigate its feasibility, recommended that the Marconi Company should build the first six stations, but they were not to own them. They were to be in England, Egypt, East Africa, South Africa, India, and Singapore, and they would cost £60,000 each. Only six out of eighteen stations, but it looked to many people like the beginning of a monopoly.

Godfrey Isaacs had a brilliant brother named Rufus, recently knighted, who had become Attorney-General in Asquith's Liberal Government. He had left school at 14, tried to settle down in the family fruit-broking business, then run away to sea. A few years later, we find him as a jobber on the Stock Exchange. Suddenly he was 'hammered' for £8,000, tried to emigrate to Panama, thought better of it and began to read for the Bar. As a barrister, he was believed to have earned £50,000 a year. And here he was, in 1910, Attorney-General at the age of 52—and two years later, the first Attorney-General to be in the Cabinet.

Marconi shares were 6s. 3d. in 1908; in August 1911 they had shot up to £2 8s. 9d.; by December they were £3 6s. 3d.; in March 1912 they were £6 15s., and in April, £9. Then they fell. Why? There was gossip: it was rumoured that two members of the Cabinet, Rufus Isaacs and Lloyd George, and the Postmaster-General, Herbert Samuel, had bought Marconi shares while the Committee was still sitting. So had Lord Murray of Elibank, who was Patronage Secretary to the Treasury. Rufus Isaacs was said to have made more than £160,000 and Samuel £250,000. The Isaacs brothers and Samuel were Jews, and the whole issue became clouded with a peculiarly British kind of anti-semitism; also with vicious party politics, for his opponents hated Lloyd George—he had been pro-Boer, had brought in the 1909 Finance Act, and National

A Clean Puddle

Insurance—the elements of what would one day be called the Welfare State.

Wilfred Ramage Lawson, editor of the weekly *Outlook*, published a whole series of articles on the Marconi case, concentrating on the three Jews—men, he said curiously, 'of the same *nationality*', as if they all came from a state called Israel. The *National Review* thought the Ministers concerned should be punished as the corrupt ministers of the South Sea Bubble had been punished. The *Eye-Witness*, a weekly founded by Hilaire Belloc and edited by Cecil Chesterton, G. K.'s brother, took up the attack, which was continued by Cecil's successor, Charles Granville.

What nobody could understand was why the accused were so silent. Were there no grounds for libel? Was it beneath the dignity of ministers to reply to newspaper gossip? Yes, it was: Rufus Isaacs and Samuel had privately agreed with Prime Minister Asquith that they would not issue writs for libel: to do so would only raise the *Eye-Witness*'s circulation.

On 11 October 1912, the Commons debated whether a Select Committee of inquiry should be appointed; and the Attorney-General took the opportunity of saying that he knew nothing about the Marconi contract, which had been awarded three months before he joined the Cabinet. Winston Churchill, then Home Secretary, confined himself to saying that he thought it 'very undesirable to give Government patronage to foreigners' anyway.

The Select Committee began sitting on 25 October, and it included Sir Frederick Banbury, M.P., a banker and a former Member of the Stock Exchange. It was never very clear whether the ministers were being accused of speculating with 'inside knowledge', or of corruptly placing a Government contract, or both. The Select Committee decided to appoint a Technical Committee known as the Parker Committee. Both Committees were beset with difficulties. Charles Granville, now theoretically editing the *Eye-Witness*, could not be found: he was said to have absconded to Tangier while 'awaiting trial on charges of fraud, embezzlement and bigamy'. Lord Murray of Elibank could not attend because he was in Bogotá, investigating business opportunities for Lord Cowdray.

Lloyd George said he was 'in a perfect fog' about what he had done; he seemed to remember telling Rufus Isaacs that he had 'bought a bear', if that was the right term. He told the Select Com-

131

mittee that his salary as Chancellor of the Exchequer was £5,000 a year, that his investments brought in another £400 a year and that the only property he owned was his house in Wales which had cost £2,000. It was pertinently asked whether anything as speculative as Marconi shares could really be called an investment; and somebody was unkind enough to remember that Lloyd George, while electioneering in 1900, had attacked Joseph Chamberlain because his family had an interest in B.S.A. and Boer War arms contracts.

In France, *Le Matin*, claiming 'inside knowledge', had taken up the Marconi Scandal: Sir Rufus had bought 10,000 shares when they were £2, and sold 2,000 to Elibank and Lloyd George; they had planned to sell half to reduce the price of the other half. This naturally filtered back to Britain. By now hecklers, both at political meetings and in the Commons, were shouting 'Marconi!' as a term of abuse against Liberals. A Mr. Powell, editor of the *Financial News*, said he had heard that Winston Churchill had some Marconi shares too: Churchill denied 'this insulting charge'. The *Daily Express* created a temporary diversion with a 'Mystery of Missing Stockbroker' story: where was Charles Edwin Fenner, Elibank's broker, who had been a partner in the bankrupt firm of Montmorency & Co.? His books—also missing— were believed to contain 'interesting details of Marconi transactions'.

The inquiry raised an important point of company law: did the buyers think they were buying shares in *American* Marconi? If so, the shares had been privately issued, and therefore (by company law at that time) no prospectus was necessary, and 'dealing before allotment' was not illegal.

Cecil Chesterton, now editing the *New Witness* (with the cricketing poet J. C. Squire as his sub-editor), went on attacking Godfrey Isaacs. He was 'gold-mad'—he had promoted companies to prospect for gold in Wales, to quarry granite in Caernarvon, find silver in Ireland, run motor taxi-cab services; and had not most of them ended in liquidation? Isaacs had 'a ghastly record' of 'swindling'.

This was it: now Godfrey Isaacs *must* bring an action for libel, and he did. At the Old Bailey on 29 April 1912, Cecil Chesterton was charged with criminal libel. Throughout the trial he seemed, or affected to be, unable to understand legal points. Isaacs was represented by F. E. Smith (Rufus's friend and Bar colleague) and Edward Carson, who stressed Godfrey Isaacs' impeccable record: he might not always have shown sound judgement, but nobody had impugned his honesty: he had risked his own money, and lost a good deal of it.

Hilaire Belloc, in evidence, said: 'Cosmopolitan finance is a dangerous power': he would oppose it whether it were Jewish or not. But there was evidence that both the *Eye-Witness* and *New-Witness* had maintained a policy of anti-semitism. The Judge, in his summing up, plainly thought Chesterton guilty of 'ignorance of business' and 'racial prejudice'. The jury, out for only five minutes, returned a verdict of guilty. Chesterton, fined £100 with costs, had clearly expected to be sent to prison, and told reporters that the lightness of his sentence was 'a victory for clean government'.

The Committee's report, when it came, was hopelessly divided into majority, minority, and an isolated report which agreed with nobody else; most of the disagreements were party political ones, and at one point a Mr. Falconer, a Liberal, rewrote three-quarters of the report by proposing amendments to almost everything.

All through the summer of 1913 press comment went on and on. *The Times* had six consecutive leading articles on Marconi. One of them remarked wickedly that 'the Ministers had stepped into a puddle believing it to be a *clean* puddle'. Another paper thought that the Committee's report was like 'caning the whole of the Sixth Form'.

'We find,' the Report said, 'that the rumours current in the City of London as to the connection between Ministers and Marconi shares, however recklessly and inaccurately expressed, arose chiefly from distorted accounts of Ministerial dealings in the shares of the American Marconi Company . . .

'We are of opinion that the persistence of rumours and suspicions has been largely due to the reticence of Ministers . . . We regard that reticence as a grave error of judgement and as wanting in frankness and in respect for the House of Commons.'

The Report pleased nobody. *The Times* thought it whitewashed the Ministers and blackened the Committee. It had also blackened the Liberal party: Rufus Isaacs was said to be near nervous prostration, and Lloyd George, according to Frank Owen's biography, 'lost weight, lost vitality, fell ill again, and his black hair grew grey'.

A Commons debate on the Report (in which all the Tories voted against the Ministers) found that Ministers had been 'indiscreet' but that the charges against them were 'wholly devoid of foundation'. The Lords held their own inquiry on Lord Murray of Elibank, who said he had refused to appear before the Select Committee because he did not want Liberal Party Funds transactions to be made public. He had, after all, practically been accused of gambling with them in the course of his duty to increase them by wise investment. His Peers let him off with a warning; and to his credit, he paid the debts of Montmorency & Co., left by the absconding Mr. Fenner, out of his own pocket: they amounted to £40,000.

Now it was the Stock Exchange's turn. The Committee for General Purposes held its own inquiry into that part of the scandal which intimately concerned them. Fortunately most of the mud had been slung at the Government, but the Stock Exchange was bound to be slightly spattered, and the old evil of 'dealing before allotment' had come up again. There *had* been irregularities in the flotation of the shares of the Marconi Telegraph Company of America; and in November 1913 the Committee summoned before it Heybourn & Croft, a jobbing firm, and several firms of stockbrokers, including Billett, Campbell & Grenfell, brokers to the Marconi Company.

On examination, the brokers were found to be blameless, in the circumstances; and the jobbers were awarded the maximum penalty; Messrs. Heybourn, Croft, and William Bagster Jr., all partners, were suspended from membership and forbidden to enter the Stock Exchange for five years.

The Committee then passed the following resolution: 'The Committee condemns in the strongest terms the manner and method of the introduction of the shares of the Marconi Telegraph Company of America in the Stock Exchange, and they give notice that all introductions of this character will render members concerned in them liable to be dealt with under the Disciplinary Rules'.

Herbert Asquith felt obliged to support his Ministers, even though it meant saving the political life of Lloyd George, his greatest rival, who was unlikely to love him for it. If he had demanded the resignation of both Ministers, it might have been thought that they were guilty (Frances Donaldson, author of the only recent survey of the case, thinks that 'they all decided to bluff it out'). Lloyd George, three years later, became Prime Minister and a national hero who led his country to victory. Rufus Isaacs, two months after the inquiry, was made Lord Chief Justice, and went on to become a baron, president of the Anglo-French Loan commission to the United States, special ambassador to Washington, Viceroy of India, and the first commoner since Wellington to be created a marquess.

# 16

## We Don't Want to Lose You

'This is to certify that Twenty-Five Pounds five per cent War Stock, 1929–1947, has been inscribed in the Post Office Register of Government Stock in the name of Alan Jenkins.'

—from the author's personal archives

War—on what scale nobody, at the end of 1913, could have foreseen —was less than nine months away. A Royal Flying Corps had been formed, and Italian pilots had shown in Libya that it was possible to bomb military objectives from the air. There was a Franco-British Naval Agreement, and a new Balkan League. France had extended conscription from two to three years. One Zeppelin had flown over London, another, the *Deutschland*, had crashed. Britain had a new class of battleship, beginning with H.M.S. *Dreadnought*, launched in 1906, turbine-driven and capable of 21 knots; and the Navy was going over to oil.

Before the European lights go out, let us take a last look at the Stock Exchange as it was in the summer of 1914. If you entered the House from Capel Court, the Consols market was in front of you, with the Colonial market on your left, and just beyond it, the American and Canadian Rails. On your right were Indian Rails, Mexican and Uruguayan Bonds, and other Foreign Rails. In the middle were foreign government stocks. If you entered from Throgmorton Street you would immediately see South African mines, the Kaffir group, and nearby, on the left, British Columbian, Australian, and West African mines (the old 'Jungle Market').

Daily *Official Lists* show that in 1914 about 4,500 securities were quoted. The total value of all quoted stocks and shares was about £11,000 million. Of this, transport and public utilities accounted for over £1,500 million, 80 per cent of it rails, but only ½ per cent water

135

boards. Industrials, broadly classified in the *Official List* as 'commercial and industrial', 'breweries and distilleries', and 'iron, coal and steel', represented about 8 per cent. Gilt-edged, we saw in Chapter 14, represented 10 per cent, half of which was British Government stocks. British banks relied on Consols for most of their £190 million of investments, but life assurance companies had only about one per cent of their money in Government stocks. It has been estimated (from estate duty sources) that private investors—perhaps 600,000 of them—held from £150 to £200 million of gilt-edged stocks, an average of £300 a head.

The effect of war—in particular the First World War—on the stock market has been likened to 'a bludgeon descending on a watch'. The watch is not only stopped, but smashed. Armaments, army clothing and equipment, and shipping shares do well, but in most other respects it is as if 'earthquakes, explosions, assassinations, fraud, failures, death, devastation and disasters' had all happened at once. The words are F. E. Armstrong's, and from 4 August 1914 onwards most of them were true. The next four years were to relegate the City of London to only second place as a world financial capital, and the London Stock Exchange, in importance measured by volume of business, second to Wall Street; or perhaps 'second *only* to Wall Street' is a more graceful way of expressing it. It was to emerge, however, with its integrity and international reputation as high as ever.

If the Stock Exchange had too many eggs in one basket, that basket was its international business. The first result of war in 1914, even a few weeks before it was declared, was acute anxiety about the solvency of various accounts, since many member firms had taken it upon themselves to arrange financing for their clients.

On 25 July, the Vienna Stock Exchange, panicked by Serajevo and the impending war with Serbia, which was only four days away, suspended dealing. During the next week all Europe's Stock Exchanges except London and Paris closed, and then Paris announced that there would be no settlements for a month. In London prices fell sharply, and jobbers refused to deal. On 28 July seven firms were 'hammered'. What could they do? If brokers had bought stock for Continental clients, they could not be paid. If they had borrowed from the bank, there was every likelihood that the bank would call in the loan, as several European banks were already doing.

The Committee for General Purposes had an all-night meeting on 30 July, and in the morning announced that the Exchange would be closed until further notice and settlements were postponed until 1 September. The Government extended Bank Holiday by two days, and a very quick Act of Parliament confirmed by law the Stock Exchange decision to postpone all payments for a month, which in practice became three months.

Some firms, such as de Zoete & Gorton, took the decision that never again would they undertake financing operations. The Committee asked for full information about borrowings by members, and found that they totalled £81 million for the London Stock Exchange and £11 million for provincial exchanges. The Government stepped in with a relief scheme by which joint-stock banks agreed not to press Stock Exchange members for repayment, and the Bank of England offered to back lenders up to 60 per cent of their collateral. Everybody was asked not to press anybody else for payment until a year after the end of the war, whenever that should be; and there were few members of the Stock Exchange who shared the optimism of the popular press that it would be 'all over by Christmas'.

The Stock Exchange, conservative by nature, suddenly showed its national characteristic of adaptability to wholesale change, as it had already shown a talent for rapid improvisation. 'Business as usual' as a slogan could not be fully implemented while the House was closed, but it was found possible, without any official disapproval, to continue dealings in the 'Street', and also by using the Extel tape system which was now connected to most offices. 'Brokers gave indications of what they wished to do,' says a contemporary account, 'leaving their special telephone number, so that propositions could be made'. Within a week after war was declared, the Exchange Telegraph Company had offered this service (known as the 'challenge system') free as long as the House was closed.

However, this tended to keep prices down, and a number of jobbers in the Consols, Colonial and Canadian markets agreed to accept prices as at 30 August as minimal. But this did not really work with the 'challenge' system, and certain other members, led by Wedd, Jefferson & Co., pointed out its unfairness to some of their number in a letter to the Committee. The result was a ruling that dealing in Trustee stocks should be for cash only, options should be suspended, and members should follow a list of recommended prices. This also

137

was unpopular, because it was possible for individual dealers to sell outside the House at lower prices; but minimum prices were officially in force, with one or two alterations, for the next two years.

Gradually the American market disappeared. The British Government needed dollars to finance both its own and its Allies' war efforts, and holders of American securities were encouraged, indeed coerced, to sell them and invest in British stocks.

Home markets shrank, due partly to Government requisitioning (railway branch lines, for example, were dismantled and sent to the battlefields in France and Flanders); and about £1,000 million worth of securities vanished from the House.

War news, true or false, caused the expected fluctuations; but by the end of 1914 there was enough optimism around to keep prices well above the recommended minima. Really bad news could have caused prices to fall dangerously; there was a constant risk of clients in neutral countries selling out in London, and an equal risk of (knowingly or unknowingly) 'trading with the enemy'.

When would it be safe to reopen the Stock Exchange? The Committee at first thought it could be done in November; the Chancellor of the Exchequer was not sure. Meetings were held with the Bank of England and the Treasury. Finally, on Christmas Eve, a set of temporary regulations was published which, if observed, would enable the House to resume business on 4 January 1915. It would be closed on Saturdays to relieve pressure on the depleted staffs of the banks. Minimum prices would continue for at least a month, bargains must be for cash, arbitrage was forbidden, and evidence must be provided that all business was free from any 'enemy alien' taint. Already both the Committee and the Treasury were coming round to the idea that minimum prices were paralyzing business, and gradually, over the next eighteen months, one category of securities after another was exempted. On the same day, 4 January 1915, a new list was published—*The Daily Supplementary List of Securities not Officially Quoted*. One of the temporary wartime regulations was that all bargains had to be marked and recorded, and this could not be done without the second list as well.

Meanwhile, a committee chaired by Lord St. Aldwyn had been set up to regulate new issues. Everything, foreign or domestic, had to be 'advisable in the national interest'. There were said to be nearly 1,400 applications to float new enterprises in February 1915. One of them was for rebuilding shelled towns in Belgium, whether during or after the war was not clear. Permission was apparently given for new film production companies, but not for building cinemas (then generally called picture houses) to show them in. As the war grew tougher, so did the Treasury, and very few new issues saw the light of day before the Armistice.

How was a World War to be financed? How long could such a war be expected to continue? There was no previous experience to go on. The only certainty was that money would have to be borrowed on a scale never before imagined. Three years was the longest period anyone could conceive in November 1914, when the Government announced £350 million of 3½% at 95, repayable 1925/28. As an additional and perhaps unprecedented incentive, the Bank of England offered to lend subscribers the issue price, on the security of the stock itself, at 1% below Bank Rate. The loan was a great success, but, as one economist has put it, 'this may have been one of those occasions when the Departments helped'.

Ypres, Neuve Chapelle, Aisne, Loos; in April, the beginning of the Gallipoli blunder; the first use of poison gas and *flammenwerfer;* the British Isles blockaded, the sinking of the *Lusitania*. And in June 1915, a second War Loan, 4½% 1925/45 issued at par, again with new incentives. Small savers could buy it at post offices in amounts as small as £25 bonds or five-shilling vouchers. There were conversion options from existing loans, and subscribers were guaranteed the right to convert into any new loan at par, if a new loan were issued on still better terms. All this was very popular with the investing public, but was criticized by economists as bad housekeeping: was the Government really so hard up that it had to resort to borrowing on bad terms and throwing gratuities to old customers? The answer was that it worked: it raised more money than the whole of Consols, and realized a sum only a few million pounds less than the whole National Debt in 1914.

In 1917 came the famous 5% War Loan, issued at 95 and repayable 1929/47, or, if subscribers preferred, a 4% 1929/42 stock tax-free. Income tax was not then the monster to be legitimately avoided that it is today, and this alternative loan was a flop. The 5% loan—tax-free for foreign investors—was the largest-ever success, raising over £2,000 million. The Chancellor of the Exchequer, Bonar Law, urged the public to borrow from their banks and invest in 5 per cents. The public, who, with the general shortage of goods had little else to spend their money on, responded magnificently; and the Stock Exchange was busier, with its depleted membership, than it had been for years.

The timing of the 5% War Loan was skiful. The war was going as badly as ever, there was a rumour that 'we're short of shells', the U-boat war was intensified, the French army was said to be mutinying; but Lloyd George was Prime Minister, and the entry of America into the war on the Allied side was now inevitable. Above all, saving was patriotic, and encouraged by the most efficient propaganda machine the world had seen, directed by Lord Northcliffe, owner of *The Times, Daily Mail,* and a string of magazines.

It is at this point that Horatio Bottomley re-enters our story. More than thirty years before, Bottomley had briefly owned the Catherine Street Publishing Association, which, among other papers, had published *Youth,* a boys' magazine whose sub-editor had been Alfred Harmsworth, the future Northcliffe. At the beginning of the war, Bottomley, who had gone bankrupt for £233,000 in 1911 but still somehow managed to race his horses in Belgium, announced to all and sundry that he would 'break with the sordid past' and place his talents at the disposal of his country.

Those talents were public speaking and journalism, both patriotic in a way that appealed to the best and the worst in a mob audience, and both very highly paid. His recruiting meetings, stage-managed by Charles B. Cochran, had made him 'next to Kitchener, the most influential man today'. He was paid £50 per speech. Northcliffe commissioned articles from him at £100–£150 each (many of them ghost-written by freelances, who were paid only £25). Some of these appeared in the new *Sunday Pictorial,* which had been launched in 1915.

Soon Bottomley was turning his attention to Government stocks. His company-promoting days were over, and his name had for years been mud on the Stock Exchange; but his war propaganda, it could not be denied, had a certain usefulness as long as he did not touch anything but War Loan. There had already been some trouble with *John Bull,* which was now running a City Supplement puffing some companies and denigrating others by dark hints about 'discrepancies in their accounts'.

The *John Bull* War Loan Club came to grief when it was found to be illegal under the Lottery Act. In 1918, however, Bottomley turned this into a 'Premium Bond Club' for buying War Savings Certificates. In a few weeks at least £100,000 was subscribed, if the figures may be trusted; and it has been estimated that nearly £900,000 passed through his hands altogether. At any rate, he was able to pay his creditors, get his discharge from bankruptcy, and win back his seat in the Commons. Meanwhile his War Stock Consolation Draw offered 'consolation shares' to *John Bull* readers who had not won prizes in the War Stock Combination. It was, however, the Victory Bond Club that really upset the Stock Exchange and brought about Bottomley's final downfall, as we shall see later.

One of the worst features of civilian life in the First World War was the 'hate' campaign, encouraged by Northcliffe and implemented by Bottomley in speeches and articles, against anyone with a German name. The Stock Exchange has always had members with German, Austrian, Dutch, and Jewish names which, to the unsophisticated insular patriot of 1914–1918, sounded German. It was not enough to be a British subject, or for one's family to have lived in Britain for generations: spy-mania was rampant.

Theodore Althaus, later to become senior partner in the stock-broking firm of Pember & Boyle, a mild-mannered man who had been a master at Wellington College before being picked by Lord Roths-child for a City career, stood on the Floor of the House one day in 1917, reading a War Office telegram informing him that his 22-year-old son Frederick had been killed in action. As he did so, a fellow-Member rushed up to him and shouted: 'Why don't you get back to Germany, you dirty Hun?' Useless for Mr. Althaus to protest that he had no reason to be ashamed of his name, or to change it to an English one, as some Members had done. The telegram in fact was an appalling mistake: Frederick Althaus had been badly wounded but was very much alive, as he is today, in his late seventies, silk-hatted, with a white carnation in his buttonhole, Member and former Deputy-Chairman of the Council of the Stock Exchange and a 'father of the House' (i.e. a member for more than fifty years).

After this incident, Althaus Senior was persecuted no more; but others were excluded from the House altogether—the Committee actually asked them to stay away for the duration, and a number of members styling themselves the Anti-German Union succeeded in preventing many of them from being re-elected. In 1918 a new rule was brought in stipulating that every ex-enemy alien must have been resident in Britain or a dominion for ten years, and naturalized for five, before he could be eligible for membership.

Those Members and clerks who were of military age had gone to war with as much patriotism, but far less panoply, than there had been in the Boer War. This time there was no community singing, no post-horns, no flag-flapping, no burning of effigies of the Kaiser. Within a week after the declaration of war in 1914, Major Robert White of Govett, Sons & Co. was raising a Stock Exchange Battalion of Royal Fusiliers, and by the end of the month there were 1,600 volunteers. Casualties were exceptionally heavy, and the War Memorial which used to be part of the West wall of the old House contains some 400 names including two V.Cs, C. H. Frisby and A. C. Herring.

Meanwhile women had invaded the City to replace the men at the Front. Some broking firms actually had a lady clerk, and it had been found that women were not too frail to operate typewriters or to man telephone switchboards; and those of them who were over 30 were rewarded with the vote in 1918.

The Armistice came, with President Wilson's Fourteen Points, and at last the Peace of Versailles, that passed all understanding, followed immediately by Keynes on its *Economic Consequences*. The Government, said the Cunliffe Committee on 'Currency and Foreign Exchanges after the War', must stop borrowing and start trying to reduce the National Debt. It tried a Victory Loan in 1919: you had the choice of 4% Funding Loan 1960/90 at 80, or 4% Victory Bonds at 85. Money was tight, and the scheme was not a great success. It was temporarily boosted by the irrepressible Bottomley, who started a completely unauthorized Victory Bond Club, appealing to everyone's patriotism, and operated, not this time from *John Bull*, but from Bottomley's own flat at 26 King Street.

Bottomley said he was aiming to raise £100 million. The Bonds cost £5 each, but the Club offered ⅕ shares at £1 each. It promised the return of all subscriptions on demand, and guaranteed that *all* interest would be devoted to the prize fund, with no deductions for postage, printing, or administration. Was there any administration? There seemed to be no organization for dealing with complaints or even with dud cheques; a few forged tickets appeared, and some subscribers got their money back three times over; there were no records to show whether any prizes were awarded at all.

142

The old rogue was losing his grip; he was meanwhile buying ailing newspapers and losing money on them; and supporting a new political party dedicated to 'keeping faith with ex-servicemen' and 'introducing business principles into the Government—including the issue of Premium Bonds'. At one point he was said to have bought £500,000 of Victory Bonds at 85 himself, and had to sell at a loss when the price fell to 73.

Suddenly there appeared, in January 1920, a Thrift Prize Bond Club, with its headquarters in Paris. The Victory Bond Club was merged with it: anyone holding £10 certificates in the old club was invited to send another £5 and exchange his certificates for £15 French Credit National Bonds. As these French Bonds cost £9 on the market, Bottomley made a profit of £6 on each, and he went to Paris and collected the money personally in a suitcase.

It was a libel action against an old enemy, Reuben Bigland, that finally brought him down. In 1921 Odhams Press had cold feet and gave him a golden handshake of £25,000; and next year he was sentenced to seven years' penal servitude for fraudulent conversion. He had blackened the name of Victory Bonds, and it is to the credit of the Stock Exchange that, even if they could not prevent his activities, they refused to have anything to do with him.

# 17

# Growing Up

'The game of professional investment is intolerably boring
and overexacting to anyone who is entirely exempt from
the gambling instinct; whilst he who has it must pay to
this propensity the appropriate toll.'

—J. M. KEYNES, *The General
Theory of Employment,
Interest and Money*

It took a long time after the war for the Stock Exchange to 'get back
to normal', if there was such a thing as 'normalcy' any more. Their
problems were at first domestic and constitutional. Relations with
provincial stock exchanges were not too good. In 1918 provincial
brokers formed a British Shareholders Trust Ltd. Why, they asked,
should issuing houses use only London brokers for new issues?
British Shareholders Trust Ltd. aimed to be an issuing house itself,
so that provincial brokers could have a slice of the business. It did
not work, because the Committee of the London Stock Exchange
immediately forbade its members to split commissions with anyone
who belonged to the Trust; but it was eventually to bring the Council
of Associated Stock Exchanges closer to London by airing certain
grievances.

One effect of the war had been the enforced closing of ranks in the
money market generally. The City was developing a greater sense of
responsibility; it had got used to a measure of control; perhaps
*laissez-faire* and *caveat emptor* were on their way out? Before 1914,
says W. S. Wareham, Head of the Quotations Department of the
Stock Exchange, 'members could and did deal in securities they
chose without restraint; the official Stock Exchange view appears to
have been that the only important thing about a security was whether
or not it was freely marketable'. In 1919 the Committee ruled that a
new issue must be made either with a prospectus, or with an advertisement, giving the same basic information, in at least two

144

national morning newspapers. (There was still, be it noted, no real control over what was said in the prospectus.)

This was followed by an attempt to exercise control over the admission of securities to the market: 'The rules regarding permission to deal, which were issued in 1921 to meet the Treasury's financial supervision when the Stock Exchange was re-opened after the war, allowed the members to deal in virtually all securities but only on conditions, i.e. if they were quoted on other recognized exchanges or if specific permission for the bargains had been obtained'. Now that the temporary wartime regulations had been repealed, this meant some control of the securities in the *Supplementary List* as well.

By the spring of 1919, the City was trying to get back some of its old 'arbitrage' business with the Empire and America, despite exchange difficulties. Account dealing was not generally allowed for another three years. The mood of the country, and still more of the Stock Exchange, was restless. 'The pent-up demand and shortages created by the war,' remembers one veteran Member, 'offered great scope for financial mergers, flotations and recapitalizations'. Inevitably there was a boom—and it was in industrials.

About £400 million of new issues came on to the market during 1919 and 1920—coal mines, steel, textiles, car manufacturers (the Twenties were rich in new brands of car, and any schoolboy could reel off a list of a couple of dozen) and car accessories, such as unsplinterable glass for windscreens—while established concerns such as Vickers, Dunlop, Levers, and J. Lyons sought fresh capital. The Stock Exchange had not been so busy since 1914; and yet not so busy that it could not find time to play roulette in the House, a practice which the Committee had to forbid in 1920.

Gilt-edged securities were not quite the same bastion of defence they had been; was anything? Poor Soames Forsyte, still droppin' his final 'g's, dazed by the post-war world, reflected: 'Things were unsettled, people in a funk or in a hurry, but here was London and the Thames, and out there the British Empire, and the ends of the earth. "Consols are goin' up!" He shouldn't be a bit surprised. It was the breed that counted.' And at the reading of Timothy's will (he had just died at the age of 101) old Gradman, Soames's clerk, gleefully worked it out that Timothy's £150,000 of Consols, 'even with income tax at 2 per cent', would be worth £8 million in the year 2020.

The industrial boom was of course followed by a slump, and names like Bevan and Hatry were beginning to be heard. More brokers, keeping just on the right side of 'advertising', began to send out 'Investment Suggestions' to their clients. They included industrial and oil shares, which would never have happened before the war.

One such list, put out in October 1920 by de Zoete & Gorton, is divided into Trustee Stocks (English), which included Government stocks, home rails, India, Australia, and the Gold Coast; Foreign Stocks; a special category of 'English, Colonial & Foreign Railway' Stocks; and Miscellaneous, which lumped together clearing banks, insurance, shipping, tobacco, oils, and the Maypole Dairy. Dividend dates, price, yield, and 'remarks' are given for each security. In an era of Trusts and Marriage Settlements, brokers still had difficulty in persuading Trustees to include ordinary shares and foreign government bonds.

Advertising by 'outside' brokers and bucket shops was rife at the time, and in 1922 the Committee, while still forbidding publicity for individual members, undertook regular cooperative advertising in London and provincial papers, inviting investors to write in for a list of reputable brokers. As these lists included only members of the London Stock Exchange, the provincial exchanges objected; and an uneasy solution was reached by advertising in London papers only.

During the slump there occurred the failure of a large and respected firm of brokers, Ellis & Co. (established 1778). The companies involved included British Glass Industries Ltd. (incidentally, a Hatry flotation), Amalgamated Industrials, and the City Equitable Fire Insurance Co. The senior partner of Ellis & Co. was Gerard Lee Bevan, who was also the Chairman of City Equitable and a director of several other companies. In the spring of 1922 he was 52; he had been a partner in Ellis & Co. since 1894; and he had disappeared, leaving unanswered the question of a balance sheet in which, it was alleged, some non-existent assets had been included.

With a mixture of moral disapproval and envy, newspaper readers noted that, although he had a fashionable address at 21 Upper Grosvenor Street, W.1., he had been living in a suite at the Carlton Hotel 'with a young Frenchwoman'. He had left London by air on 8 February, and it took nearly five months to trace him to Vienna, where he had arrived in disguise with *another* young Frenchwoman and a forged passport in the name of 'Léon Vernier, of Lille'.

In Vienna he had been arrested for false registration and assaulting a policeman, who had tried to prevent Bevan from taking aspirin, thinking he meant to commit suicide. The penalty for this was three days' imprisonment which, on appeal, was changed to two months' hard labour. It took about a month to extradite him; on 1 September he appeared at Guildhall Police Court, and was sent for trial on 24 October.

Bevan's claim that he had 'a complete answer to all charges' took several weeks to unravel and refute. The ramifications of his Commercial Bank Group were almost impossible for the jury to understand; but the bankruptcy of Ellis & Co. could only have come about by bad management as well as criminal activity. There was evidence of 'meaningless Board meetings' entirely dominated by Bevan, and the jury added a rider to their verdict of Guilty—that 'the offences of Bevan had been rendered possible through the failure of other directors to carry out their duties properly'. A *Times* leader, on 6 December, regretted the effect of the case on the reputation of the City.

There was a fair amount of speculation in foreign currencies during these years. The famous example, of course, was Maynard Keynes. He had begun in 1919, Sir Roy Harrod tells us, 'buying and selling foreign currencies forward in large quantities. His operations included the rupee, the dollar, the French franc, the mark, the lira, and the Dutch florin. Broadly, he tended to be a bull of dollars and a bear of the European currencies.' This was the man who, on holiday in Algeria, had undertipped a shoeshine boy who thereupon threw stones at him. 'I will not be a party,' Keynes said, 'to debasing the currency.'

Keynes has often been instanced as one of the greatest gamblers on the Stock Exchange. Was it really gambling? Let us examine his technique. 'His selection,' Roy Harrod says, 'was based on two main considerations; first, the prospects of the business in the country in question, having regard to the general economic circumstances, and secondly, the balance-sheet of the company. He laid great stress on the latter. Careful scrutiny of the balance-sheet was more valuable than all the inside information in the world. The laws of arithmetic were more reliable than the winds of rumour. Having chosen his stocks carefully, he was entirely unwilling to be frightened out of them by short-term reverses. Nor did he take quick gains.'

147

But this was Keynes in his responsible position, after 1924, as First Bursar in charge of King's College (Cambridge) investments, which he managed with spectacular success, 'buying low' for long-term growth and sticking to his choices even in bad times. There was always a conflict between his own investments and those of King's. The accusation that he used inside information gained while he was at the Treasury was probably false. It is said that his decisions were all made in bed, in the half-hour before he got up, with no help beyond information from his broker, the City pages of the newspapers, and his own judgment.

At Easter 1920 he came a cropper (with his own speculations). He made £22,000 profit on francs, but £8,000 losses on dollars. By May, he was almost ruined: he had lost £13,125, and had to borrow £5,000 to keep his account open with his brokers, O. T. Falk. Whatever unease he may have felt at the way in which stock exchanges then operated, he had been brought up to believe that successful speculation benefited the community: it 'tended to reduce market fluctuations; it provided a trustworthy finger-post for producers and consumers; it enabled the whole economic system to function more smoothly and efficiently'.

The market recovered slowly after the slump. There was a small boom in tea shares in 1924; a Greek 7% Refugee Loan floated by the League of Nations, which opened at six points premium and met an outstanding demand; and a new boom in rubber shares during the summer of 1925.

Banks and insurance companies had large holdings in quoted securities; and Professor Morgan estimates that in 1924 'private individuals held some £2,000 million of quoted government securities'. Investment trusts were making a comeback, with more ordinary shares, more industrial, less government stock. In the House itself, the rules against ex-enemy nationals was slightly relaxed; and in the same year, 1925, the Provincial Brokers' Stock Exchange, with members in a hundred different towns, ranging from Douglas, Isle of Man, to St. Helier, Jersey, was recognized as a properly constituted stock exchange.

In 1926 came the biggest promotion of the Twenties, Imperial Chemical Industries, uniting Brunner, Mond, United Alkali, Nobel, and British Dyestuffs. It had a bad image with the pacifist generation of the 1930s, who believed that it manufactured poison gas and that it was therefore a cartel of 'merchants of death', but it was a pointer to the future of industry. That year also saw the issue of 4% Consols, which survives today.

The General Strike, which from nearly half a century later looks such a cataclysm, the very edge of revolution, in fact lasted only nine days. On 6 May 1926, the Committee debated whether to close the Stock Exchange; and decided not to. The day before, a single-sheet *Times* found space to say 'Prices opened lower, but there was no pressure to sell'. Next day, under the headline 'Calm Markets: General Decline in Prices', it was noted that Gilts and Home Rails were down, and speculative shares such as goldmines were 'steady'. *The Times* was up to four pages again, and 'the spirit exhibited by both employers and employed in the City yesterday was splendid. The difficulties of transport had very little effect on attendances at offices.' In the House 'many members and clerks' were 'free to take up various voluntary duties connected with the national emergency, including service in the ranks of the branch of the Special Constabulary that has been formed under the auspices of the Stock Exchange'. Gilts, however, had fallen slightly.

On 8 May, there was 'little change' and 'complete confidence in the outcome'; and by 11 May there was once again 'a firm tone'. The boom trend of the later Twenties had scarcely been rippled by an unprecedented confrontation between management and labour. New companies were being born every week. It has been estimated that in 1928 alone, 284 companies issued £117 million of shares, and 40 per cent of them (mostly small ventures) failed within the next three years.

The word 'bucket shop' was no longer Stock Exchange jargon: every newspaper reader, in these years, knew roughly what it meant— a suspect firm outside the Stock Exchange which was under no official supervision and advertised for business. Unfortunately such firms, to the uninitiated, were extraordinarily difficult to distinguish from perfectly legitimate 'outside' brokers who simply did not happen to be Members of the House. The House was, at this time, extremely difficult and expensive to get into: nominations, like any other commodity, were subject to the law of supply and demand, and at one point in 1927 a nomination could cost over £4,000.

We are approaching the 'dirt track boom' of 1928–29, which inspired a London evening newspaper cartoonist to show a sketch of the Stock Exchange with the caption: 'The Earth is the Lord's and the *foolness* thereof'. A retired Member recalls that 'jobbers in this market were daily being invited to cocktail parties "up West" to see the prodigies coming to market'. Clearly the general public had no idea that bucket shops and respectable members of the Stock Exchange were two different things. 'Thieves' Kitchen' was another synonym for the Stock Exchange, used by every bus-conductor.

There is a depressing similarity between the share-pusher of the 1920s and his coffee-house counterpart during the South Sea Bubble two centuries before. He has a 'good address' near Throgmorton Street, and a splendid title containing words like 'Trust', 'City of London', 'British'. He is 'in the know'; he has enormous mailing lists of people known to be investors. He is adept at writing a literate and convincing prospectus. He sends out 'information bulletins', only different from those sent out by sound broking firms in the inflated prospects of the shares he is selling. For a full study of share-pushing, we shall have to wait until the Board of Trade Report 1937, but it is all happening in the years 1926–29, and will continue, despite legislation, into the 1930s.

What could the Stock Exchange do? Nothing, as long as it suffered so much competition from outside dealers whose stock-in-trade was so often in unquoted securities. There were two Companies Acts (1928 and 1929) which stipulated that more information about unquoted companies must be given in prospectuses, and making illegal certain weird practices such as the selling of shares by door-to-door travellers who might also, for all anyone knew, be carrying a handy line in lavatory brushes. And in August 1929, on the brink of the Hatry crash, the Committee of the Stock Exchange made some highly important new rules about quotations. Among them, all share certificates must carry a director's signature (to prevent forgery); and every shareholder of a quoted company must be sent a copy of the company's balance sheet and profit and loss account *at least a week before the annual general meeting*, and a copy must simultaneously go to the Share and Loan Department of the Stock Exchange.

Forgery played a crucial role in the Hatry crash; but there is another disaster we must look at first. Crashes are always preceded by booms, and the boom on Wall Street in the 1920s was to end in a kind of earthquake that not only shook London and all other financial capitals, but whose tremors were to be felt all through the

1930s. Wall Street, Hatry, Kreuger, Britain's abandonment of the Gold Standard, were all interrelated; and there are men with long memories on the London Stock Exchange today who say: 'That was when we really began to grow up'.

# 18

## Animated Dealings

---

'Just around the corner
There's a rainbow in the sky:
Mr. Herbert Hoover says now's the time to buy—
So let's have another cup of coffee,
And let's have another piece of pie!'
—American popular song (*circa* 1929)

'On 3 September 1929,' says Professor J. K. Galbraith, 'by common consent, the great bull market of the 1920s came to an end.' Only nine months before, in his message on the State of the Nation, President Hoover had said that America 'could regard the present with satisfaction and anticipate the future with optimism'. Even Bernard Baruch, adviser to several Presidents, had told a reporter that 'the economic condition of the world seems on the verge of a great forward movement'. It has been estimated that only $1\frac{1}{2}$ million out of a population of 120 million Americans had any active association with the stock market: and it is fair to assume that most of them were in New York.

People in those days believed in Financial Wizards. What did Financial Wizards themselves believe in? Well, J. Pierpont Morgan was said to follow the guidance of an astrologer named Evangeline Adams. Ivar Kreuger, the Swedish Match King, in one of his rare interviews, said that the secret of his success was 'silence, more silence and still more silence'. Three years later his reasons became clear when he shot himself in his Paris flat. John Raskob, a director of General Motors, wrote an article in *Ladies' Home Journal* saying it was patriotic to invest money: 'Everybody ought to be rich', he wrote, and everybody could do it by saving 15 dollars a month and investing them in 'sound common stocks', which would produce 80,000 dollars at the end of twenty years.

Television was about to arrive: it was only three years since poor Baird had demonstrated his apparatus, but he had shown that it could reproduce colour as well—why not invest in it *now*? 'The commercial possibilities of this new art defy imagination,' said a prospectus. (It is only fair to add that sober New York brokers were advising their clients that both radio and aviation must still be regarded as 'spice'.) There were, of course, solid-sounding Investment Trusts, one of which, Anglo-American Shares Inc., had two British peers on its board.

Speculation was a national hobby, like betting or filling in the pools. There were stories of a rich man's chauffeur, a broker's valet, a hospital nurse who had listened to the delirium of a patient, cleaning up sums of up to 30,000 dollars by acting swiftly on tips. Alexander Dana Noyes, financial editor of the *New York Times*, was almost the only warning voice, who saw that the boom was being swollen by manipulation. What was about to happen was due to a complex of international monetary causes, but only partly so: looking back on it, Professor Irving Fisher of Yale said it was as much due to the mob psychology of panic: 'It was not, primarily, that the price level of the market was unsoundly high . . . the fall in the market was very largely due to the psychology by which it went down *because it went down*'.

There were warning signs as early as 25 March, when there was heavy selling of speculative shares such as Commercial Solvents, Wright Aero, and American Railway Express, and on this and the following day nearly 8¾ million shares changed hands on the New York Stock Exchange. But Average Investor didn't want to know. Brokers' offices were so crowded that they had to open more offices, some of them on transatlantic liners. On 12 August, the *Ile de France* sailed for Europe, and among the passengers was Irving Berlin the song-writer, who seized the occasion to sell his 1,000 shares of Paramount-Famous-Lasky—which went bankrupt soon afterwards.

The *Wall Street Journal* tried, in a very odd way, to rally confidence on 11 September: 'Don't part with your illusions: when they are gone you may still exist, but you have ceased to live'. The stock market, it went on, was 'but a mirror which provides an image of the underlying or fundamental economic situation'. And John D. Rockefeller was trying to calm everyone down by saying: 'My son and I have for some days been purchasing sound common stocks'.

Comedian Eddie Cantor cracked back: 'Sure—who else has any money?'

Then came the rumours—new ones every day: worst of all, the rumours about banks—even *they* were selling. Companies bought their own shares. Investment trusts bought shares in other investment trusts. And into all this came, from London, the news of the Hatry crash. Did this prick the bubble of Wall Street and cause the final disaster, or was it the other way round? Was Kreuger right when he said (although his own shares were regarded almost as gilt-edged in New York) that London would always be safer than New York, where it was 'risky to introduce securities, because once the New York operators start working on paper, their quotations lose all relationship to real value?' To some people, he claimed to have foreseen it all.

The Hatry news reached New York on 20 September. On balance, it would seem that Wall Street hurt Hatry a great deal more than Hatry hurt Wall Street. At most, Hatry—the full extent of whose muddle was anyway not yet known—increased the general gloom.

How did all this appear in London? On 22 October, the day after so many sales (6,091,870) took place in New York that the ticker-tape was an hour behind, *The Times* noticed 'a more than usually protracted Street market yesterday'. On Thursday 24 October, when 'panic' was the only possible word you could use, 12,894,650 shares changed hands in New York; but there were some for which no buyers could be found. This was the day when the suicide reports began, and anyone seen on top of a high building was assumed to be about to jump off. By midday eleven speculators had done just that. (Yet the overall suicide figures for October 1929 in New York were lower than usual, and it was easy to blame the crash for them all.) There was one authenticated case of two speculators jumping hand in hand from a window of the Ritz 'because they had a joint account'; which possibly started the then current sick joke about hotel reception clerks asking people: 'Do you want the room for sleeping in or jumping from?'

In London, *The Times* of 25 October reported 'animated dealings' in New York; prices of leading American shares had fallen by 'several dollars', and in London, International Nickel, Hydro-Electric, Brazilian Traction, and Canadian Pacific had declined 7 to 12 dollars, and Columbia Graphophone had fallen 4 points. Wheat, cotton, coffee, and rubber were 'weak in sympathy'; there was a 'general weakness in Americans', while Gilts had 'hardened'. The leading article, all 2,000 words of it, was about the Motor Show.

Not until 28 October did *The Times* devote a first leader to the subject. It was called 'The Great Gamble', and, not yet fully aware of the Hatry glass house at which other people might throw stones, it wagged a smug finger at American speculation, which 'diverted capital from more serious enterprises' (hang on a moment: didn't Walpole say something awfully like that?). It noted that the 'market capitalization of one motor-car company alone exceeded by a big margin the total pre-war National Debt of Great Britain'. However, 'with the cheapening of money in America, money will gradually become cheaper elsewhere, and pave the way for a reduction in Bank Rate in this country'. The City Editor observed mildly: 'In Wall Street it is believed that the crisis is over'.

Over? Next day, 29 October, has gone down in history as the worst on any stock market. Huge blocks of shares were sold as job lots: an Exchange messenger boy is said to have offered a dollar a share for a block, and got it. In the first half hour of trading, sales were going at an estimated rate of 33 million a day (the actual number of recorded sales was 16,410,030). From the visitors' gallery at Wall Street, the turmoil was watched by Winston Churchill, and there were some who said that it was partly his fault for having, as Chancellor of the Exchequer in 1925, returned Britain to the Gold Standard.

This was reported in London as 'further collapse on Wall Street', and the London Stock Exchange, beginning to tear its hair over Hatry, admitted to being 'unsettled'. By 2 November it seemed to *The Times* City Editor, 'hysteria has disappeared', and the American economist Stuart Chase was reported as saying: 'We have probably three years more of prosperity ahead of us before we enter the cyclic tailspin which has occurred in the eleventh year of the four great previous periods of commercial prosperity'.

Two days later, the British Labour Government, with fine psychological timing, announced a new Conversion Loan (5% 1944–64), which at once began to do well. 'A brighter tone' prevailed: Gilts were reassuring.

In New York, there was further selling, and on 13 November the ticker again ran over an hour late. London reported a 'weak tone'.

but Gilts and Foreign Government Bonds were 'firm'. Commodities fell slightly; so did industrials such as British-American Tobacco, HMV, and Royal Dutch. The 5% Conversion was still doing fine. By the beginning of December, the City was anxious to scotch rumours of 'large open positions'; it was however true that many speculators had been badly hit by American shares, and 'have had to sell securities to repay loans to bankers and others'. In New York, Evelyn Laye, opening in *Bitter Sweet*, heard that she had lost £10,000 overnight.

On New Year's Eve, the *Banker's Magazine* published figures showing that the prices of all stocks and shares had fallen continuously during the past year. Taking 365 representative securities, valued at £6,719,828,000 on 17 December, there had been a decrease of £349,775,000, or 4.9 per cent. London had not suffered too badly.

London's problem was not speculation and the resultant panic, which it had better means of controlling than New York, but unsound company promotion. Not that New York didn't have that, too; but the 1929 crash, upsetting every other Stock Exchange in the world, sending money rates up everywhere, suddenly tightening credit, revealed some special areas of weakness, and pushed two big operators—Hatry at once, Kreuger in a year or two—towards their downfall.

London, at this time, was a big market for American shares: because of the time difference between London and New York, dealing went on long after the House had officially closed for the day—either in Shorter's Court, in the street, or at home by telephone. (Even today, if the Dow Jones index falls ten points, London generally comes down a few points in sympathy.) But in 1929 there was more than sympathy, in a world accustomed to a perpetual money crisis, amid the booms and slumps, with trade stagnation and rising unemployment.

Professor Galbraith sees Clarence Charles Hatry as 'one of those curiously un-English figures with whom the English periodically find themselves unable to cope'. What, one wonders, is so un-English about a company-promoter who gets into a jam and stoops, in panic, to forgery? Veterans of the City do not remember Hatry quite like that. 'Of course he broke *the code*, you know,' one is told. 'Brilliant ideas—but over-ambitious. Should have gone bankrupt like an honest man. Had some pretty hairy people round him—even

156

in the middle of the trial, they used to ring us up for loans to keep his 'good' companies going—they got abusive towards the end—we were glad we never touched them.'

Hatry, who did himself well, moved in expensive if not aristocratic social circles, and liked to entertain celebrities such as Arnold Bennett on his yacht at week-ends, was now just 40. His specialities were local government stocks and large amalgamations which could be called 'rationalization of industry'. One of these, British Glass Industries (1919), went wrong in 1926 and was bought cheap by Canning Town Glass Ltd. The confusingly-named Commercial Corporation of London went into liquidation. Yet his Drapery & General Investment Trust (1927) survived to become part of Debenhams; Corporation & General Securities (1926) issued £37 million of municipal loans, and no harm done; and Allied Ironfounders (1929) survived until 1969 when it was acquired by Glynwed Ltd. In the last case, Hatry tried to move too fast: having united a large number of iron and steel companies, aiming at about three-fifths of the whole industry, he failed to raise the necessary capital, fell back on market-rigging to boost the shares, and robbed Peter to pay Paul; all this while Wall Street was beginning to collapse and money was getting dearer.

There was also trouble in his Austin Friars Trust, one of whose concerns, Photomaton, had been formed to market a then revolutionary invention for taking 'instant' portrait photographs. It was now proliferating into other countries, following the pattern, very popular at the time, of selling the patent rights country by country through locally-financed companies. New ideas, at this time, were bandwagons on which it was very easy to persuade people to climb.

But the most dangerous trouble of all was in thrifty places like Swindon and Dundee. So it came about that in September 1929, Hatry was charged with 'conspiring with John Gialdini and other persons unknown to forge and utter valuable securities purporting to be bearer scrip certificates relating to part of the authorized issue of Borough of Swindon 4¾% Redeemable Stock' and other stocks. With him were three associates named Daniels, Tabor, and Dixon. Mr. Gialdini had vanished.

To their credit, the remaining four had given themselves up. On 19 September the Governor of the Bank of England, Montagu Norman, told the Chairman of the Stock Exchange Committee, Sir

Archibald Campbell, what had happened. The speed, decisiveness and thoroughness with which the Stock Exchange then acted wrote some of the best pages in its history. It had to protect both investors and itself, for its honour was again at stake, to an extent it had not known since the Whitaker Wright crash thirty years before; and it did so with a very real measure of self-sacrifice (including salary cuts for Stock Exchange staff for three months).

Next day the Committee appointed a sub-committee of investigation, and immediately suspended dealing in Hatry shares. Settlement had to be postponed indefinitely, because nobody yet knew how much over-issuing there had been, and which certificates had been forged (Hatry himself had admitted to £1,400,000 worth). It had also to be established whether any Members of the Stock Exchange had knowingly taken part in the swindle.

Hatry's affairs took nearly five months to sort out. The sub-committee eventually reported that it had examined thirty-two broking firms and four jobbers; it concluded that, while some brokers should surely have realized that they were being involved in some very odd transactions, nobody had actually broken any Stock Exchange rules. Hatry's total deficit was found to be £13 million, and the sufferers were Members and investors alike. Hatry had practically dictated the price of his own shares, which was 'contrary to the principles on which the business of this house is based'.

The trial of Hatry and his three associates at the Old Bailey reveals some fascinating glimpses of finance nearly half a century ago. They were prosecuted by the Attorney-General, Sir William Jowitt, and defended by great names of the pre-war Bar such as Birkett, Curtis Bennett, and St. John Hutchinson. It appeared, for example, that the Austin Friars Trust had never had a balance sheet. 'Was there ever any annual meeting?' asked Mr. Justice Avory. 'No,' replied Sir Gilbert Garnsey of Price, Waterhouse & Co., who had carried out an investigation at the request of Lord Winchester, chairman of several Hatry companies. Where was Mr. Gialdini, the dominating figure in the Dundee Trust? In Italy, from which country there was no extradition. Mr. Justice Avory: 'He is—er—not now expected to return? (Laughter).'

The Attorney-General took his stand upon the honour of the City: 'In all the difficulties which this country has had to contend with, perhaps our greatest asset is that traders and businessmen in the City of London have a high, an unsurpassed, reputation for honest dealings'. The only honesty to be found in the accused was the fact that they had confessed, and Hatry himself had taken most of the blame: 'I wish to say,' his statement read, 'that there were irregularities'.

This was made much of by Birkett, for the defence. Hatry had practically bankrupted himself, putting his own money into certain companies, especially the Austin Friars Trust. There was no evidence that he had kept a nest-egg for himself. Hatry's greatest punishment would be that 'a blow had been struck at the integrity of public credit and private dealing... Hatry had hoped that, by doing a great wrong, he would do a great right'. He had also had bad luck, since his failure had coincided with 'the greatest depression in share values'. The main cause of the trouble seemed to be the Austin Friars Trust, with its liabilities of £19 million: 'the money raised for acquiring steel shares was used to meet these liabilities'.

This was quickly refuted as 'the defence of any office boy who robs the till to back a winner'. An attempt was made to fix the blame for the scrip forgery on the absent Gialdini; but it was established that Hatry, at a meeting at his house on 23 June, had brushed aside all objections and taken the decision himself. In sentencing the accused (Hatry to fourteen years, the others to lesser terms of imprisonment), Avory called the whole affair 'the most appalling frauds that have ever disfigured the commercial reputation of this country'. There had been 'wholesale forgeries of spurious securities in trustee stocks, which neither banker nor broker nor any member of the public would dream of suspecting to be otherwise than genuine'. It was this, the *Law Journal* noted on 1 February, that had created a legal precedent and merited 'condign punishment'.

The press was not slow to ask how such frauds were possible. Had not bank directors been singularly unsuspicious? Was there not some laxity and naïveté in municipal finance? 'A system under which a firm can act, as Hatry acted, as both issuer and banker for a municipality seems definitely mistaken,' said *The Times* in a 1,500-word leader. Its City Editor, however, had reassuring news from the Stock Exchange on 10 January 1930: 'The investing public will receive in full whatever is due to them'. This referred to a scheme worked out by an unofficial committee for settling uncompleted bargains made for the 26 September 1929 account. The committee members were Claude Lemon, Fred Pitman, H. L. Urling Clark, and F. S. Cokayne. 'The other purposes,' *The Times* went on, were 'to minimize trouble on the Stock Exchange, to avoid litigation, and bring to an early termination an awkward and unfortunate episode'.

It was explained, as it had been explained many times during the past weeks, that settlement had had to be postponed because of 'certain irregularities'. The wisdom and necessity of this was clear from the unofficial committee's report, which was well received at a meeting of jobbers on 14th January and a meeting of brokers on the 15th. Those of the investing public who had sold any Hatry shares would get full payment, whether the shares were 'good' or 'bad'. Brokers would get only 70 per cent. Country brokers, who had bought almost entirely for clients, would pay 40 per cent, while London buying brokers, or 'shunters' acting for country brokers, would pay 10 per cent. London buying brokers who acted for other clients would pay 42½ per cent of the amount due from them, and dealers would contribute 'on a sliding scale based on turnover'.

The total amount involved was over £1 million, and it appeared that private investors were in a small minority. Contributions made by jobbers and brokers totalled about £800,000, and the deficit of £200,000 was found from 'very generous promises' by Stock Exchange Members, some of which were 'pure gifts'. The fund of £1 million was to be vested in trustees.

The scheme was perhaps a compromise; but, the Committee for General Purposes said, it was 'the only plan which will save innocent people from becoming involved in serious trouble'; which would certainly have happened if settlement had been 'done precipitately in September'.

*The Times*, which like other newspapers had been critical of the long silence of the Stock Exchange during the trial, on 25 January made handsome amends: 'After the disclosures of the past few days there is more reason than ever to be grateful for the masterly plan contrived by Members of the Stock Exchange, which has so much diminished the area of possible litigation'. Three days later it welcomed the news 'that the Committee for General Purposes of the Stock Exchange yesterday appointed a sub-committee to inquire into the present rules and regulations governing the grant of permission to deal in securities. There have been some foolish criticisms lately of the supposed inertia and incapacity of the Stock Exchange Committee, but every well-informed person realizes that these criticisms could only have been made in ignorance of the true facts.'

In fact, several important alterations to the quotation rules had come into force on 1 November 1929. (The Stock Exchange has always been a little ahead of Companies Acts in sealing off loopholes.) One of them, we saw in the last chapter, was the revolutionary requirement that share certificates should bear the signature of a director. The sub-committee had little to add to the 1929 amendments, and while forgery became less likely, the City had to wait nearly ten more years for legislation which would really stop share-pushing. However, a further internal reform was the setting up of a Records Department which kept files on all financial operations and who was doing them; and this, together with the new Permission to Deal Rules, made for what the police call 'suspicious alertness'.

When Clarence Hatry eventually came out of prison, where he was prison librarian and devoted some time to gardening, he published a remarkable book, *Light Out of Darkness*, in which he proposed to solve the world's problems by huge transferences of population from poor countries to rich ones, from crowded ones to spacious ones. 'Brilliant ideas—but over ambitious'.

# 19

## Protecting the Public

---

'I have built my enterprise on the firmest ground that can
be found—the foolishness of people.'

—IVAR KREUGER

Fathers of the House (those who have been Members for fifty years
or more) look back on the Hatry Crash as 'a healthy shock'. 'We
stopped being a sort of private, easy-going club and became professionals,' they tend to say. 'We took, much more seriously, our
duty to maintain a free and orderly market. There must be no more
Hatrys. There must be much more information. We needed to raise
our general financial and accounting standards, and take our place
alongside the Treasury, the Bank of England, and the Board of Trade
in joint efforts to protect investors. We needed to grow up into the
national institution we believe we are today.'

That the new rules and laws had teeth was shown in the case of
Lord Kylsant, who in 1931 went to prison for six months for technically 'drawing up and circulating a prospectus, the contents of
which he knew to be false in an important particular'. At 68, he
controlled the largest shipping organization in the world, which he
had built up by amalgamating Royal Mail Packet with most of its
competitors in the South American refrigerated meat trade; Elder-
Dempster with Union-Castle the Coast Lines group, the White Star,
and eventually Harland & Wolff.

It has been argued that Kylsant was the 'fall guy' who hadn't read
his own small print. But he had failed to appreciate that directors'
names on a prospectus meant, in law, that they took responsibility,
'collectively and individually', for every statement in it. (This point of
British company law still frightens Americans, who think it would be
unenforceable in their own country).

162

These were slump years, in which we find the stock market still searching for a complete code of conduct, seeking even more information on securities, and yet perhaps fearing too many new rules which might inhibit business. In September 1931, after a suspension since 20 June, Britain went off the Gold Standard. A week before, foreign countries had been withdrawing gold from the Bank of England at an alarming rate. On 19 September the Stock Exchange announced that it would open on Saturdays, to show willing to do its bit in trying to revive trade. The first Saturday morning saw the heavy dumping of British Government securities from abroad, with a sharp fall in prices. On Sunday the 20th, the Committee decided to close the House on the following day to prevent speculation; and Bank Rate shot up to 6 per cent. The Cabinet rushed through a bill to suspend the Gold Standard; it was passed on the 21st; and 'business as usual' was resumed on the 23rd under temporary regulations (no contangos, no options until further notice).

The worst was over; things could only get better. There was no inflation after all; and we had a National Government headed by Ramsay Macdonald. On the first night of Noël Coward's patriotic *Cavalcade*, the audience rose spontaneously, even tearfully, and sang the National Anthem (as Malcolm Muggeridge wickedly said in *The Thirties*): 'God save our gracious Pound'.

How were Consols? Doing fine; the only stable thing in a shaking universe. Five per cent War Loan, regarded almost as Gibraltar, had dropped 14 points during those fearful days in September 1931, but Consols only 2½. Next year came the biggest-ever conversion—of 5 per cent into 3½ per cent War Loan.

Unit trusts were coming back (the first British one had been in 1868), first from America, and then in 1931 came 'M & G'—Municipal & General Securities, the first of the British unit trusts we know today, followed by several others. They were—and are—an attractive proposition for the small investor who wants safety and is happy to leave the choice of securities to professionals. But the General Purposes Committee of the Stock Exchange saw at once that there was a risk of bucket shop 'trusts' which could take both Members and investors for a ride unless they conformed to the Companies Acts; and they set up a special sub-committee to study unit trusts and establish criteria by which they could qualify for recognition.

March 1932 brought together into the news two strange personal-

163

ities, one British, one Swedish, with perhaps only one thing in common: both seem genuinely to have believed that there was a future in investing in Russia.

Martin Coles Harman had begun his City career in 1902, when he was 16, with Lazard Bros. the merchant bankers at £48 per annum. He had left Lazards in 1924 and put his own savings into the Rock Investment Co. Ltd., whose securities he claimed were 'nearly all' quoted on the Stock Exchange. His interests were in oil, gold, artificial silk, machinery, and rubber, some in Russia, some in Korea; and his group had £14 million capital.

He had also attracted a certain amount of publicity by buying Lundy Island for £16,000, and had been summoned in 1930 for unlawfully issuing 'pieces of metal of the value of one halfpenny'; 50,000 of which had been made for him by The Mint (Birmingham) Ltd., contrary to the 1870 Coinage Act. The coins bore a puffin (the symbol of Lundy) on one side, and his own head on the other. Paranoia has seldom taken so endearing a form. Later, he issued his own postage stamps for tourists.

Harman's defence was that Lundy was 'outside the Realm'; it was 'a vest-pocket-sized self-governing Dominion', paying no rates, taxes, or customs duties. He was thus above the law. The prosecution, having done more homework, showed that Lundy had been part of England since 1321, and came for electoral purposes under the constituency of Torrington, North Devon. Harman was fined £5.

In 1932 he failed with liabilities of £500,000, and was not discharged from bankruptcy for eight years. Simultaneously he was sued by Morris & Jones Ltd., wholesale grocers, of Liverpool, for 'applying moneys of the company in the purchase of shares and debentures in other companies', to wit, his own. It appeared that after August 1928, when he had been appointed to the finance committee of Morris & Jones, he had sold their Government securities (including £138,000 of War Bonds) and reinvested the money in Rock Investment Co. Ltd.

Harman maintained that he had foreseen a fall in Gilts, and that the future lay in industrials, especially in Russia. What he had not foreseen was Wall Street and Hatry, both of which he blamed for his own failure. He had been very successful with Lena Goldfields, in Russia, until the new Five Year Plan, which had reversed previous Soviet policy and now discouraged foreign investors. It was not absolutely clear whether he had rigged the market for his own shares.

He lost the action, and for the next few years was seldom out of the news as his affairs were cleared up. He was actually convicted, in 1933, of 'fraudulent conspiracy' in connection with Chosen (Korea) Corporation Stock, and after a seventeen-day trial spent eighteen months in Wormwood Scrubs. Eventually he reestablished himself in business at 65 Broad Street Avenue, E.C.2., wrote letters to *The Times* on such subjects as the inadequate dimensions of prison cells, and sea-birds, of which, on Lundy, he had gained considerable knowledge, and which was good publicity for the island anyway. So was the prize of 'four fat bullocks or £250' which he offered for a swimming race from the Devon coast to Lundy in 1952: it was won by Captain Abdel Rehim of Egypt. Harman died two years later leaving £23,000.

The shares of Kreuger & Toll, part of the international financial empire of Ivar Kreuger, the Swedish Match King, were regarded almost as gilt-edged in New York, but rather speculative in London. Kreuger, with his clammy handshake and funereal suits, his mistresses, his strange love of chocolate soufflé and caviare in that order, and his twenty-room apartment in the Place Vendôme 'so that he could see Napoleon out of the window', has been called many things. To *The Economist* he was 'a man of great constructive intelligence and wide vision'; to the *New Statesman* 'a very Puritan of finance'; to Maynard Keynes 'the greatest financial intelligence of his time' who had a mission to 'create a canal between countries with abundance of capital and those in bitter need of it'.

He had successfully speculated in Czarist bonds (for there was still some hope, at this time, that Russia would eventually repay pre-1917 debts). Then he had grown to fear Russia (whose matches were competing with his own) and to see Hitler as a bulwark of European security, and, in the middle of the Wall Street crash, had announced a German loan of 125 million dollars.

He lent money to governments; he was Herbert Hoover's friend; he was essential to the 1930 Hague Conference on reparations, as a link between Germany and her creditors; in Russia, Ilya Ehrenburg wrote a strangely prophetic novel whose central character, Olsson, a Swedish industrialist, died of a heart-attack in a Paris flat. That book was found beside Kreuger when he shot himself on Saturday 12 March 1932.

To lessen stock exchange panics everywhere, his suicide was not announced for some hours. In London and Stockholm, there were men who thought they had some idea of the reason. At the request of the Swedish Government, Price Waterhouse & Co. were already examining his affairs. On 13 April it was revealed that he had supervised the counterfeiting of 142 million dollars' worth of Italian Government securities, forging the signatures of Italian officials himself (and spelling one of them, 'G. Boselli', in three different ways). Price Waterhouse alone wrote fifty-seven reports on Kreuger's world financial manipulations dating back to 1917; bribes and blackmail and market-rigging all stood revealed. His book-keeping, Price Waterhouse reported, was 'so childish that anyone with a rudimentary knowledge of book-keeping could see that the books were being falsified'.

The Kreuger affair was another shock to the London stock market: the City had lent Kreuger money, and also lent money to others on the security of his shares, now almost worthless. It was another salutary warning, and at least enabled the City to preen itself on being stabler than New York. In America and Sweden, it led to reforms in accountancy and company law.

The term 'public relations' was not generally known in 1933, but it is in this year that the Committee for General Purposes published 5,000 copies of a booklet, *The Work of the Stock Exchange* by Sir Stephen Killik, explaining the stock market to the general public. The 'image' of finance in general had taken a series of beatings on both sides of the Atlantic: Professor Galbraith finds that it was a distrust of morals more than of power, and that it was centred on the stock market.

There was, however, an excessive care for reputation in the case of Blennerhassett, v. Novelty Sales Services Ltd. Mr. W. L. R. P. S. Blennerhassett, in the summer of 1932, found himself the object of much ragging by other Members of the Stock Exchange. It was the height of the yo-yo craze, and an advertisement headed 'Beware of the yo-yo!' appeared in the *Evening Standard*. The copy featured a 'Mr. Blennerhassett, as worthy a citizen as any that ever ate lobster at Pimm's, or holed putt at Walton Heath,' who had become a complete drop-out and had had to be 'taken away' owing to his obsession with the yo-yo. The *Evening Standard* apologized, but Mr. Blennerhassett was determined to sue.

He was cross-examined by Sir Patrick Hastings, K.C. Was not Blennerhassett an accepted 'funny name'? Had not W. S. Gilbert and Mark Twain both invented comic characters of that name? Had he no sense of humour? Was not the Stock Exchange the home of practical jokes?—'The Stock Exchange has been very depressed lately. I was the first joke that had happened for a long time.' An alderman of the City of London testified that he had believed that the Blennerhassett in the advertisement referred to a real person, and that Mr. Blennerhassett might have been thought to have broken the House rule against advertising.

The copy-writer of the advertisement testified that the name Blennerhassett was a standing joke among his children, and that was what had given him the idea. He himself had never heard of the real Mr. Blennerhassett. The jury by this time were rocking with laughter, and the judge did not ask them for a verdict: case dismissed with costs.

But more serious matters were afoot. All through these years of depression the Stock Exchange was progressing towards new measures for the prevention of fraud. The sub-committee on unit trusts gave an interim report on 12 December 1935, which was approved by the General Purposes Committee and sent to the Treasury and the Board of Trade. The Board of Trade at once began to frame suitable legislation. 'The protection of the public,' said the report, could only be assured by 'legislation which could be universally enforced'. In February 1936 the Government appointed the Anderson Committee to consider the whole question; and one of its members was R. P. Wilkinson, Deputy-Chairman of the Stock Exchange and Chairman of the Sub-Committee on Fixed Trusts.

Another committee, the Bodkin Committee, was at work on measures to eliminate share-pushing, and there was also a Foreign Transactions Advisory Committee. Wilkinson was a member of all of them, and he and other members of his firm, de Zoete & Gorton, went so far as to act as 'decoys' in order to find out how bucket shops worked. 'Often a bucket shop would appear to be beyond suspicion with all settlements being made through a bank. Confidence was established by offering British Government stocks at below market prices, and an ultra-conservative policy would be adopted when reviewing investments. Then, after a few weeks or months, a modest speculation which showed a profit would be encouraged, and this was usually settled by cheque. The next move would be to offer a larger holding and the customer would be told not to take too much of the stock as it would be speculative. A sharp increase in price would then take place (in most instances the securities were unquoted) and following this . . . the trap would open' and the customer was given the impression that 'such a magnificent opportunity could not be missed'.

This was what O. Henry would call 'gentle grafting'; but often, 'once he had parted with his money the investor never heard from the bucket shop again'. One such operator is said to have spent £50,000 on 'bait' before fleeing with £1 million to a South American country from which there was no extradition.

Perhaps the meanest swindle of all was to approach people who had received compensation for industrial accidents. Thus a blind man, who had £4,000 yielding an income on which he and his family were solely dependent, was fleeced of every penny he had.

All the work of the three committees was at last embodied in the Prevention of Fraud (Investments) Act which, although passed in 1939, did not actually come into force until 1944, during the war. By this Act stockbroking was confined to institutions recognized by the Board of Trade, or to licensed firms and individuals, and again restricted advertising, with stiff penalties for offenders—a maximum fine of £500 or two years' imprisonment or both. Thus bucket shops— of which there were believed to be as many as 800—were forced out of business.

The case of Mr. Garabed Bishirgian deserves a brief note. In January 1936 he and two associates, J. H. Howeson and Louis Hardy, were charged with having issued, in September 1934, a false prospectus of James & Shakespeare Ltd. The three men were defended respectively by Sir Patrick Hastings, Sir William Jowitt, and Walter Monckton. The affair, known at the time as the Pepper Trade Crisis or Bishirgian's Corner in Pepper, barely touched the Stock Exchange, for pepper is a commodity, not a security. But Bishirgian was both a director of James & Shakespeare and also a member of Bishirgian & Co., outside brokers; and he was good at getting highly-respected names to join his boards of directors.

It was said in his defence that his firm stood to lose £750,000, and he had already lost £90,000 before the prospectus was issued. Why should he buy so much pepper? 'What could a person do with 11,000 tons of pepper?' asked the Attorney-General, Sir Thomas Inskip.

'Would he go on buying or selling? If the latter, the inevitable consequence would be that prices would sag and the bottom drop out of the market.' Mr. Howeson was described as 'a world figure in tin', and the company also dealt in shellac. Was it merely a sin of omission that there was no mention of pepper in the prospectus? Cull & Co., the bankers who provided the underwriting, had been told only of shellac.

The case of Lord Kylsant was mentioned once or twice: both he and Bishirgian had been charged under Section 84 of the Larceny Act. Kylsant's offence was that he had shown figures as annual profits which had in fact been brought forward from reserves. Bishirgian, in his prospectus, had suppressed facts about certain 'forward contracts'; and he too was convicted. Things were getting really tough for all but the most scrupulous company promoters.

As the decade approached its close, and the war clouds gathered, the Stock Exchange worked steadily at its domestic affairs, especially at its relations with provincial (which it traditionally called 'country') stock exchanges. There was, it must be admitted, a certain amount of friction—not only between London and 'the country', but between brokers and jobbers.

London could argue that 'the country' had no uniform constitution or 'code of laws'. Way back in the 1890s there had been strenuous efforts to achieve this, and the Council of Associated Stock Exchanges had very nearly succeeded. Birmingham, Leeds, Liverpool, Manchester, and Sheffield had agreed in principle on a code, but Edinburgh and Glasgow had found it impracticable, though desirable. So, for the time being, they had agreed to differ. It is curious to reflect that the total membership of the twenty-two stock exchanges in the country in 1939 was only about 1,000. The London Stock Exchange, at this time, had a membership of just over 4,000 (about 2,500 brokers and 1,500 jobbers—and this marked a great change from twenty years before, when there had been rather more jobbers than brokers).

The provincial exchanges needed access to London markets, and yet London to some extent regarded their members as competitors: a subcommittee in 1939 reported that the 'damage' of provincial jobbing in particular had 'continued to grow'. Yet London could hardly do without the business brought to them by the provinces. Provincial brokers however could legitimately complain that in new issues from London they were overlooked in favour of London brokers; and there were endless arguments about commission-splitting. It was to take another thirty years before all these problems were ironed out; but a big step forward was taken in 1939 by the foundation of an Advisory Committee of Stock Exchanges, which brought London, the Council of Associated Stock Exchanges, and the Provincial Brokers Stock Exchange closer together.

There was also an important change in the rules in 1939 by which partnerships could be turned into private (unlimited) companies and become corporate (as well as individual) members of the Stock Exchange.

The reasons for this were given in the 1939 Report of the Committee for General Purposes: 'the severity and inequity of the effects of existing methods of direct taxation on violently fluctuating incomes . . . of Members of the Stock Exchange. In the case of jobbers the position has been made worse by the liability incurred to pay on unrealized and frequently unrealizable profits arising out of writing up book values to the market prices for the purpose of arriving at a taxable income'.

A new toy had appeared in the House (installed on 16 January) called the Trans Lux indicator, which 'conveys dividend and other important announcements by passing the information across a screen illuminated for the purpose'. The first announcement to appear was the Cow & Gate dividend, which 'was at once construed by Members as a "bull" point'. It was about the last recorded joke before the war.

So the 1930s came to an end, and so did a number of old ideas. After 1929, what some people called the 'patent market' collapsed (Photomaton had been a typical example): magic company formulae, inventions, processes, gambles—often based on perfectly sound ideas, such as unbreakable gramophone records, which were not yet commercially viable. The crash of the Credit Anstalt Bank, an associate concern of the Rothschilds in Vienna, seemed to have spoilt for a long time the Governor of the Bank of England, Montague Norman's, idea of 'borrowing short and lending long', especially lending to foreign countries. Merchant banks turned their eyes away from overseas and looked homeward. Chain stores became popular, and Rothschilds surprised everybody by a new issue of Woolworths shares. But they were not good times; and after Munich there was little or no reason for optimism.

170

# 20

# Business not Quite as Usual

'My rule was always to do the business of the day in
the day.'

—THE DUKE OF WELLINGTON

The Stock Exchange had been making plans for what was politely
called 'an emergency' for two or three years, both collectively and
individually. The 1939 Report told all Members, in February, that
'the Stock Exchange will be expected, so far as circumstances permit,
*to carry on its business*'. At the same time, Members should 'give
precedence to National Service' (conscription had been introduced
soon after the Munich Settlement). This meant the calling up of many
clerks, who should 'not be withdrawn by their employers', and
engaging 'temporary unauthorized or Settling Room clerks'.

Individual firms installed extra telephone lines in partners' country
or suburban houses in case 'evacuation' should become necessary;
and arranged Air Raid Precautions and Fire-Watching schemes for
their City premises, often in cooperation with other firms, and staff
were trained by professional A.R.P. Officers. 'Even a mortuary
was provided,' a veteran remembers, 'on an erroneous but reasonable
assumption that some people would die of heart failure under the
stress of heavy bombardment'. Older Members, of course, joined
'Dad's Army'.

There was a shadow plan for the Stock Exchange, the Bank of
England and other institutions to evacuate to Denham film studios,
Buckinghamshire, and many firms quickly bought or rented houses
around the village; but the move *en masse* was never needed. The
important thing was that, unlike 1914, everyone was prepared.

On 30 August 1939, the Government ordered the evacuation of

171

children from London, fearing immediate air-raids if war were declared. The Stock Exchange Committee immediately announced that the House would be closed that day—not in panic, but to ease the enormous transport problem. In 1914 the Stock Exchange had been closed for five months: in 1939 it reopened within a week. The closure on 1 September had shown the old tendency towards street dealing, and it was better to stay in the House (except during air raids, when it was always closed because of its glass roof).

The Second World War was taken calmly by the Stock Exchange. There was no huge overseas market to lose, though £525 million of American securities in British hands were requisitioned by the Government; and the Government fixed temporary minimum prices for its own securities. The same temporary regulations were applied as in 1914—bargains for cash only, no options, and no permission to deal in new issues without Treasury and Committee approval.

On 12 September the Treasury set up a Capital Issues Committee chaired by Lord Kennet, of which the Deputy Chairman of the Stock Exchange, R. P. Wilkinson, was a member. Among other things, it made it compulsory for brokers for new issues to consult the Government Broker about *when* to deal. These measures, together with Government price controls, rationing, taxation (especially 100 per cent Excess Profits Tax, which had the effect of eliminating speculation), and exchange control kept interest rates low.

In the Second World War, remembering what had happened in 1914–18, the Government felt it did not have to offer one bargain package of stock after another, assisted by Mr. Bottomley or someone like him. In March 1940 there was a 'general purpose' issue, suitable for all sizes of investor, of £300 million of 3% War Loan, 1955–59. It took a long time to sell; small investors especially were unenthusiastic, and it looked as if price control wasn't working. By the time the Government needed another issue, in the summer of 1940, the Germans were overrunning France and invasion was expected at any moment. However, an issue of 2½% National War Bonds was fairly successful, and was followed by others. There were also 3% Savings Bonds in December 1940.

This programme was unspectacular, but it worked: 'a definite policy was adopted that the medium/long term rate was to be 3% and short money 2½% and loans were issued at par. So successful was this policy', comments one firm of brokers specializing in Government securities, 'after the initial difficulties that the yield on Consols 2½% fell from 4% in 1939 to under 3% by 1945, despite an enormous increase in the National Debt'. A glance at the *Official List* in March 1939 shows that the aggregate nominal value of British Funds was about £7,000 million. In April 1945 the figure was nearly £11,900 million.

'Despite falling bombs and the wail of sirens,' wrote F. E. Armstrong at the end of the war, 'Members have attended the City each day, and with the exception that for one week when the leaden roof of the old Dutch Church in Austin Friars was blown by enemy bombs on to the floor of the House, Members have had access to the Stock Exchange. *The List of Officially Quoted Securities* has appeared with unfailing regularity ... *The Supplementary List* ... has also appeared daily. To save paper, quotations of many securities in which there was little public interest were dropped.'

As men went off to the armed Services, women replaced them in many offices, as clerks and accountants; and when they left for 'more essential' war work, married women took their places. They were not, however, seen on the Floor of the House.

The Advisory Committee of Stock Exchanges continued, during the war, to iron out problems such as commission rates for various classes of agent, and the vexed question of 'country jobbing', by which certain provincial firms were by-passing London and dealing mainly with provincial stock exchanges. New and amended rules were made which improved relations all round.

The Prevention of Fraud (Investments) Act was not yet in force, though the Stock Exchange was pressing for it to become law; and just before it did, the Government in 1943 set up a new committee under Lord Cohen to deal with the further reform of company law. The Stock Exchange was again represented on it by the Deputy Chairman, R. P. Wilkinson; and it met amid the constant thundering of V1 and V2 missiles until its work was completed in 1945. The results of that work were seen in the 1948 Companies Act.

But the great constitutional change in the Stock Exchange during the war years took place only six weeks before V.E. Day, in March 1945. Dual Control between Trustees and Managers (representing the Proprietors) and the Committee (representing the Members) had been a problem since the very beginning of the Stock Exchange in its 1802 home, and its abolition had been urged many times, most of all in the Report of the 1878 Royal Commission. But that was nearly seventy years ago! Why had it taken so long? The reason for ending Dual Control now, in 1945, was not that there was much conflict of interest between the two governing bodies; it was rather that such conflict had almost disappeared. For one thing, nearly all Members were now Proprietors as well, and held very few shares. Talks had been going on for three years, and although the two bodies were merged into the 'Council of the Stock Exchange' with effect from 1 March 1945, it was not confirmed as a permanent body until March 1948, so that this radical change could be ratified by the vote of all Members.

The Council henceforth was to consist of nine Trustees and Managers as foundation members, and thirty to thirty-six ordinary Members elected by ballot, together with the Government Broker. There was also provision for the gradual retirement of foundation members, and the virtual abolition of the shareholding qualification.

It had been a very different war from its predecessors. Patriotism itself had become a quieter market. No Charlie Clarke to wave flags, no persecution of Members with German names, no special Stock Exchange Regiment. Yet in 1945 it was recorded that there were some 1,250 Members and over 1,000 clerks in the Forces; 228 names were added to the roll of honour on the Stock Exchange War Memorial; and there were about 300 military decorations.

# 21

# The Post-war World

---

'You young fellas under forty—you haven't seen a real
bear market.'

—New York banker, quoted in
*The Money Game* by 'ADAM SMITH'

August 1945 gave us two apparently unconnected phenomena. The
first was an atomic bomb which dropped on Hiroshima, killed 91,000
people, and demonstrated a new power—confirmed almost immediately by the establishment of Harwell Atomic Research Centre—
in which money would sooner or later have to be invested: for one
thing, atomic power could be used to generate electricity. The
second was the return of the Labour Government, committed to
nationalization on an unprecedented scale. The Labour Party and
the City have never been head over heels in love; and Labour's
overwhelming majority was described at the time as 'a major shock
to investment psychology'. It had one useful effect, however: it
prevented a runaway Stock Exchange boom followed by another
1929.

Nationalization—first of the Bank of England, then of civil
aviation, coal, electricity, transport, the health service, gas, and
(in 1950) steel—was not unpleasing to the investor who was prepared to regard State industries as a new kind of gilt-edged, guaranteed Government stock. 'Institutional' investors, private investors
and trustees alike were rearranging their portfolios. Insurance
companies and others had willy-nilly bought Government securities
during the war, and were now wondering if they had not got too
many eggs in one kind of basket. Most thoughtful broking firms had
foreseen the growth of this institutional business, and were building
up statistical departments and picking the specialist brains of

175

accountants and investment analysts; and it was now prudent thinking to include a proportion of equities in all funds. But some of these industrial equities were about to be reduced by nationalization, leaving fewer alternatives.

Nationalization was to mean the issue of more than £2,000 million of Government stock to compensate the former owners, with another £1,400 million for gas and electricity. In October 1946 Dr. Dalton, the new Chancellor, announced that 3% Local Loans would be redeemed on 1 January 1947, but stockholders could convert to 2½% Treasury Stock if they wished. Both gas and electricity almost disappeared during the fuel crisis of early 1947, which coincided with the severest winter for fifty-three years; and following Dr. Dalton's Budget leak in September, we had a new Chancellor, Sir Stafford Cripps, the personification of austerity, who was however to reverse Dr. Dalton's 'cheap money' policy.

Nationalization of the railways took a long time to carry out, and it was 1948 before Transport 3% Stock 1978/88 was issued. This happened on New Year's Day, forcing the Stock Exchange to open on one of its traditional holidays.

Since May 1947 the *Official* and *Supplementary Lists* had been combined. This had come about because of stricter Quotation rules. There had been odd cases of certain old-established companies which had been granted an official quotation at a time when there were only minimal requirements to comply with; and younger companies which, having complied with the stringent 1930 rules, were still relegated to the Unofficial List. Some companies found themselves uncomfortably in *both* Lists. The Secretary of the Share and Loan Department explained it thus in 1949: 'What had happened was that the Permission to Deal Rules, which embodied new issues *control*, had absorbed the old Quotation Rules which only embodied *formalities*. The Stock Exchange, instead of just buying and selling securities, had developed standards of integrity and of disclosure, and had compelled not only its own Members but also everyone else connected with company promotion to comply with them.'

In 1948 the new constitution of the Stock Exchange, with a single Council and the reduction of the shareholding qualification to *one* share, came into effect. Having decided to stop being an exclusive club with an uncomfortably un-clublike organization, it now set itself on a more democratic path while adopting the organization of a club, with an elected management committee. The only things now missing from the 1878 Commission Report, besides the Visitors' Gallery, was incorporation, which still has not yet happened and is nowadays considered hardly worth discussing.

Next year sterling was devalued, the Labour Government was re-elected, and the market, fearing limitation of dividends, was depressed. However, the nationalization of steel in 1950 brought plenty of business to the Stock Exchange, as did the denationalization of steel two years later when the Tories were back in power. But they were frustrating years. The Capital Issues Committee still restricted issues according to the economic situation, and this went on until 1959. Even if you had the money, it was difficult to spend it: you had to have a licence to do anything. Successive Chancellors (of either Party) restricted dividends, taxed profits and encouraged 'ploughing back'.

A further measure of public protection was introduced in 1950 in the establishment of a Compensation Fund set up by Members for the—nowadays very rare—emergency caused by the failure, death or negligence of a Member.

In 1951 the celebrations marking the 150th anniversary of the laying of the Foundation Stone reached a climax with a visit by King George VI and Queen Elizabeth—the second royal occasion in three years, for in 1949 Princess Elizabeth with the Duke of Edinburgh had lunched with the Chairman, Sir Henry Urling Clark, and the Council and then walked through the Market.

The Stock Exchange, having for good reasons eschewed advertising (other than 'generic' advertising), began to think in terms of public relations, a convenient term which embraces all kinds of publicity but cannot be accused of aggressive promotion, and concentrates on the provision of information and the elimination of error. A committee on publicity had been discussing this since 1949, after a sharp attack on the Stock Exchange by a Cabinet Minister, Herbert Morrison, and in November 1953 the long (seventy-five years) awaited Visitors' Gallery was opened, and a film, *My Word is My Bond*, was made in 1958. The committee had taken the advice of a leading international advertising agency, The J. Walter Thompson Co. Ltd., which now has a public relations subsidiary known as Lexington International Ltd. This was all very new for the

City; but the really revolutionary step was the provision of attractive girls to show and explain to visitors what was happening on the Floor. It had been going on in New York for many years, but the application of the 'air hostess' system (to avoid some such expression as 'girl guides') was the subject of hilarious press comment at the time. The Stock Exchange, they implied, was not only with it, but way out. In 1957 a resident public relations officer was appointed; and he became the nucleus of a full-sized public relations department supplying information to the Press, TV, radio, and the general public.

Commercial television was about to burst upon Britain; all it needed was capital. Today new companies hardly ever seek a quotation straight away: the usual stages are private company, unquoted public company, and then quotation. Independent Television in 1955 broke through those customs, and the companies concerned sought, and got, immediate quotations.

The stock market was approaching its first post-war boomlet. In 1959 new issues within Britain, after several years of rigid control, were almost completely derestricted. After only £255 million of new issues in 1958, there were £435 million in 1959. Credit was easier; so was the tax on profits. It was reckoned that in 1965, the year of Corporation Tax, new issues totalled about eleven times what they had been in 1939.

For several chapters we have failed to inquire after the welfare of the Small Investor. In 1959 there was a survey to try to find out who he—or she—was. It revealed that he 'is far more likely to be a man than a woman. He is probably a member of the lower middle class, or possibly the upper working class.' He had left school at 16, and was married with one child who would soon be earning. His pay was (1959) about £17 a week, he probably had a bank account, had insured his life, was buying his own house, reckoned to save (and invest) £100 a year. He might switch from shares to a building society.

This picture was enhanced by a second survey, commissioned by the Stock Exchange from the British Market Research Bureau Ltd., whose results were published in 1966. It found that 2½ million people invest directly on the Stock Exchange, while 22½ million are indirect investors through life insurance and pension schemes. Of the 2½ million direct investors, 1,800,000 (72%) have money in industrial and commercial stocks and shares. The typical investor acquired his first shares before he was 40 (usually on the advice of his bank manager) and did so because he wanted either growth or income. Only 6 per cent of investors were interested in short-term speculation. Our typical investor was (by a 14 per cent margin) more likely to be a man (though if he lived in America he would be outnumbered by a 1 per cent majority of women); nearly half of all shareholders are in the middle income group, and more than half of them are over 50.

The 1959–60 'boomlet' led to an organization change in the transfer of securities. Under the old system, both buyer and seller had to fill in a form which was signed by all owners, whose signatures had to be witnessed, and the 'deed' had to be sent to the company with the share certificate, which had to be cancelled and a new one issued. The new system, which only became law in 1963 with the Stock Transfer Act, greatly simplified this procedure and speeded up transactions.

Meanwhile the Stock Exchange was again examining its membership rules and qualifications. Until August 1957, there had been a waiting list of authorized clerks, all of whom had served at least four years on the Floor, and who could be elected without nomination. This list was closed from 1960, and all new Members were required to buy nominations until 1969 when the system was abolished.

The influence of the 'institutions' was pushing the Stock Exchange towards a world of sophisticated, specialized knowledge—the world, not of 'who you know' but 'what you know'. A candidate now must have a proposer and seconder, but he must also have at least three years' training with a member firm. The stringent filter of examinations was now not far away, although it was possible for a man with valuable business or professional experience (say, as an actuary or a chartered accountant) to by-pass the training period.

More and more it was a world of experts and specialists—and of mechanization. It used to take twelve hours for the central Settlement Department to put through the paper work to link original seller and ultimate buyer. Computerization of the centralized Delivery and Settlement Departments has now greatly speeded this work. This is the result of the extended use of modern techniques, whose revolutionary influence on the Stock Exchange dates from the early 1960s.

The threads of the future were being pulled together about this time. We have seen previous efforts to bring 'country' exchanges nearer to London (or the other way round, if you are viewing London from the provinces); and 1962 saw the appointment of a Coordination Committee to start what Sir Martin Wilkinson has called 'nearly eleven years of chat' to bring about a closer relationship, and finally union, between London, the Associated Stock Exchanges, and the Provincial Brokers' Stock Exchange. The first result was the 'Federation of Stock Exchanges in Great Britain and Ireland', born in 1965 and drawn from all three bodies. The rest we shall see later.

Meanwhile, although Britain's membership of the Common Market was still a remote possibility, the Stock Exchange was drawing nearer to Europe, certain firms were opening branches abroad, and London now regularly met its Continental opposite numbers in the Fédération Internationale des Bourses de Valeurs (F.I.B.V. or International Federation of Stock Exchanges), officially set up in 1961, but whose spirit dated back to the 1930s, when Continental stock exchanges used to meet under the aegis of the International Chamber of Commerce. It was the signing of the Treaty of Rome that revived this internationalism.

In 1957, W. S. Wareham, now Head of the Quotations Department, and Frederick Althaus, then a Deputy-Chairman of the Council, were invited, together with representatives of the Zurich Stock Exchange, to join an Assembly in Paris, under the presidency of Pierre Sellier, Syndic (Chairman) of the Paris Bourse. They began to discuss long-term questions such as the transfer of capital, taxation of securities, collection of dividends, and problems of stolen securities. Vienna joined in 1959, and Madrid in 1960, to be followed by Johannesburg, Copenhagen, New York, and Toronto. In 1961, the Assembly was held for the first time in London, where it took the historic decision to form a Federation with its own constitution and secretariat.

This year, 1961, also saw one of the biggest leaps forward in the Stock Exchange's long history: the decision, not merely to rebuild, but to have an entirely new building which, along with the BP, Kleinwort Benson, and other towers, has given the City a skyline that no Londoner would have imagined a decade ago. This was not an easy decision to take. At a time of poor turnover and low profitability, it looked horribly expensive; and it meant altering the Deed of Settlement, which needed a 75 per cent majority in favour. Professor Lord Llewelyn Davies, FRIBA, and Mr. H. Fitzroy Robinson,

FRIBA, were appointed Associate Architects, with Trollope & Colls Ltd. as main contractors. The foundation stone was laid by the Queen Mother on 14 November 1967 and the new building was opened by the Queen on 8 November 1972.

The chief problem of building on the existing site was how to maintain a Trading Floor while it was going on, and this was achieved by careful phasing of demolition and construction. All brokers were asked how many telephones they would require in the new building: their telephones would be near, but not actually on, the Market Floor. Jobbers would have telephones from their offices direct to their pitches. They were also asked to choose between three types of pitch. In the old Market jobbers traditionally pitched their stands around pillars. There are no pillars in the new building: instead, there are rings of seats, inside which jobbers' clerks and telephonists work.

The total area which has been redeveloped is 62,858 square feet, and the 26-storey Stock Exchange Tower is 321 feet high. Four storeys contain air conditioning and heating plant. The upper storeys accommodate the Council and Administrative Offices; the middle storeys are let to member firms, and until the opening of the new floor in 1973 the lower ones housed part of the Temporary Market. At 23,330 square feet, the new Market is slightly smaller in area than the old one. There is a new Public Relations Block with a much larger Visitors' Gallery.

Just how dense accommodation in the City is becoming, both above and below ground, can be seen from the fact that the foundations of the Tower, which extend 40 feet below street level, are at one point within five feet of a Tube railway tunnel.

One of the most urgent reasons for rebuilding was that the telephone systems were seriously overburdened. In the old Market there were two: the Post Office Call Room and the Bartholomew House system operated by Exchange Telegraph. In the new building, as we have seen, all Member Firms operating in London have a communication point within the Market area. Connected, and interconnected, through the Stock Exchange automatic switchboard, they are like a small town within a city.

There is an entirely new Market Price Display Service. More than 1,200 television receivers have been installed in some 250 offices around the City, and each of them can display information on 22 channels. The system is linked to a Ferranti computer.

The new paging system, specially designed by Modern Telephones Ltd., is one of the fastest in the world and can handle 1,200 calls per minute. There are 1,500 receivers, remotely controlled from 280 points, and the system could be expanded to 4,000 receivers if necessary. This is perhaps the greatest change noticed by older Members. From 1801 until 1970, the usual method of calling a Member on the Floor was the stentorian voice of a 'waiter' (so-called from coffee-house days) or a flashing number above a Member's stand. Now Members carry pocket 'bleepers'—small microwave radios by which they can be reached anywhere on the Floor, or (theoretically at least) in neighbouring pubs and cafés.

# 22

# Big Battalions

'The engine which drives Enterprise is not Thrift, but
Profit.'

—J. M. KEYNES, *Treatise on Money*

For many years, the City has been looking across the Atlantic at
the Securities and Exchange Commission in America, established in
the Thirties to ensure that there should never be another 1929, and
wondering whether Britain ought to have a similar independent
statutory body for protecting the investor. In June 1962 the Company
Law Committee, on which the Stock Exchange was represented and
to which it gave evidence, reported that such a body would not suit
Britain. American lawyers they had interviewed confirmed that the
United States had no single Stock Exchange like the London Stock
Exchange whose controls (even though Federation was still ten years
away) operated throughout the whole country.

Another profound difference was that most American new issues
were not listed, whereas in Britain it was compulsory. 'We are not
persuaded', the Committee reported, choosing its words carefully,
'that a system of control on the U.S. model would work as well in
this country as the more flexible, though perhaps theoretically less
perfect, system which has grown up here over the years'. The Committee recommended instead closer cooperation between the Board
of Trade and other bodies concerned with the protection of the
investor.

In London we feel that only people who know the business inside
out can really run the Stock Exchange. The New York Stock Exchange exists to sell shares, and until recently carried on its letterheads
the slogan 'Own Your Own Share of American Business'. The

British Stock Exchange exists *to provide a market*. A speech by Lord Ritchie of Dundee (Chairman 1959–65) made this abundantly clear: 'We in London', he said, 'have no intention of establishing a monopoly . . . Our aim is to maintain a fair and free market and to make its facilities known as widely as possible to anyone who may want to use them.' He went on to praise 'our unique Jobbing system' and 'the Broker-Client relationship' for which there was 'no substitute'. However, 'because we do not think it our function to embark on a high-pressure selling campaign, it must not be thought that we do not wish to encourage new investors'.

The word 'flexibility' is much used by Stock Exchange people. The Stock Exchange can make or alter rules much more quickly than the principles behind those rules can become company law. And those rules are often more stringent than company law: thus the Companies Act of 1967 requires a company seeking quotation to provide profit statements for the last five years, but the Stock Exchange wants to see them for the last ten, and a great deal more about trading prospects too. However, there are glaring exceptions to this: North Sea Gas, for instance.

The fear of 'limiting our flexibility' is one of the reasons given for abandoning the old 1878 idea of 'incorporation by Royal Charter': 'if we were incorporated, for example, we couldn't have joined the Take-Over Panel'. Incorporation would mean paid management, instead of the often burdensome unpaid work undertaken by members of the Council. Incorporation, finally, might lead to monopoly, which is almost the condition of the Paris Bourse.

This is perhaps the place to take a look at the Stock Exchange as a self-governing body. Its Council, immensely strengthened by having become a single body in 1948, has to run the Stock Exchange to the satisfaction of the Government, other City institutions (in particular the Bank of England), commerce, industry, and the private investor. Confidence and integrity are of paramount importance. The Stock Exchange must therefore be governed by men with the greatest possible experience of, and contact with, merchant banks, clearing banks, investment trusts, insurance companies, accountants, and lawyers; men, too, who have managed their own member firms well.

The Council of the Stock Exchange, kept flexible by the election of members for limited periods only (so that the whole Council can change within a decade) has a civil service executive to carry out its policies. It is led by a Chairman (by custom a broker) and two Deputies, one of whom (by custom) is a jobber, and one a broker. These three, all unpaid, form an executive committee which meets every day with the Secretary-General and the Secretary to the Council. Deputies serve for three years only, so that there is a 'bank' of men with experience of the Chairman's Room and its problems, and a constant supply of fresh thinking. The Chairman is re-elected each year during his term of office, and his re-election to the Council comes up every three years.

In the last twenty-five years the Chairman has become more of a public figure than ever before. He must sometimes appear at short notice on television to represent the Stock Exchange. He must make policy speeches, notably at the annual Bankers' Dinner in the City. Obviously he must be a man who is 'good on his feet'. The type of leadership expected of him has changed over the years. He guides rather than initiates; nevertheless each Chairman tends to exercise his influence in certain particular directions during his 'reign'.

Thus Sir John Braithwaite (Chairman 1949–59, during the difficult post-war years) concentrated on public relations, chairing the first Public Relations Committee himself, and eventually handing over to Frederick Althaus. His public relations policy—to defend the good name of the Stock Exchange rather than to stimulate the sale of securities—remains the same today. In Sir John's time, amid much other progress, the Rules were drastically revised, and the Compensation Fund was set up.

Lord Ritchie of Dundee (Chairman 1959–65) had the worrying task of overseeing the commencement of re-building of the Stock Exchange, with the tricky negotiation of freeholds of properties required (especially 54–61 Threadneedle Street, without which the whole project might have foundered). In his 'reign', too, the new, simpler, quicker Transfer System was born; the requirements for quotation were made stricter, largely as a result of a personal letter from the Chairman to all quoted companies asking them to sign an undertaking; and progress towards a United Stock Exchange was greatly helped by his Chairmanship of the Coordination Committee in 1962. To Sir Martin Wilkinson (Chairman 1965–73) fell the tasks of progressing these initiatives, of guiding the Stock Exchange through the boulder-strewn paths of the Take-over Code at home, and of taking it into the international sphere.

Meanwhile London and 'the country' were drawing steadily closer together. In an Interim Report of February 1964, the Committee on the Coordination of the Stock Exchanges showed that the 'country' was full of ideas. Amid much down-to-earth stuff about commission, a common standard for quotation, dealing arrangements and branch offices, it came up with a proposal that there should be a written Entrance Examination for candidates for membership; and this was implemented seven years later.

The date 25 March 1973 was that on which the Federation of Stock Exchanges in Great Britain and Ireland became *The* Stock Exchange. The Constitution and Rules of the London Stock Exchange have been modified in line with the new proposals, and members of the other Stock Exchanges became members of the enlarged organization. These other Stock Exchanges—some of them already the result of amalgamations—are the Midlands and Western, Northern, Scottish, Irish, Belfast, and Provincial Brokers Stock Exchanges. All members pay the same subscription, and all new candidates for membership are admitted on the same terms. The assets and liabilities of individual Exchanges are those of the Stock Exchange, and former Compensation Funds have been merged into a single fund. For the time being at least, each Exchange will keep its own trading floor.

The National Council has forty-six members, thirty-five of whom were the London Stock Exchange Council. (This proportion will continue for an interim period of nine years.) It is responsible for discipline and regulations governing quotations, but the regional units will handle disputes subject to appeal, and will grant quotations under the agreed rules.

In the 'eleven years of chat' that have brought us to this point, there have been difficulties, fears, and apparent anomalies. The driving force towards a United Stock Exchange in recent years has been described as the desire 'to allow British brokers to present a united front to the Common Market'. British, did we say? But is not Ireland a foreign country? And if Dublin, why not Paris? Could this be the beginning of an all-European, later a World, Stock Exchange?

Moreover, there were twelve women members of the 'country' Stock Exchanges, and the London Stock Exchange had always set its face against women members: as recently as 1971 London (led, it is said, by younger members) had voted against them. Is it fair to say, as some do, that they have been smuggled in by the back door?

One positive advantage of the United Stock Exchange is that it removes restrictions which have prevented London brokers from opening offices in provincial centres. At the same time it gives provincial brokers direct access to the London Market. Most opponents of the scheme were smaller brokers who feared annihilation by 'big boys'. As for branch offices, one or two London brokers before the amalgamation found that they did not pay, and they generated too many small deals which jammed up settlement procedures.

Could the U.S.E. lead to a concentration of *all* jobbing in London? Or will it go the other way? In the increasing competition and general speeding up of business under the new organization, it might equally happen that a London broker might deal with a Glasgow jobber. What seems certain is that efficiency will be the winning factor. Another possibility is that London may become an international market, while 'country' floors specialize in home and regional shares, and cater for the smaller investor.

This is how it appears from London. How does it appear from the country? 'The all-important consideration for us,' says a leading Scottish broker, 'is access to the London Market. Whatever our differences, most of us knew that we really needed U.S.E. Up to ten years ago we operated on split commission with London—but London found it didn't really pay.

'In many ways, we like to think, the provincial exchanges were a ginger group. We were *ahead* of London in some things—compensation funds, for example, and new rules about commission. Then London probably feared it would have to underwrite provincial failures'. Not that failures were many; but there was a spectacular case in Scotland which must have worried London a lot.

The old Federation rule that no provincial broker could have a branch office within twenty-five miles of London has of course gone; and yet there seems to be no great rush to come to London. The reverse fear—London opening branches in the provinces, by takeover if necessary—seems to have been a source of considerable anxiety, and the Federation had a rule against it. London's anxieties were mainly about provincial accounting standards.

The provinces were by no means unanimously in favour of the jobbing system. Twenty years ago, that same Scottish broker admits, many people were definitely against it. But majority opinion has now

187

come round to the London view that it is the only way to get a truly stable market. As for London jobbers, it seems probable that some of them at least (whatever they may profess) would secretly like a little more competition; and those that do not will want to be represented on provincial floors.

The Scots were the first to 'regionalize' their Stock Exchanges by amalgamating Glasgow and Edinburgh in 1964. They have recently (April 1971) rebuilt the interior of the Scottish Stock Exchange in Glasgow while preserving the Franco-Venetian façade which dates from 1844, and made a twenty-minute documentary film of their own, *Capital at Work*.

'London is more flexible than we are,' continues our Scottish broker. 'Nowadays people come into the London Stock Exchange from other careers—say, after five years in insurance. The specialized expertise is useful, but continuity is still important, and clients don't like too many new faces.'

There is also the difficulty and expense, from the 'country' viewpoint, of setting up a Settlement Office in London; and it seems unlikely that more than half a dozen provincial members would be either willing or able to have a London branch.

Under the U.S.E. system, one-man firms will not be permitted— and this can only benefit the investor, who needs to be able to refer to Mr. B. if Mr. A. is not available. 'The distances of provincial cities from London could still present problems, in spite of modern transport and communications,' our Scottish broker concludes; 'that's why it is important for us to pick the right people to express our views in London'. Thus it is significant that the Secretary of the Federation of Stock Exchanges in Great Britain and Ireland, Norman Kemp, was formerly Secretary of the old Edinburgh Stock Exchange. In a word: 'No more introspection! We're closing our ranks, as we approach the E.E.C., in order to go out together for really big business.'

In this prospect of big business, and in the future of the Stock Exchange generally, the International Federation is slowly but surely playing its part. Already in 1963, at a meeting in Paris, they were discussing the amount of information available to shareholders and to the investing public; and the Working Committee was asked to consider ways of providing more informative accounts, better information about companies' activities, and more details about the activities of Stock Exchanges themselves. After further meetings in Vienna, Berlin, and Geneva, they began to work out possible standards for admission to listing; and in 1966 the New York Stock Exchange became a full member of the Federation.

The degree of cooperation was greater than anyone expected. Take, for example, the question of printing Bearer Securities. The British representatives had always emphasized the importance of the steel engraved plate printing process to eliminate the possibility of forgery (remember Kreuger!) which has been made easier by developments in lithographic and other photographic methods; and this view was supported by most leading European Security Printers and also by the New York Stock Exchange.

In Britain, we put Her Majesty and Arthur Wellesley on our five-pound notes. The New York Stock Exchange goes further, and requires its listed companies to include a human face and figure on all share certificates. Thus it has come about that Hugh Hefner, chairman of the magazine group, has put Willy Rey, 23-year-old Playmate of the Month for February 1971, across the centre of Playboy Enterprises common stock certificates. Nude, naturally.

In October 1967, the Federation recommended standards to ensure that accounting documents are audited by qualified and independent persons; and at Hamburg, in January 1970, subjects discussed included take-over bids, taxation of securities, and institutional investment.

In all this, the quiet and diplomatic efficiency of W. S. Wareham, Head of the Quotations Department, has been crucial. 'We are the only European Stock Exchange who are completely masters in our own house,' he says; and there have been many delegations from foreign stock exchanges to see how we work. 'We are listened to. The international investor has confidence in London. We may have had battles over harmonizing our standards and reaching a good settlement system, and our international network is still loosely organized; but it is early days yet, and the time is not yet ripe for any attempt to apply international disciplinary powers.'

Mr. Wareham has also been extremely active in what has become known as the City Code. In July 1967, following public criticism of certain take-over transactions, the Stock Exchange, in consultation with the Bank of England, asked the Issuing Houses Association to revive the City Working Party (first set up in 1959) in order to re-examine the rules governing such transactions. The Confederation of British Industry and the National Association of Pension Funds were also invited to join the discussions.

The Working Party completely rewrote the code of practice in relation to take-overs and mergers, in the form of a set of general principles and a number of more specific rules. This led to the establishment of the Take-Over Panel, with Mr. Iain Fraser as Director-General and Mr. Wareham as his Deputy.

Take-overs are probably the most difficult situations for Average Investor to understand. He perhaps visualizes a take-over as a prehistoric lizard, devoured by a larger lizard, who in turn may be swallowed by a reptile of monstrous size, the whole process happening in jungle conditions; and he is not at all sure that he is ultimately going to benefit from it. He noted the failure of I.C.I. to take over Courtaulds back in 1962; he reads headlines like 'Who's Nibbling At Rank-Hovis-McDougall?' on the City page of his newspaper; he may have heard of the old Rule 29 which said 'It is undesirable to fetter the market', and wondered how it could be reconciled with Rules 30–33 which tried to 'fetter the market' in order to prevent 'inside dealing'. His mail is full of communications from offeror and offeree, each accusing the other of inefficient management. What, unless he is a professional speculator, is he to think?

The principles of the Take-Over Code go back to a document of 1959 entitled 'Notes on Amalgamations of British Businesses'. It is designed to ensure that all relevant information is made available to shareholders, that they have enough time to reach a decision, that they all receive the same treatment, that minorities are not oppressed, that the market is a fair one and accompanied by disclosure of dealings by the bidders, and that the biddees do not make major changes in their assets or financial position in the face of the bid without prior approval of the shareholders in general meeting.

The Code is not written in precise legal language, which could impede legitimate business. Nor is it a rigid system like the professional code of conduct of the General Medical Council.

The vast majority of mergers and take-overs are settled peacefully and are conducted without criticism. It is of course the exceptions that hit the headlines. The Stock Exchange is concerned, as it has been in its rules for the admission of securities to quotation, both with the efficiency of the market and the highest standards of conduct, and believes that the key to this is 'self regulation' or voluntary self-discipline. This very British idea seems in practice to work very well.

'The cynicism which sometimes arose on the question of whether a voluntary system such as the Panel operates would work,' said Lord Shawcross, Chairman of the Panel, in his 1971 annual report, 'is now less often heard, and a number of foreign countries including Japan, Sweden, and France, have sent representatives of Government or of Stock Exchanges to study just how the system does operate. Indeed, the Basle Stock Exchange has proposed that arrangements broadly similar to our own should be adopted officially for all Swiss Stock Exchanges, and in Germany, a voluntary code of conduct has been introduced to deal with "insider" transactions.'

The Panel, which can and does meet at a few hours' notice, is not concerned with the question of whether an offer is adequate or not; that is for the shareholders of the 'offeree' company to decide—if they can. A take-over must have a reason, not an excuse. The first version of the Code came into force in March 1968. In its first year, the Panel considered about 575 take-over situations, and the loopholes still to be covered were revealed. The second version appeared in April 1969, and stressed that the spirit, as well as the letter, of the Code must be obeyed. It tightened up still further the rules about profit forecasts, making directors personally responsible for them, and defined the terms used. It made it abundantly clear that if, in the Panel's opinion, a member of the Stock Exchange has broken the Code, then he will be disciplined by the Stock Exchange. The Panel itself had now been strengthened, and there was an appeal committee chaired by Lord Pearce. (Incidentally, it is interesting to note the tricky ethical position of Panel members, some of whom wear two or three different hats in the City, and must not use any highly confidential information gained under any of them.)

The third, and latest, version of the Code, published in February 1972, was the result of City Working Party discussions based on some 1,200 cases. It was only necessary to convene the full Panel in sixteen cases. The appeal was used only twice—and one of these cases was that of Pergamon Press. One rule—the old Rule 30—was found to be unenforceable: it had tried to prevent dealings by the bidder in shares of the company he wished to take over after he had decided to make an approach. For the bidder can always say that he

191

had not actually decided to make an approach. Thus the Code is not yet perfect; but—the great advantage of this system against one dependent on company law—new rules can be made very quickly to close loopholes. The City will bend over backwards to make the Code work, rather than be 'fettered' by legal control such as the Securities and Exchange Commission exercises in America.

There is obviously a limit to the size of a group produced by a take-over or series of take-overs, and that is set by the Monopolies Commission. Are such huge groups really necessary? The answer usually given to this is that what counts is efficiency, and that, as we enter the Common Market, we enter 'the age of the big battalions'.

We need them to compete in Europe, just as we need international groups. Objections to the system are usually political, not financial; and if the small investor feels left out of it all, he can trust the wisdom of the large professional and institutional investors whose voice is powerful. 'In a free-enterprise society', Stock Exchange people say, 'we have to respect rights of ownership. It's the *user* of the market-place who ultimately calls the tune.'

# 23

## Stockbroker Country

'I've made many mistakes and miscalculations ... on
days when I'm wearing a tight collar.'

—PAUL GETTY, *How To Be Rich*

'Your Client has sold 1,000 XYZ Shares for the current account.
He requests you to effect a contango on his behalf. For what reasons
may he want to do this? What type of contango would you effect?
Can you assure your Client you *can* contango?'

'What do you think is the outlook for U.K. industrial share prices
over the next year or so and why? Name an industry whose shares
you expect to do well and one whose shares you expect to do badly;
explain why in each case.'

'Discuss the reasons for applying "Discounted Cash Flow" to assess
the profitability of a new project.'

'Explain how the following items will be treated for Estate
Duty ...'

These questions are taken from the 1971 Examinations of the
Federation of Stock Exchanges in Great Britain and Ireland. There
are four three-hour papers—on Stock Exchange Practice, the
Technique of Investment, the Interpretation of Company Reports
and Accounts, and Taxation. Unless he has certain special qualifications (such as being a Chartered Accountant), the candidate for
membership of the Stock Exchange must sit this examination. He
must also be at least 21; be proposed and seconded by Members of
not less than four years' standing and with not less than two years'
personal knowledge of the candidate; have completed three years'
training with a Member Firm; be prepared to pay an entrance fee of
£1,050 and a subscription of £262·50 on election and annually
thereafter; be elected by the Council by three-quarters majority;

acquire one Stock Exchange share (price 5p); and be prepared to pay £1,000 into a Nomination Redemption Fund.

The old-boy net is waning; you no longer drift into stockbroking because you have failed on the stage. 'It isn't an easy money business, as so many people used to think,' says Sir Martin Wilkinson, the former Chairman. 'Nor is it a club any more, though you have to be able to get on with people. We rather like a candidate who's been in some other City job first. You must, nowadays, have an absolutely professional attitude and ability: you must be able to deal with the big institutions who are now the leading investors, to talk with real *knowledge*, if you're a broker'.

One firm of brokers, Pember & Boyle, who specialize in Government stocks, says: 'Half our partners are family and friends. The remainder have worked their way up through the firm. There's no doubt that examinations show the trend towards professionalism. We look for young men with talent—they may be ex-Army, or actuaries, or with some other specialist qualification; but they must be trained people, all-rounders, of top quality. Nowadays it's smart to be able to say, in your brochure, "*not* a family firm".'

Frederick Althaus, CBE, senior partner of Pember & Boyle, is of the old school—Rugby, Balliol, joined his father's firm. Harry da Costa, a jobber in his early fifties, was educated at the Coopers' Company's School in the East End, matriculated at 15 and joined Lumsden & Co., brokers, as an office boy at 12s. 6d. a week. 'We had no central delivery then—I had to dash about everywhere in the rain'. After being promoted to stamp-licking and ledger-keeping, he joined A. L. Goodday, a jobbing firm as 'general blue-button and clerk'. He became an authorized clerk and eventually a partner until his firm merged with Durlachers. In 1960, Harry took the plunge and for a time went into business on his own, boldly reversing a trend. The number of jobbing firms has declined from 250 (pre-war) to 99 (1960), and now there are only 21 (in London). Mergers, retirements, and keen competition have taken their toll.

The diminishing number of jobbing firms does not mean that they are dying out. The jobbing system, unique to Britain, makes for a stable market. It has sometimes been suggested that it could be replaced by a computer; but no Member really believes this. 'You can use a machine to match bargains,' one is told; 'but for dealing there is no substitute for eyeball-to-eyeball confrontation.'

Harry da Costa lives at Wonersh, Surrey. It is, you could say, in the stockbroker belt; which reminds us that we have forgotten to point out, in this book, that stockbrokers are people. They don't just play golf; they play the oboe, they marry ballet-dancers, they do abstract sculpture, they belong to the National Rose Society, and one Member of the Council, Nicholas Goodison, is an authority on the history of English furniture and barometers and has written two major books on them. It would seem to have been Osbert Lancaster who invented the term Stockbroker Tudor to describe a half-timbered house built in the 1920s in which stockbrokers are said to live. I have never met one who did; but I know two Members of the Stock Exchange, a broker and a jobber, who live in *genuine* Tudor.

The Economist's Advisory Group, in *An Economic Study of the City of London*, solemnly analysed the private addresses of Members of the London Stock Exchange and found that the overwhelming majority of them live in South-West and West London, with Surrey, Essex, Sussex, and Kent close behind. This research was carried a stage further by John Hollis, Head of the Stock Exchange Public Relations Department, who found a thick cluster of them along the Inner Circle Line, especially Sloane Square and Kings Road, Chelsea, followed by Hampstead and Belgravia-Pimlico.

But this is retrograde, Southern English thinking; for the stockbroker belt is no longer around London, but within commuting distance of all the principal cities of Britain.

What, as we face Europe and the future, are Members of the Stock Exchange thinking and talking about? Women Members, advertising, V.A.T., the possible listing of the bigger broking and jobbing firms, even more computerization.

Women Members are here to stay. (*The Times* of 27 March 1973 recorded their first appearance and spoke of 'this fallen bastion of City misogyny'.) It used to be said that life on the Floor of the House was too rough for them, that they would never actually deal themselves, but send their clerks instead. Yet women on the Floor at Liverpool Stock Exchange never excited any comment. Now, in London, there are coarse jests about which jobbing firm will produce the first topless dealer.

It could even turn out that women make better stockbrokers than men. William Baker, a professor at the University of California, found that *personality traits* were more important than anything else in the broker's equipment—'an approach to buying and selling which is almost feminine—an intuitive reaction . . .'

The present position about advertising is that brokers may advertise in journals which 'circulate mainly overseas'. There has been a hint that they may also be allowed to advertise in certain investment magazines. Some Members complain that merchant banks, who offer stockbroking as a service, advertise, and that this is unfair competition. Others—probably those with smaller businesses—fear that only 'the big boys' would profit from it. Behind all this is the genuine horror of a possible return to 'bucket shop' standards unless advertising is rigorously controlled.

There has been a little anxiety about 'computer dealing systems'. These are mechanized services offered by certain merchant banks which, at first glance, would seem to threaten the Stock Exchange by eliminating the usual client-broker-jobber channel of communication and commission. So far, the Stock Exchange has actually welcomed this competition (which, it is felt, cannot affect more than 4 per cent of total turnover) and has brought down commission rates on gilt-edged securities. There are four such systems in America, where anyway the structure of the market (spread between cities up to 3,000 miles apart) is different; but experience so far suggests that computer dealing has not been a runaway success.

Pessimists are wondering whether the British Stock Exchange's undoubted superiority in size (its turnover is bigger than the combined turnover of the Brussels, Frankfurt, Amsterdam, Paris, and Zürich stock exchanges), in practice, and in service will really be appreciated in a Continent where most other financial institutions have more in common with each other than they have with the City of London. 'Continental markets are subject to manipulation,' City Editors hint darkly; or—'the French are not very share-conscious'.

Against this, it is perhaps consoling to note that (at the time of writing) several leading French companies with a combined capitalization of about £2,000 million are said to be seeking quotation in London, among them the Compagnie Générale d'Electricité, Rhône-Poulenc (chemicals), and Air Liquide (the French equivalent of British Oxygen). And in November 1971, Milan Stock Exchange cabled the Chairman of the London Stock Exchange expressing the hope that *Dictum Meum Pactum* (My Word Is My Bond), the motto of the British Stock Exchange, would be adopted by all Common Market stock exchanges 'as a symbol of seriousness'.

'We *can* lead,' say the optimists—and they are mostly on the inside, and should know. 'Over the last ten years nothing has been done by countries already in E.E.C. to create a capital market. There have been many delegations from abroad to study our system'.

During the past decade, the Stock Exchange has worked hard at its image and, through its Public Relations Department, has received conducted parties from schools and delegations of overseas businessmen; made films which have been shown in the Stock Exchange's own cinema and borrowed through film libraries about 900 times a year; given lecture courses and published leaflets covering every aspect of the stock market.

One highly imaginative way of appealing to youth is the Stock Exchange Finance Game. Each participating school is given a theoretical £25,000 to invest in a portfolio of stocks and shares (not more than £2,500 in any one holding), forms an investment team (usually at sixth-form level), and is sent the *Stock Exchange Official List* every day. It has about eight weeks to maximize its profits. The team can seek advice (by post, not telephone) from the Stock Exchange Central Broker, and the Stock Exchange computer works out their valuations, allowing for commission, stamp duty, and taxation. The winning team is awarded individual money prizes and an all-in prize for the school.

'There are still a few people who think of us as a sort of betting shop,' Sir Martin Wilkinson says. Among them is the worst kind of small investor. 'The bane of our lives,' a stockbroker told me wearily, 'is the chap who rings up out of the blue and says: "I've just won a hundred quid. What do you think of R.T.Z.?"'

To this chap, the Stock Exchange would reply, almost with one voice: 'Get your priorities right. If you're a family man, don't buy equities until you have started buying your house through a mortgage covered by life assurance, have made adequate provision for your dependants and have, say, £500 salted away in a building society or something equally safe. *Then* you can think about investing, and if you're wise you'll start with unit trusts, where the investing is done for you by professionals. It won't give you a gamble, but you'll be glad of the dividends coming in.'

Does it all sound rather dull? No more Bubbles, Hatrys, bucket shops, Wall Street Crashes, overnight fortunes? Instead, investment analysts, computers, codes, rules? It must be fifteen years since anyone was debagged on the Floor of the House. Mind you, the City can still be fooled: in January 1970, a merchant bank invested a million pounds in a mining company called E. J. Austin International after being shown 'a grey sludge', allegedly from the San Jacintho foothills of California, which when chemically treated yielded copper and silver. It was eventually established that cuprous chloride and silver nitrate had been brought to the site 'from other sources' a few days before. The sort of thing that used to happen in the Kaffir Circus eighty years ago . . .

The word 'panic' has only appeared once in a City page headline in the past three years, and even then it wasn't justified. 'Inflation has helped to remove some of the basis of panic,' one jobber told me. 'People are more sophisticated nowadays. The Department of Trade, the financial press, company law, more information, more controls— they all help to keep your nerves steady. And we have safeguards like the compensation fund for failures—which hardly ever happen nowadays, anyway—there aren't many industries that look after their customers like that . . . Panic? Well, if President Kennedy had been killed on a Thursday, instead of a Friday night after Wall Street had closed . . . And the Cuba confrontation—that was really dangerous, there was a lot of selling; but jobbers bought and made money—I reasoned that if Russia and America went to war, we'd all be finished anyway, so I might as well be optimistic!'

But still the greatest optimism I have encountered, during the writing of this book, is that of an octogenarian White Russian, a client of a well-known 'country broker' who holds, like my late father, some stock in the City of Nikolaev. He is patiently waiting, he says, for 'the Soviet Experiment' to end, whereupon, he firmly believes, Czarist bonds will become redeemable.

\* \* \* \* \* \*

So the story which began in the White Sea ice-packs, continued in the coffee-houses, through Gorgonzola Hall to the 26-storey tower (from whose top you can almost see the Common Market on a clear day), which bestrides Throgmorton and Threadneedle Streets in London and now includes every Stock Exchange in the British

Isles, is more than four centuries old. It is not ended, and will not be ended as long as we and our colleague countries in Europe remain what are called property-owning democracies. It is one of the great strengths of the City of London, that Square Mile of financial expertise whose total resources are truly formidable, and whose word—no cliché, this—really is its bond.

# Acknowledgments

I should like to thank the Chairman and Council of the Stock Exchange, the Stock Exchange Public Relations Department, Mr. C. D. Morley, CBE, Secretary of the Stock Exchange 1949–65 and Secretary-General 1965–71; and many individual Members for their help, advice, and information in the writing of this book.

Among many books consulted, I must acknowledge my debt to three standard works—*The Stock Exchange: Its History and Functions* by Professor E. Victor Morgan and W. A. Thomas (Elek Books, 1969) for economic history; *The Book of the Stock Exchange* by F. E. Armstrong (Sir Isaac Pitman & Sons Ltd., 1957); and *A History of the Stock Exchange* by Charles Duguid (Grant Richards, 1902). This last book is almost the only source of information on the daily life of the House in the last two decades of the nineteenth century.

In the Guildhall Library, London, I found a strange account of *Chancellor's Voyage to Muscovy* (translated from Clement Adam's seventeenth century Latin, edited by Edmund Goldsmid, and privately printed in Edinburgh in 1886); and made liberal use of files of *The Times* and *Financial Times*.

Other books and publications which were helpful in varying degrees included:

*Report of the Royal Commission on the Stock Exchange*, (1878)
*The South Sea Bubble* Lewis Melville, (Daniel O'Connor, 1921)
*The Railway King* R. S. Lambert, (Geo. Allen & Unwin, 1934)

*Acknowledgments*

*The Thirties* Malcolm Muggeridge, (Hamish Hamilton, 1940)
*English Social History* G. M. Trevelyan, (Longmans, 1942)
*The Bank of England* Sir John Clapham, (C.U.P., 1944)
*Mrs. Beeton and Her Husband* Nancy Spain, (Collins, 1948)
*The Smith of Smiths* Hesketh Pearson, (Penguin Books, 1948)
*The English Middle-Classes* Roy Lewis and Angus Maude, (Phoenix House, 1949)
*The Life of John Maynard Keynes* Sir Roy Harrod, (Macmillan, 1951)
*A Book of Trials* Sir Travers Humphreys, (Heinemann, 1953)
*Hatred, Ridicule and Contempt* Joseph Dean, (Constable, 1953)
*The Great Crash* J. K. Galbraith, (Hamish Hamilton, 1955)
*Horatio Bottomley* Julian Symons, (Cresset Press, 1955)
*Lloyd's of London* D. E. W. Gibb, (Macmillan, 1957)
*How To Be Rich* Paul Getty, (W. H. Allen, 1961)
*Kreuger: Genius and Swindler* Robert Shaplen, (André Deutsch, 1961)
*The Marconi Scandal* Frances Donaldson, (Hart-Davis, 1962)
*The Rothschilds* Frederic Morton, (Atheneum, New York, 1962)
*De Zoete & Gorton: A History* (privately circulated, 1963)
*The Life of Charlotte Brontë* Mrs. Gaskell, (Dent's Everyman, 1966)
*The Gilt-Edged Market* Eric Chalmers, (W. O. Griffith & Sons Ltd., privately circulated, 1967)
*The Meaning of Investment in an Age of Plenty* Louis Ginsburg, (Harrap, 1968)
*Stockbroking Today* J. Dundas Hamilton, (Macmillan, 1968)
*The Money Game* 'Adam Smith', (Michael Joseph, 1968)
*The Great Barnato* Stanley Jackson, (Heinemann, 1970)
*The Three Crowns* (staff magazine of Coutts & Co.), Autumn 1971
*The Stock Exchange Journal*, 1969–72
*The Forsyte Saga* John Galsworthy (Heinemann)

# Index